Spiritual Entrepreneurs

Where Religion Lives

Kristy Nabhan-Warren, *editor*

Where Religion Lives publishes ethnographies of religious life.
The series features the methods of religious studies along with
anthropological approaches to lived religion. The religious studies
perspective encompasses attention to historical contingency,
theory, religious doctrine and texts, and religious practitioners'
intimate, personal narratives. The series also highlights the critical
realities of migration and transnationalism.

Spiritual Entrepreneurs

Florida's Faith-Based Prisons
and the American Carceral State

∙∙∙

BRAD STODDARD

The University of North Carolina Press Chapel Hill

This book was published with the assistance of the Anniversary Fund of the University of North Carolina Press.

The University of North Carolina Press has been a member of the Green Press Initiative since 2003.

Library of Congress Cataloging-in-Publication Data
Names: Stoddard, Brad, author.
Title: Spiritual entrepreneurs : Florida's faith-based prisons
    and the American carceral state / Brad Stoddard.
Other titles: Where religion lives.
Description: Chapel Hill : The University of North Carolina Press, [2021] |
    Series: Where religion lives | Includes bibliographical references
    and index.
Identifiers: LCCN 2020038285 | ISBN 9781469663074 (cloth) |
    ISBN 9781469663081 (paperback) | ISBN 9781469663098 (ebook)
Subjects: LCSH: Church work with prisoners—Florida. | Prisoners—
    Religious life—Florida. | Criminals—Rehabilitation—Florida. |
    Faith-based human services—Florida. | Evangelicalism—Florida.
Classification: LCC BV4465 .S76 2021 | DDC 365/.34—dc23
LC record available at https://lccn.loc.gov/2020038285

Cover illustration: Drawing of prison door © iStock.com/Zdenek Sasek.

For Stacy Lane Stoddard

Contents

Acknowledgments

Almost a decade has passed since I first learned about Florida's faith- and character-based correctional institutions (FCBIs) and since I first directed my attention to this project. Since then, I have interacted with numerous people who offered support, time, patience, and insights to help make this book possible.

My mentors at Florida State University (FSU) have been with me since this topic first caught my attention, and I would like to thank Amanda Porterfield, John Corrigan, Michael McVicar, and Martin Kavka for offering feedback, direction, and criticisms at multiple stages in this project. I would also like to thank my dear friend Stephen Tripodi (mentor, conversation partner, and drinking buddy) from FSU's College of Social Work and his amazing family. My colleagues from FSU continue to inspire me with their intellectual curiosity, work ethics, and critical insights. I am particularly grateful to Tara Baldrick-Morrone, Cara Burnidge, Emily Suzanne Clark, Mike Graziano, and Adam Park.

As I worked on and refined this book, I benefited from the feedback I received at a couple dozen conferences where I presented my research on FCBIs, including conferences at the American Academy of Religion, the American Historical Association, the American Society of Church History, the John C. Danforth Center for Religion and Politics, the Society for the Scientific Study of Religion, and various colleges and universities. My work benefited from feedback I received from formal respondents but also from fellow panelists who either modeled scholarship or directly commented on my work.

While I have not presented my work on FCBIs at a meeting of the North American Association for the Study of Religion (NAASR), the colleagues I met primarily through my association with NAASR helped me in numerous ways. Chief among them are Craig Martin, who read various versions of this book and who provided important feedback, and Russell McCutcheon, who challenged me to think about the sociopolitical work that results from socialization efforts in FCBIs. I would also like to thank all the members of NAASR's executive committee, particularly Dennis LoRusso, who read some of the manuscript and who always pushed me to identify my terms in clear and accessible language. My term as NAASR president is approaching its end, but it has been a joy to work with Rebekka King (vice president) and Martie Smith Roberts (executive secretary and treasurer) over the past three years. Former NAASR president Greg Alles deserves special thanks for his guidance, advice, and everything he did both for me and for the Religious Studies department at McDaniel College.

Researching this project took me to prisons across the State of Florida, but I also conducted archival research in several locations where archivists and librarians proved to be generous and patient. I am particularly indebted to the staff at the Southern Baptist Convention Historical Library and Archives for their generous research grant and for making me feel welcome while I researched in their archives. I also extend my appreciation to the staff at the State Archives of Florida and to Jim Baggett from the Birmingham Public Library. I would also like to thank the American Academy of Religion, Florida State University, and McDaniel College for funding this research.

The bulk of this book relies on ethnographic research I conducted in Florida's Department of Corrections (DOC). Without the DOC's help, this book literally would not exist. Retired former secretary Louie Wainwright is a legend of sorts in the world of corrections, and after searching the state of Florida, I found him living in a retirement community not far from me. After spending countless hours in archives and researching public DOC documents online, I developed a history of the DOC and an opinion of Wainwright, and my project benefited tremendously as I talked to Wainwright about his tenure as head of Florida's DOC and about the history of the DOC itself. I am also grateful to the DOC staff for allowing me to research in Florida's FCBIs. Most people try to stay out of prison, but I wanted desperately to get in. I thought this project died when the DOC declined my initial request to research inside its prisons; however, with the help and support of former DOC secretary Michael Crews and former Head Chaplain Alex Taylor, the DOC approved my second research proposal, and with few exceptions, the DOC staff has since been fantastic to work with. I specifically want to thank all the wardens, assistant wardens, correctional officers, classification officers, chaplains, and other DOC employees who supported my research. I am particularly grateful to Warden James Coker and Chaplain Steve Fox from Wakulla Correctional Institution (CI) for granting me unprecedented access to research in Wakulla CI. It was serendipitous that the world's largest faith-based correctional facility was only a half hour from my home, but without the support of Crews, Taylor, Coker, and Fox, it would not have mattered.

This project also benefited from the volunteers (particularly Allison De-Foor, Ike Griffin, Hugh MacMillan, and Bob and Mary Rumbley) who shared their stories and made me feel welcome in their classes, homes, reentry facilities, coffee shops, and other places we interacted. Florida's faith-based correctional facilities would not exist without the support of volunteers, and without their stories, this project would be incomplete.

I want to offer a special thanks, first, to Sean McCloud, who generously offered to read the manuscript and who provided extensive feedback that helped me shape this book (no, seriously, thank you, Sean!). Second, I am particularly indebted to the people who are the subject of this book—the incarcerated people themselves. They provided handshakes, support, encouragement, and accommodation, and they shared their stories to help a comparably privileged graduate student get even the remotest glimpse of life inside prison. When I think of the incarcerated, I think of a phrase I heard regularly inside the prisons: "Hurt people *hurt people*." Their stories were painful to hear, as they typically included histories of abuse, neglect, and substance abuse. Hurt people *hurt people*. I came to believe that some of the incarcerated do need to be detained, but most of them do not. Not to diminish their crimes, but they are also victims, both of circumstance and of mass incarceration, and in most countries (or in the United States forty years ago) they would be free. Instead, they are incarcerated in an under-funded prison system that, much like their families and society itself, views them as burdens to be managed instead of individuals worthy of our respect. Many of them will die in prison, but most will not. In either case, I wish them well and thank them for their generosity and support.

This book was a work-in-progress for many years as I wrote and rewrote every chapter. During that time, I shared my work with some of my undergraduate students who expressed interest in the project. These interactions proved true the old cliché that students can be the best teachers. A couple dozen incarcerated students at Maryland Correctional Institution for Women read and commented on an earlier draft of this manuscript. They were fascinated by FCBIs and they were also interested in my scholarship. Their feedback was particularly important, as they challenged me to clarify several topics and as they encouraged me to think about the differences between life in FCBIs and the lives they live in a conventional women's prison. I would also like to thank my students from REL 2265 at McDaniel College (Abby Blankenship, Patricia Dixon, I'kea Horton, Allison Isidore, Becca McDonald, Angel Petty, Courtney Shumaker, and Kathalyn Urquizo) who read and commented on one of the chapters.

Over the past several years I had the honor of participating in several seminars and workshops where we discussed our work. The Young Scholars of American Religion proved particularly fruitful, where, led by mentors Laura Levitt and Jim Bennett, the group helped me sharpen my project. The Emerging Scholars Program at the University of Virginia was similarly fruitful, where Mike Graziano and Heather Mellquist Lehto read a version of the introduction and offered incredibly valuable feedback. I also want to thank Michael Altman and the rest of the Department of Religious Studies at the University of Alabama for organizing the American Examples workshops, of which I was a member of the 2020–21 cohort. At one of our meetings, I workshopped a version of one of my chapters. Steven Ramey led the entire cohort in an extensive discussion about the chapter. The insights I gained from this discussion not only benefited the specific chapter but spilled over into the rest of the book.

Special thanks to Kristy Nabhan-Warren for expressing interest in the project and to Elaine Maisner from the University of North Carolina (UNC) Press for patiently guiding me through the review and editorial processes. Elaine's advice combined with insights from three generous readers to make this a better book. Thank you, also, to the entire editorial and marketing team at UNC Press.

Finally, I am thankful and grateful for my family, including my mother, my in-laws, my Aunt Louise and Uncle Jerry, and my extended family in multiple states. I include in this group my adopted family in Rodgers Forge, who would indulge my academic ramblings when I wanted to discuss them but who usually helped me escape this project and focus on other important topics like local craft beer releases and food. I am particularly indebted, however, to my wife and children. Perhaps it's a cliché to say "Without so and so this project would not have been possible," but this is definitely applicable to this book, as without the support of Stacy, Ryder, and Addison, I would still probably work in the financial industry on the other side of the country. Ten years ago, Stacy and I lived in our favorite city in the world, I had a lucrative job, and our children were thriving in their schools. I do not recall the exact moment I told Stacy that I wanted to leave it all and apply to graduate school so I could complete my doctorate and teach Religious Studies, but I do remember that she was always 100 percent supportive.

That support has never wavered. I owe her more than words can describe, not only for moving across the country (twice), but for her patience, love, support, and understanding for the countless times I retreated to my office or to a local coffee shop so I could read, study, grade, write lectures, or work on this book. I want to thank Stacy, to whom this book is dedicated, for sharing this journey.

Spiritual Entrepreneurs

Introduction

The Not-So-Subtle Hand of God

· ·

Gerald Mathers stood before some eighty incarcerated felons in the chapel at Wakulla Correctional Institution (CI) in Crawfordville, Florida, pausing for a moment before he delivered his sermon. He scanned the audience, where he saw what by now were familiar faces—convicted murderers, rapists, money launderers, pedophiles, drug dealers, and thieves gathered for their weekly worship service with Mathers, a Christian who volunteers at the prison. Mathers knew the men quite well, as he worked with them intermittently as counselor and mentor for several years. As a result of his familiarity—and his unquestioning belief in their sincerity—he had no doubt that these were some of the most devout Christians he had ever met.[1]

He was also familiar with this particular prison, as he walked through its gates dozens if not hundreds of times and as he had spent numerous hours inside the facility. When he finally spoke, Mathers reflected on the prison itself.

"Wakulla Correctional," he said. "Faith-based! *Praaaaiiiiissssseeee God!*" The incarcerated men in the room responded with a loud chorus of "Amen" as arms extended into the air.

"You're in a faith-based prison," he continued.

You ever think about what it took to create a faith-based prison? You ever think about the history of prisons and how only *now* we're getting faith-based prisons? You ever think about the Enemy and about how He's attacking the world? You think about the homosexualing and the drug use and the fornication, and you might just think Satan is winning. But then you think about a *faith! based! prison!*, and you just *know* that God is in charge! *People* can't give you salvation; *only God can do that*! *People* can't make a faith-based prison; *only God can make a faith-based prison*! If you ever wonder who is winning and who is charge, you remember that you're *lucky enough* to live in a faith-based prison, and then you remember that this is evidence of God's divine plan and justice and omnipotence. Pray with me!

Every head in the room bent down.

Capable of housing 1,397 incarcerated men, Wakulla CI is the world's largest faith-based prison, or as Florida's Department of Corrections (DOC) now calls it, a faith- and character-based institution (FCBI).[2] It is also the flagship FCBI in Florida's larger FCBI program, which currently includes three faith- and character-based prisons and thirty-two faith- and character-based correctional dormitories.[3] Roughly half the states in the nation operate faith-based correctional institutions, but they pale in comparison with Florida's more expansive FCBI program. The state of Florida owns and administers these facilities, but in terms of religious programs and programming, prison administrators largely defer to the Christian volunteers and to the incarcerated themselves who run the bulk of the classes and worship services. This arrangement allows volunteers like Mathers to preach with minimal state interference. Perhaps this freedom to "preach the gospel" in a state-owned space is what inspired Mathers on this particular day.

Mathers and like-minded supporters of this novel penological experiment argue that FCBIs not only are the result of divine intervention but are part of God's larger plan to rally the faithful before Armageddon. They see the not-so-subtle hand of God in the walls that surround the incarcerated, in the correctional officers who provide discipline in FCBIs, and in the broader administrative and political structures that created the most extensive faith-based correctional system in human history.

Florida's FCBIs are but one piece of what the authors of a recent report termed "the quiet revolution" that began in the mid-1990s when various levels of government successfully began to reallocate taxpayer funds from state-run welfare and social service programs into faith-based organizations (FBOs) tasked with "tackling society's toughest problems."[4] Though the report's authors overstate their success, they are essentially correct when they highlight that the recipients of government-funded social services today are more likely to receive faith-based services than in previous decades. This "revolution" began in earnest with 1996's Charitable Choice legislation, which not only required the federal government to partner with FBOs to provide social services but also allowed FBOs to provide these services in religious or "sectarian" settings where the FBO retains "control over the definition, development, practice, and expression of its religious beliefs."[5] Charitable Choice also extended to FBOs religious exemptions that allowed religious organizations to discriminate in their hiring practices. In other words, Charitable Choice allowed FBOs to use government funds to provide social services on their terms and in their facilities to recipients of their choice. FBOs also have greater flexibility in their hiring practices, as theological considerations at least partially replace employee rights.[6]

The provisions outlined in Charitable Choice provided the foundation for a new level of partnerships between FBOs and government from the federal to the local. President George W. Bush extended these partnerships several years later when he created the White House Office of Faith-Based and Community Initiatives, which similarly sought to reallocate government-run social services to FBOs and private organizations.[7] Presidents Barack Obama and Donald Trump modified and renamed the program, leaving intact its basic administrative structure and mission.

Charitable Choice and the White House's attempts to empower FBOs are but two examples of "the quiet revolution." This "revolution" impacted some states more than others, with states like Florida leading the movement's vanguard. Florida's FCBIs—and the hundreds of faith-based dorms, prisons, reentry programs, and crime-prevention programs common in most states—are but a few of the examples and evidence of this "revolution's" success. Other examples include government-funded faith-based drug prevention and treatment programs, pregnancy prevention and counseling programs, adoption programs, voucher programs that provide funding for religious education, homeless centers, and soup kitchens, among many others. Proponents of "the quiet revolution" envision a future where seemingly private organizations and FBOs provide most, if not all, of the nation's social services. In this model of state-sanctioned socialization, the government helps create and sustain a "market" of social services where recipients exercise their ability to "shop" for their preferred form of social-service provider.[8] Market logics allow them to choose a faith-based social service provider, who may or may not receive government funding. This overt mingling of religion and government, however, has caused many to question or even to deny "the quiet revolution's" legality.[9]

Over the past several decades, the U.S. Supreme Court's legal decisions combined with congressional legislation to clarify the legal framework for state-funded religious social services. Understandably, the idea of government-funded religious social services seemingly contradicts the popular notion of "separation of church and state"; however, as legal scholars Ira Lupu and Robert Tuttle wrote, "Simplistic metaphors about church-state separation" fail to capture or adequately describe the historical relationship between religion, church, FBOs, and state.[10] Scholars have noted that government-funded religious social services in the United States predate the founding of the nation itself and that they have existed throughout U.S. history.[11] Several legal scholars summarized this history when they described the "'mutual dependence' of faith-based providers and government agencies" that existed since the nation's founding, when the government provided funding for religious orphanages, hospitals, and other groups operating with religious mandates.[12] The government continued to fund religious organizations or organizations with religious components from the nation's founding to the present. While government-funded religious social services have a longer genealogy, "the quiet revolution" is relatively new as it seeks to expand considerably FBOs' involvement in the delivery of social services while closing or curtailing government-run social services, it encourages FBOs to highlight the religious components and aspects of their services, and it empowers FBOs' autonomy in areas traditionally regulated by the government.

Despite the growing trend to empower faith-based social service providers, scholarship has not adequately addressed this topic. Theologians and politicians have espoused the virtues of the FBO movement, lawyers and legal scholars have addressed its legality, and sympathetic social scientists claim to have persuasively demonstrated that FBOs are more effective social service providers than traditional government-run programs. The occasional critic has questioned these studies, but their dissents have not stifled the larger movement. Qualitative analyses of "the quiet revolution," however, are largely absent. This book helps fill that void.[13]

Spiritual Entrepreneurs provides a critical ethnography and history of Florida's FCBIs as a case study to explore "the quiet revolution's" history, development, impact, and implications.[14] It situates the history of FCBIs within the larger contexts of mass incarceration, the New Christian Right's (NCR) political activism, and neoliberal reforms that accompanied mass incarceration and that members of both major political parties supported.[15] This convergence reinforced an imagined binary between the government and the private and it selectively privileged the latter—with religion and faith as necessary or essential components—at the expense of the former. Prison reformers, prison administrators, and politicians who wanted to curtail mass incarceration accepted this imagined binary as fact, and they created FCBIs that replicate this underlying logic.

Drawing from archival research and from extensive ethnographic research inside Florida's FCBIs, this book disagrees with many of the proponents of Florida's FCBIs who argue that these facilities are, in the words of at least one proponent, "guerrilla attacks" on mass incarceration.[16] Where the proponents of FCBIs argue that faith-based correctional facilities are rational or evidenced-based responses to the problem of mass incarceration and to the rampant immorality that fuels it, the history of mass incarceration and FCBIs suggests that both the "problem" and the "solution" share an underlying neoliberal ideology that renders it disingenuous to consider one without the other.[17]

Despite the focus on FCBIs, this book is not about religion per se, nor is it a book about faith or faith-based reforms. Scholarship has repeatedly and persuasively argued that contemporary notions of "religion" and "faith" (and their imagined opposite—the "secular") are relatively recent historical inventions, themselves the products of larger political, economic, sociocultural, and ideological forces.[18] Instead of treating "religion," "faith," and "secularity" as fixed and stable categories, this book explores the implications of the categories "religion" and "faith" in the neoliberal era.[19] Specifically, this book uses the example of Florida's FCBIs to argue, first, that the category of "faith-based reform" is an extension of neoliberal logics, and second, that faith-based reforms function to empower neoliberal economic, political, and sociocultural policies as they replicate the neoliberal epistemologies that favor an imagined private, that create alternatively regulated spheres of state-sanctioned socialization, and that favor allegedly market-based solutions to the nation's economic and social problems (like crime and mass incarceration). FCBIs help create neoliberal subjects and subjectivities as they motivate the faith-based initiative's supporters to prioritize and create an imagined and faith-saturated private sphere at the expense of the government-dominated public sphere. They also create notions of subjectivity and citizenship that replicate neoliberalism's market-driven epistemologies and then teach the incarcerated to embrace these notions as the ideal model of rehabilitation, desistance, and sociopolitical life more broadly.[20]

To demonstrate these claims, this book explores dominant FCBI culture as it is lived and practiced in FCBIs, particularly in the chapel, in classrooms and classes, in study groups, and in other places I accessed routinely over the course of my research. It documents the people who introduce into Florida's FCBIs the ideas that constitute the dominant core, and it follows their message into the prisons via the incarcerated people who embrace and perpetuate it.

This research occurred under the watchful eyes of a combination of chaplains, correctional officers, volunteers, and incarcerated instructors (called "inmate facilitators" in FCBIs) who seemingly share a similar understanding of FCBIs, their mission, and the desired culture. At least one of the aforementioned authority figures was present in almost every room I entered in an FCBI and overheard almost every conversation I had inside them (with the exception of private interviews and discussions), limiting my ability to capture some of the more mundane acts of resistance as incarcerated men and women attempt to subvert the dominant culture described in this book. While I describe the ways that people attempt to subvert dominant FCBI rules and culture in FCBIs, I document these subversions intermittently in the chapters that rely more heavily on ethnographic research where these subversive moments are rarely the focus. Instead, I document these acts of rebellion and disagreement within the context of larger narratives. In short, power is exercised at multiple levels in FCBIs, often to competing ends. My research confirms that multiple subcultures exist in FCBIs; however, due to a combination of factors (including my status as a "free man" combined with the watchful eyes of authority figures), *Spiritual Entrepreneurs* focuses on the dominant culture in FCBIs, which as demonstrated in this book is common and quite stable in every FCBI I entered.

Critical Ethnography

While historical analysis is important to this book, a large portion of the research is based on traditional ethnographic methods such as observation, discussions, and interviews. All of these research protocols invite their own problems. As Peter Metcalf and many other scholars have observed, ethnographic research and participant observation are inherently subjective, partial, and interpretive.[21] These potential problems are not unique to ethnography, as every scholar relies on partial data to construct the narratives relevant to their research agendas, although critics disproportionately level this criticism against ethnographers.

Drawing largely from traditional ethnographic methods, *Spiritual Entrepreneurs* provides a historical analysis and critical ethnography of Florida's FCBIs. Scholars have long used the term "critical ethnography" to describe their work, although they disagree on the meaning and ultimate goal of critical ethnography.[22] Critical ethnography (or as H. L. Goodall Jr. termed it, new ethnography)[23] differs from older, conventional ethnography, which attempts to describe and interpret culture and cultural meanings.[24] According to Jim Thomas, critical ethnographers differ from conventional ethnographers as they "describe, analyze, and open to scrutiny otherwise hidden agendas, power centers, and assumptions that inhibit, repress, and constrain. Critical scholarship requires that commonsense assumptions be questioned."[25] To achieve these goals, sociologist George Noblit contends that critical ethnography calls the researcher to consider how the ethnographer's research is complicit in "acts of domination" that enable or perpetuate oppression.[26]

Collectively, these scholars share a common assumption that critical ethnography should expose oppression and advance social justice.[27] This approach to critical ethnography, however, shares the positivist assumption that social justice has a discreet and achievable outcome, independent from relations of power that manufacture regimes of liberation. Drawing from Michel Foucault, this book recognizes that discourses of social justice and liberation are themselves historically contingent. Instead of using critical ethnography to advance a particular notion of social justice, this book uses critical ethnography to explore hidden regimes of power that the proponents of FCBIs ignore or do not acknowledge.

Admittedly, I tell a story about FCBIs that does not resemble any version of FCBIs as expressed by my informants and interlocutors. To account for the discrepancy, recall that I approached this project interested first and foremost in the faith-based initiative and "the quiet revolution," with particular interest in its history and implications.[28] I am and remain deeply indebted to every person who met with me and who invited me into their homes, services, workshops, worship services, revivals, prisons, cellblocks, dorms, and churches.

These relationships, however, do not require me to simply repeat their stories. I agree with Bruce Lincoln, who wrote that scholarship begins with critical inquiry.[29] That is, scholarship begins when we depart from the stories our research subjects tell about themselves. If I have succeeded in this project, the incarcerated people who live in FCBIs will read this book and hear their stories, voices, and histories. Additionally, scholars or other interested parties will read this book and think about the implications of these stories, voices, and histories.

The ethnographic component of my research ended in 2015 when I moved from Florida, although I returned for several weeks in 2018 to conduct additional archival research, to interview more volunteers and prison administrators, and to visit some of the FCBIs. I returned, however, to find a DOC that was not as receptive to my research. In the intervening years, many of my contacts had retired from the DOC, including many of the chaplains, the head chaplain, and the secretary himself. The new secretary declined my interview request, and the head chaplain consented to an interview only after I submitted a new research proposal that listed, in advance, the questions I intended to ask. The DOC approved the interview, but the free-flow conversations I experienced with numerous DOC employees proved to be remnants of the past as the head chaplain could only answer the vetted questions. The DOC also barred me from entering any prisons or from interviewing prison administrators, with the exception of one chaplain I previously interviewed. While I was not able to reenter the prisons, the information I gathered on this trip reminded me that Florida's FCBIs are perpetually a work in progress as FCBIs evolve based on numerous factors.

As such, this book provides a snapshot of FCBIs from 2013 to 2015. During this period, the DOC gave me permission to "visit Tomoka, Wakulla, and Lawtey Correctional Institutions' Faith and Character-based Programs, and possibly other institutions as well." As I interpreted this approval letter—and as DOC chaplains and administrators interpreted it—for the first and only time (to my knowledge), the DOC allowed a researcher to enter all its FCBIs. While I was not able to visit every FCBI, I attended hundreds of programs, classes, workshops, meetings, seminars, and worship services for almost every religious group in FCBIs. I interviewed incarcerated men and women, senior DOC administrators, and FCBI administrators. Correctional officers also talked to me and contributed to my research, as did elected politicians and dozens of volunteers who talked to me inside the prisons and who met with me in their homes, coffee shops, restaurants, churches, and the reentry homes they operate for the formerly incarcerated. I have not entered an FCBI since August 2015, and while some aspects of FCBIs have changed, research suggests the "core" of the program (as described in this book) remains intact.[30] The FCBI program would not function without it.

American Exceptionalisms

The historical analysis and ethnographic research combine to track the intersection of several larger trends that collectively underlie both the "problem" of mass incarceration and the "solution" that is FCBIs. First, this book explores the intersection and mutual constitution of "tough-on-crime" politics and conservative Christianity.[31] By most standards used to measure religiosity, the United States consistently ranks as one of the more religious nations in the modern world. Our commitment to religion, we often hear, is not a recent development; rather, it is part of the rich heritage we inherit from America's colonial past. The authors of a recent survey of American religiosity expressed as much when they wrote, "From the beginning of the Colonial period, religion has been a major factor in shaping the identity and values of the American people. Despite predictions that the United States would follow Europe's path toward widespread secularization, the U.S. population remains highly religious in its beliefs and practices, and religion continues to play a prominent role in American public life."[32] The authors of this study would have little problem finding scholars of American religious history and Supreme Court justices who would readily agree that comparably high levels of religiosity are part and parcel an inseparable element of the American experiment.[33]

Another, seemingly unrelated, form of American exceptionalism has a much shorter genealogy that most interested parties date back to the late 1970s or early 1980s when Americans criminalized more behaviors, created longer prison sentences for convicted criminals, curtailed the rehabilitative prison model, and created both a culture and an economy centered on what is commonly termed the tough-on-crime approach to criminal justice. Proponents of these changes argued that they were logical and necessary steps to stem rampant criminality that swept the United States since the early 1960s, when rising crime rates combined with student demonstrations, high-profile assassinations, race riots, and civil unrest more broadly to create a criminality-induced culture of fear with no historical precedent in America's collective memory.[34] Americans were scared, and they were prepared to take decisive action to "reclaim the streets" and to "restore order," as they often said. The phrases "law and order" and "tough on crime" became more than catchphrases reporters used to summarize this new American attitude; they became campaign slogans and the basis of myriad new laws designed to literally capture criminals and detain them for extended periods of time in American prisons.[35] Americans not only wanted criminals to do longer time, they wanted criminals to do "harder" time, so they leveraged numerous opportunities to make the experience of "doing time" in American prisons more difficult and unpleasant. Where America previously punished criminals *with* prison, a growing majority of Americans additionally wanted to punish criminals *in* prison. As history demonstrated, their efforts were wildly successful.

From 1925 to 1972, the United States averaged 110 incarcerated people in its federal and state prisons per 100,000 Americans, peaking in 1939 at 149 per 100,000.[36] In 2007, however, several decades after the first significant tough-on-crime laws, the United States created the highest per capita prison population in human history, as it incarcerated 767 people per 100,000, almost five times the global average of 144 per 100,000,[37] and "five to ten times higher than rates in Western Europe and other democracies."[38] In comparison, over half of the world's countries and territories incarcerate fewer than 150 people per 100,000.[39] Many countries incarcerate substantially less, such as Japan, which incarcerates forty-one people per 100,000.[40] To find comparable incarceration rates to those in the United States, one has to look to countries like Rwanda and Russia, which incarcerate 492 and 474 people per 100,000, respectively.[41]

As a result of mass incarceration, the United States, which comprises less than 5 percent of the world's population, incarcerates almost 25 percent of the world's prisoners,[42] including roughly one-third of the world's female prisoners.[43] As these statistics suggest, our plans to incarcerate more offenders for longer periods of time created an almost unprecedented regime of incarceration. Scholars often refer to this regime as the carceral state.[44]

By conventional notions of religiosity, the United States, then, is one of the more deeply religious modern or industrialized nations, and it incarcerates the world's largest per capita inmate population. Admittedly, scholars have long acknowledged the compatibility of tough-on-crime politics and conservative theologies, but this book locates this compatibility within a third factor—the larger economic, political, and sociocultural transformations often termed neoliberalism.[45]

Neoliberalism

As political theorist Wendy Brown argued, "neoliberalism" is an elusive concept that its critics often deploy primarily to criticize the economic and political changes that began in earnest in the 1980s.[46] David Harvey described neoliberal political theory when he wrote that neoliberalism assumes that "human well-being can best be advanced by liberating individual entrepreneurial freedoms and skills within an institutional framework characterized by strong private property rights, free markets, and free trade."[47] Scholars like Dennis LoRusso criticize Harvey for theorizing neoliberalism as a coherent ideology, suggesting instead that we should explore "the myriad contested and dynamic social processes that fall under [neoliberalism's] banner."[48] LoRusso insightfully reminds us that neoliberalism is not a self-contained ideology; rather, neoliberalism is a multivalent process that, while centered on market reforms, necessarily ripples beyond the economy into the political, social, and cultural.[49]

Michel Foucault made a similar argument in his College de France lectures when he addressed neoliberalism's emphasis on *homo oeconomicus*, or economic man. Foucault argued that neoliberal reforms developed in opposition not only to twentieth-century economic policies but to federal social programs like the New Deal and similar government-run programs that targeted poverty, education, and segregation. In Foucault's analysis, proponents of neoliberalism—while focused on economic reforms—are concerned with larger political, ideological, and sociocultural struggles as they reform not only economic policy but the social and political institutions and policies that conflict with neoliberal logics.[50] Wendy Brown described the transformations that accompany neoliberalism when she wrote that "market principles become governing principles applied by and to the state, but also circulating through institutions and entities across society—schools, workplaces, clinics, etc."[51] Neoliberalism pervades everyday life as it transforms institutions like schools, churches, legal bodies, prisons, and other socializing agents who absorb, replicate, and disseminate neoliberal thought. In short, neoliberalism's market logics are not just confined to an imagined economic sphere. Instead, they permeate social relations and socializing institutions.[52] Neoliberalism also transcends political parties as both Republicans and Democrats adopt neoliberal agendas.[53]

Neoliberalism is unapologetically pro-business, and it aims to create this market-friendly environment by shrinking the government, by reducing taxes, and by fundamentally reforming the polity's relationship to the government and economy. The emphasis on entrepreneurial freedoms, free markets, and tax cuts displaces the idea that a strong government should play a major role in statecraft and socialization. Instead, in neoliberal logics, the government defers to the market logics that are thought to advance the nation's collective interests. This smaller neoliberal government will also withdraw or largely curtail its involvement with welfare programs and the delivery of social services. Fewer welfare programs, neoliberal theory holds, will discourage welfare fraud, and by encouraging workfare over welfare, it will encourage able-bodied workers to leave welfare and to become productive, revenue-generating members of society. It will also help eliminate government waste by reallocating welfare programs from federal bureaucrats into the hands of local administrators who can maximize the benefits of social service programs. In other words, neoliberalism impacts more than the economy as it also transforms the government's relationship with two growing populations: Americans who need social services and Americans who do not adhere to neoliberal America's rules and laws.

Loïc Wacquant described in detail the havoc that neoliberal welfare policies wreaked not only on the existing poor but also on a new class of poor people forced into poverty who were unable to find jobs in the new neoliberal economy.[54] To this end, neoliberalism, he concluded, "entailed much 'creative destruction', not only of prior institutional frameworks and powers (even challenging traditional forms of state sovereignty), but also of divisions of labour, social relations, welfare provisions, technological mixes, ways of life and thought, reproductive activities, attachments to the land, and habits of the heart."[55] Part of this "creative destruction" included new social and political policies that created mass incarceration, as U.S. prisons increasingly incarcerated people who under twentieth-century liberalism received social services outside the prison. Wacquant suggests that mass incarceration at best is a symptom of American neoliberalism. At worst, it is a necessary element.

Mass incarceration presents a potential paradox for neoliberalism in the United States, as state-run correctional departments expanded while neoliberal reforms transformed and partially privatized major appendages of the U.S. government. Perhaps the greater irony is that while proponents of neoliberalism argue that deregulation and smaller governments will empower more efficient and productive market-based solutions, they ignore the extensive state efforts that helped create and sustain these allegedly deregulated spaces. Historian Quinn Slobodian noted as much when he argued that neoliberalism redeploys rather than shrinks government.[56] Instead of deregulation, neoliberalism results in alternative regimes of regulation that simultaneously empower and constrict, depending on the objects of their legislative animus. Prisons are an extension of this contradiction as the carceral state grew conterminously with the rise of neoliberalism and as prison administrators increasingly governed prisons with neoliberal principles. Today, prisons across the nation routinely subcontract (i.e., privatize) health care, food services, and rehabilitative programming. Prisons also turn the incarcerated into revenue streams through labor performed for as little as pennies per hour and by charging incarcerated people for phone calls, for items in prison canteens, and with mandatory co-pays for health care and psychological services. Many states also contract with corporations who run for-profit prisons.

As this suggests, bloated state bureaucracies accompanied mass incarceration, seemingly in contradiction with neoliberalism's preference for small government and market-based solutions. Prisons and prison administrators routinely embrace neoliberal thought, however, as they increasingly run American prisons on neoliberalism's market-friendly ideologies where prisons create new markets and new opportunities for private businesses to generate revenue from the over two million people currently incarcerated in the United States. FCBIs are extensions—and perhaps the logical culmination—of this larger trend.

Overview of the Book

Chapter 1 introduces Florida's DOC as it transformed from a government agency that considered rehabilitation its raison d'être to an agency that viewed rehabilitation as an adjunct to its larger mission of detaining and punishing sinner-criminals. This chapter locates this transformation within the larger social and political realignment that accompanied the development of neoliberalism. This chapter then explores the compatibility of neoliberal politics and conservative tough-on-crime theologies that combined to create a cycle where conservative Christians repeatedly argued not only that the state should punish sinner-criminals with more punitive criminal justice policies but that only religion or "faith" can rehabilitate criminals. Their interests at least partially coincided with the interests of senior prison administrators who began to run the DOC as a business. They wanted to reduce the DOC's budget and to provide rehabilitative programming that would reduce recidivism and make the incarcerated more manageable. Tasked with these seemingly contradictory impulses, senior prison administrators realized that faith-based reforms allowed them to achieve both goals.

Chapter 2 documents the compatibility of the "corrections as business" mindset that emerged in the DOC, neoliberal economic reforms, and anti-government theologies popular among the NCR. These factors combined to prioritize an imagined private sphere dominated by faith and faith-based reforms. This prioritization is evident in the legislation that preceded FCBIs, which not only created Florida's first faith-based correctional facilities but also articulated a religio-political ideology that prioritized privatized faith. This ideology provided the basis for the subsequent expansion of Florida's FCBIs.

Chapter 3 explores the alternative rules and policies that regulate participation in FCBIs. Proponents of FCBIs contend that FCBIs are open to all incarcerated people regardless of their religion or lack thereof. Critical analysis, however, suggests not only that participation in FCBIs is limited but that FCBIs are perhaps some of the most tightly regulated government-run spaces in Florida, where extensive participation policies impact the incarcerated, correctional staff, chaplains, and senior administrators like wardens. These spaces are logical outgrowths of neoliberal thought, which champions local government and seemingly market-based solutions.

The next two chapters take the reader inside FCBIs, where they explore the rehabilitative and educational structures that influence socialization in FCBIs. These chapters explore the regime of rehabilitation that exists in FCBIs, paying particular attention to the structures that influence rehabilitation and to the content of the rehabilitative classes that the incarcerated encounter in FCBIs. Despite the religious and racial diversity that exists in FCBIs, a common "core" permeates all FCBIs which reflects the theological concerns of the senior administrators who control the dominant narratives that emerge in these facilities. These administrators recruit and encourage like-minded volunteers who provide the bulk of the facilities' rehabilitative programming, and FCBIs primarily attract incarcerated people who embrace this core. The religious volunteers who compose this core take advantage of the opportunity to "reclaim" state spaces as they criticize identity politics, left-wing politics, and the welfare state. Instead, they teach incarcerated people to rely on God and their religious communities, regardless of the outcome. Together, these chapters highlight the compatibility of dominant Christian theologies in FCBIs and neoliberal thought, as faith-based reforms exist in a world of alternatively regulated spheres of state-sanctioned socialization. These chapters also argue that FCBIs serve neoliberal interests as they create neoliberal subjects.

Based on the ideologies outlined in chapters 4 and 5, FCBIs recruit and train religious leaders from the communities surrounding FCBIs. These volunteers harness the financial resources (and human capital) of their religious communities for the sake of encouraging and supporting religiosity. In the process, these volunteers fulfill the neoliberal goal of mobilizing "private" citizens who provide the bulk of the rehabilitative programming in FCBIs. Chapter 6 addresses these issues as it shows how volunteer labor and faith-based activism are extensions of neoliberal reforms. This book concludes with an analysis of the larger impact, first, of Florida's FCBIs, and second, of "the quiet revolution" more broadly.

1 Transitions

Hard Time and "Tough on Crime" Hit Florida

· ·

In July 1982, M. K. Sawyer, the new superintendent (warden) at Sumter Correctional Institution (SCI) in Bushnell, Florida, introduced himself to the staff and to the incarcerated when he authored two messages that appeared side by side on the first page of the *S.C.I. Sound*, a new collaborative newsletter produced jointly by the incarcerated and prison administrators.[1] To the staff, he wrote, "The Superintendent's purpose is clear and simple: support an environment that affords the inmate an opportunity to make positive time, and concomitantly affords the employee a better opportunity to pursue his career. . . . It's nice to be here at Sumter. I'm pleased with what I have seen so far—especially the Staff."[2] To the incarcerated, he wrote, "I care, I try to be fair. I want to help you make your time, not punish you for your crime. The Courts are for that. . . . My purpose is to make life safe and as pleasant as possible for you and your supervisors, I'll do whatever is legal to accomplish this from both sides of the street. Cheers! Help yourself and at least one other human being today."[3]

Superintendent Sawyer conveyed a clear message to the staff and the incarcerated, who learned that like many of the superintendents working for Florida's Department of Corrections (DOC) in the early 1980s, Sawyer supported what its proponents call the progressive prison philosophy that dominated DOC culture and policies for decades. This philosophy resulted in vocational, educational, recreational, and religious programs designed to help the incarcerated acquire the skills that would help them live crime-free lives outside the prisons. These programs had the centrifugal benefit of keeping the incarcerated busy during their incarceration, and busy people, prison administrators reasoned, were less likely to disrupt the prison or engage in violent or criminal behaviors.

At SCI, the incarcerated joined organizations including the Jaycees, Unity Gavel Club, and Toastmasters.[4] Group members met weekly, and they occasionally faced off in competitions such as chess and softball tournaments, where they shared the prison's softball field with other teams.[5] In

June 1982, for example, the men in C-Dorm defeated the men who worked in Food Service to defend their status as intramural softball champions.[6] When they were not playing softball or chess, the men also exercised, lifted weights, and participated in the SCI boxing program. The best weightlifters and boxers even participated in tournaments where the DOC transported them between facilities to compete.[7]

The men also worked in vocational programs designed to provide them with the "real world" job skills and with the work ethic that would benefit them when they leave prison. SCI had roughly ten such programs and courses of study including a drug counseling program,[8] business education classes,[9] a drafting program,[10] a welding program,[11] G.E.D. classes,[12] a cabinetry program,[13] a graphic arts program,[14] a vocational masonry program,[15] and various courses in the office occupational program.[16] Aspiring journalists also developed their journalism skills working for the *S.C.I. Sound*. The sum total of these classes and programs helped make prison life at SCI, to quote Superintendent Sawyer, "as pleasant as possible," as did the newly painted dorms, new landscaping, soda machines, and the introduction of popular fast food items at the prison canteen.

Like all of the prisons in Florida's DOC, SCI also had a thriving religious education program. Every prison in Florida has a "mission," meaning it caters to a specific demographic. Some prisons specialize in vocational programming, some focus on educational programming, and some prisons cater to the elderly. Every prison incarcerates people, however, and since everyone, the logic goes, is potentially religious, every prison has religious educational and chaplaincy programs. At SCI, these programs included religious programs such as daily religious classes in SCI's chapel where state-funded prison chaplains organized religious services, revivals, and visits from prison ministries.[17] In addition to the "interdenominational worship service" for Protestants, the chaplain at SCI also arranged services in the chapel for religious minorities including Muslims, Jehovah's Witnesses, Spanish-speakers, and Catholics.[18] The *S.C.I. Sound* partially reflected this religious diversity, as articles with titles such as "Introduction to Islam"[19] and "The Light of Truth in Islam"[20] appeared along with articles titled "Have You Met Jesus," "The Centrality of Christ in Your Life,"[21] and "What Is There in Hell That You Want?"[22] The chaplaincy program at SCI existed alongside the other programs, classes, and activities to provide the incarcerated with multiple opportunities to safely and productively serve their time.

The example of SCI is representative of the Florida DOC that Secretary Louie Wainwright created and nurtured over the course of his twenty-six-year tenure as the director of the DOC, where he worked hard to provide incarcerated men and women with a wide array of state-funded programs and services.[23] Every year in the DOC's annual reports and in various other publications like the DOC's employee newsletter, Wainwright and other senior prison administrators documented the many programs and rehabilitative opportunities that reflected what they called their progressive prison philosophy. This philosophy prioritized rehabilitation, and its proponents never apologized for spending taxpayers' money to implement it. Quite the contrary, they argued that the state should invest in rehabilitation as an insurance policy of sorts to prevent future criminal activity and to reduce the likelihood of recidivism.

Incarceration is always tied to larger notions of citizenship and to economic, political, and sociocultural trends, and Wainwright's progressive prisons resonated with and reflected the trends that emerged after the Great Depression and World War II. Wainwright's progressive prisons particularly resonated with New Deal Keynesianism, which identified both the individual and society as legitimate benefactors of government services, which harnessed the government in its efforts to benefit both individuals and society, and which relied on tax-driven bureaucracies to achieve its goals.[24] Scholar Nikolas Rose noted that the American liberalism that emerged in the 1900s relied on progressive, reformatory prisons to produce self-governing citizens, premised on the assumption that the government can help create a stable and productive polity.[25] Neoliberalism, however, rejects these ideas as it replaces liberal assumptions about the state with neoliberal skepticism about the government's ability to solve social and economic problems.

By the mid-1980s, neoliberal reforms were implemented in the United States, where they combined with other factors like the tough-on-crime ethos to jeopardize progressive prisons. Florida, Wainwright learned, was not exempt from these larger trends. When Florida's new governor Bob Martinez asked for Wainwright's resignation in 1987, it sent a powerful message that the era of Florida's progressive prisons was reaching an abrupt end.[26]

In the years that followed Wainwright's departure, Florida's DOC followed national trends as it transformed from a government agency that considered rehabilitation its raison d'être to an agency that viewed rehabilitation as an adjunct to its larger mission of detaining and punishing offenders. Subsequent DOC secretaries occasionally supported rehabilitation, but they rarely replicated Wainwright's passion, and they always had to contend with larger political and cultural environments where "tough on crime" combined with growing DOC budgets to drastically reduce the rehabilitative, vocational, and educational programs that were once common.

Religious programs, however, not only were immune from the larger trend to remove rehabilitative programming, but they actually expanded to fill the emerging void. As state-run educational and vocational programs either disappeared or diminished, volunteer-driven religious educational and recreational programming flourished. According to a report by the U.S. Department of Justice, in 1991, religious activities were the most popular programs in the criminal justice system, with almost one-third of the incarcerated participating in some form of religious activity.[27] Subsequent research suggests that number has since grown.[28] While other forms of rehabilitation became scarce, religious programming not only remained, but it often grew, staffed primarily by unpaid volunteers who taught the incarcerated that personal morality rooted in Protestant religiosity offers the most effective strategy for successful desistance. In Florida, religious programming evolved into the faith- and character-based correctional institutions (FCBI) program that is the subject of this book.

A Brief History of Prisons and Prison Reform

Any attempt to write a comprehensive history of American prisons will necessarily fail, as prison administration and criminal justice are both local and varied. Not only do the nation's fifty-one correctional departments operate autonomously (every state operates its own correctional department in addition to the federal system), but trends that impact an entire state's correctional department might be largely absent in other parts of the country. Despite this diversity in American corrections, however, certain dominant trends emerge. First, the history of prisons in the United States is best characterized as a cycle of innovation and disappointment that begins when prison reformers with lofty goals believe that incarceration can help rehabilitate criminals and reduce crime. Prisons rarely produce those outcomes, prompting reformers to advocate for additional reforms intended to achieve better results, while critics lose faith in prisons' ability to reform criminals at all. Sooner or later, the cycle of reform and disappointment begins anew.

Second, over the past two hundred years, U.S. correctional departments have experimented with various types of prisons and have implemented multiple rehabilitative strategies. From the first U.S. prisons to the present, however, almost every version of the prison included religious socialization as state-sanctioned rehabilitation. Individual prisons come and go as rehabilitative regimes emerge and disappear, but religious services and educational programs are a perennial constant in the nation's protean carceral systems.

Third, changes in prisons and carceral philosophies tend to correspond to the nation's larger sociocultural, political, and economic environments. This relationship between prison reform, culture, and politics began in the wake of the American Revolution when Protestant reformers created the first modern prisons, or as they called them, penitentiaries.[29] Prior to the penitentiary movement, few criminals received lengthy prison sentences as the state's (or church's) default form of punishment. Quite the contrary, most convicted offenders received fines, received corporal punishment, or were executed. Thomas Eddy, Revolutionary-era politician and prison reformer, described the public spectacle that accompanied traditional forms of punishment when he wrote that in colonial North America, "flagellation with the cat-o'-nine tails, burning in the hand or forehead with a hot iron, [and] cropping the ears of prisoners in the pillory, were all common sights to the youngest as well as the oldest portion of the community."[30] As Eddy noted, punishment was primarily public and scarcely included prison sentences as we know them today. Instead, prisons and jails were primarily used as holding cells until trial, until execution, or to extract a confession or fine.

In the late 1700s, however, prison reformers read Enlightenment thinkers like Montesquieu, Cesare Beccaria, Jean-Jacques Rousseau, and others who clamored not only for many of the political changes that inspired the American Revolution but for changes in the administration of criminal justice. These reformers believed that traditional forms of punishment were cruel, barbaric, and ineffective, so they advocated for new and more humane methods of punishment. Some even suggested that the state create entire facilities where sinner-criminals could live in silence in monastic-like environments; communicate only with administrators, chaplains, and God; read their Bibles; recognize the errors in their ways; and become penitent both before God and before the victims of their crimes. They appropriately named these facilities penitentiaries, and they relied on the combination of forced labor and Protestant Christianity to produce self-governing citizens.

The penitentiaries never achieved the reformers' desired goals. Quite the contrary, they created new problems. Instead of fostering nurturing and rehabilitative environments, prison administrators often inflicted violence on the incarcerated, occasionally resulting in deaths. Prisons also taxed mental health, as prolonged periods of solitary confinement drove some people insane and led others to attempt suicide. Trouble then followed the formerly incarcerated outside the prisons, where large numbers of newly released men and women committed additional crimes and recidivated. Prisons also created a financial burden on the communities tasked with financing them, as new prisons cost hundreds of thousands of dollars and rarely generated a profit via forced labor.

Based on a record of failure, prison reformers and other interested parties faced an important decision: do they jettison the new experiment in state-sanctioned criminal justice or modify the facilities to achieve some other goal? State governments overwhelmingly chose the latter, and a short-term experiment became long-term state policy, as once state governments built penitentiaries, they rarely returned to earlier and traditional methods of punishment.[31]

The Jacksonian era witnessed another wave of prison reform as states built additional prisons and tried to reform existing prisons to facilitate rehabilitation. Prison reform in this period centered on the debate between two competing models of reform, both premised on the combination of religious education and forced labor. The first, the Auburn system, called for the incarcerated to labor in silence during the day and to retire at night to individual cells where they would continue to live in silence. Correctional staff, chaplains, and God were their only conversation partners. The competing system, the Pennsylvania system, similarly called for silence as incarcerated men and women labored and slept in individual cells. The Pennsylvania system was the more expensive model, as every cell had to be large enough to accommodate both a bed and a work station, complete with its own set of tools. For this reason, among others, most states preferred the Auburn system and all but a few of the prisons built during the Jacksonian period attempted to replicate it.

Both the Auburn and the Pennsylvania models failed to achieve their desired goals of rehabilitation and profit, so by the mid-1800s, prison reformers were prepared to rethink rehabilitation while critics increasingly believed the prisons should simply punish criminals and serve as deterrents for would-be criminals. The Civil War soon silenced both groups as the nation fought against Southern secession and slavery. Conversations about prison reform reemerged in the wake of the Civil War, although Northern and Southern states responded differently.

Northern states again experimented with various regimes of rehabilitation, premised on the goal of producing God-fearing capitalists. Southerners followed suit during the period of Southern Reconstruction, when northerners controlled the levers of political power in the South. When Reconstruction ended in 1877, however, every formerly Confederate state except Virginia transferred the bulk of its prisoners to convict labor camps outside the prisons.[32] Convict lease systems were the South's response to the Thirteenth Amendment to the U.S. Constitution, which outlawed race-based slavery but still classified convicts as slaves of the state. The Thirteenth Amendment states, "Neither slavery nor involuntary servitude, *except as a punishment for crime whereof the party shall have been duly convicted*, shall exist within the United States, or any place subject to their jurisdiction."[33] In other words, while the Thirteenth Amendment outlawed race-based slavery and the private ownership of slaves, it legalized crime-based slavery. In 1871, the Supreme Court of Virginia affirmed this interpretation of the Thirteenth Amendment when it wrote that a convicted felon "has, as a consequence of his crime, not only forfeited his liberty, but all his personal rights except those which the law in its humanity accords to him. He is for the time the slave of the State."[34] The Thirteenth Amendment, therefore, transferred the administration of slaves from southern slave owners to the state, who then subcontracted them back to white, wealthy southerners where convict laborers worked upwards of fourteen hours per day. For the bulk of these laborers, camp-subsidized Protestant services provided their only respite.

Convict lease systems generated substantial profits both for the camp operators and for the states and counties that leased convicted criminals. Despite their profitability, southern states began to close their convict labor camps in the early 1900s and transfer the convicted back to conventional prisons. Convict labor camps attracted negative attention not only because people increasingly viewed them as surrogates for the southern cause of race-based slavery but also because stories of prisoner abuse, torture, and even murder became common. On the eve of the Great Depression, the overwhelming majority of the South's convicts were back in brick-and-mortar prisons as states closed their convict lease systems.[35]

As prisoners returned to prisons en masse, prison reformers seemed poised to revisit the issue of rehabilitation. A series of events including World War I, the Depression, and World War II sidelined their efforts as the nation focused on other issues; however, the spirit of reform reappeared in the mid-1900s when the so-called progressive prison philosophy spread through prisons, prompting the carceral dynamics documented at the beginning of this chapter. These changes overlapped with the development of New Deal Keynesianism which called for heavy government expenditures on welfare programs and the social safety net. Progressive prisons and New Deal Keynesianism shared the common assumptions, first, that the government (and government regulation) could help stabilize society and provide for the common welfare, and second, that taxpayers would subsidize these programs. Prison administrators embraced this ideology as they lobbied the government for the capital investments that would facilitate mass rehabilitation, premised on the notion that rehabilitation translated into individuals suited to live crime-free lives in the era of liberal capitalism. While prison administrators and sympathetic politicians built rehabilitative prisons, prisons' detractors began to attack not only the rehabilitative ideal but the necessity of prisons itself.

In the 1960s and 1970s, scholars, activists, politicians, and reformers across the political spectrum criticized status-quo carceral policies and practices as they shared a common assumption that prisons did not prevent crime or prepare the incarcerated to successfully navigate twentieth-century capitalism. Their similarities stopped there, however, as some critics were ready to abolish prisons and to rethink criminal justice policies from the ground up, so to speak, while other critics wanted to expand the use of incarceration and to make life harder for the incarcerated. One side would ultimately win, although it had to wait several decades to celebrate its penultimate victories.

Prison abolitionists were on one side of this debate, where they argued that prisons were incapable of substantively reforming the convicted and that they constituted cruel and inhumane punishment.[36] To understand their position, consider that when Quakers and evangelicals built the first modern American penitentiaries in the wake of the American Revolution, they imagined the new facilities would introduce more humane methods of punishment, that the prisons would reform wayward sinner-criminals by exposing them to intense Christian socialization, and that the prison's mere existence would deter crime by providing potential criminals with a perennial reminder of the fate that followed criminal behavior. Almost two hundred years later, the prisons arguably failed on all accounts. Extended periods of incarceration did not end corporal punishment; rather, they trapped men and women inside prisons, where prison administrators routinely used corporal punishment to control and discipline them. High recidivism rates reminded prison reformers that prisons did not provide enough prosocial behaviors to reduce future criminal behaviors. The modern prison, abolitionists wagered, was a failed experiment in state-sanctioned punishment.

Michel Foucault similarly critiqued the penitentiary in *Discipline and Punish*, where he argued that modern prisons were the results of new, and perhaps more insidious, techniques of governance.[37] Along with schools, reformatories, and a host of new state-sanctioned institutions, prisons functioned to produce docile, obedient, and self-monitoring subjects. Though the Christian architects of the first modern penitentiaries claimed that they offered a more humane form of punishment, Foucault argued that the penitentiaries punished the convicts' bodies through forced labor and extensive incarceration and that they attempted to reform the criminals' soul through religious socialization. As a result, the penitentiaries extracted a greater toll on the convicts as they demanded the convicted internalize their wretchedness. Far from offering a benign reform, prisons created new and more sinister methods of punishment.

Convinced that prisons were doomed to fail, criminologists and even the federal government started writing the prison's obituary. The National Advisory Commission on Criminal Justice Standards and Goals stated as much in its 1973 report when it wrote, "The prison, the reformatory, and the jail have achieved only a shocking record of failure. There is overwhelming evidence that these institutions create crime rather than prevent it. Their very nature ensures failure."[38] Based on this insight, the Commission suggested, "In view of the bankruptcy of penal institutions, it would be a grave mistake to continue to provide new settings for the traditional approach in corrections." The Commission also suggested a ten-year moratorium on the construction of new prisons, adding that "existing institutions for juveniles should be closed."[39] Echoing this sentiment, historian David Rothman, author of the award-winning *Discovery of the Asylum*, predicted a stark change in carceral policy when he wrote, "We have been gradually escaping from institutional responses and one can foresee the period when incarceration will be used still more rarely than it is today."[40] Criminologist and law professor Norval Morris made an even bolder statement when he predicted that by the end of the twentieth century, "prison in [its current] form will become extinct, though the word may live on."[41] Collectively, these voices represented a growing consensus among some professionals in the 1970s who predicted that the experiment with incarceration was reaching its end.

While some critics wanted to abolish prisons (or drastically curtail their use), others wanted to expand prisons, to remove rehabilitative programs, and to make them more punitive. These desires, among others, paved the way for the carceral state. As political scientist Marie Gottschalk wrote, "The construction of the carceral state was the result of a complex set of historical, institutional, and political developments. No single factor explains its rise."[42] While mass incarceration is not the result of any single factor, most scholars agree that while the proverbial seeds were sown in the decades preceding the 1960s, the roots of mass incarceration lie in the 1960s. The combination of the racialization of crime, urban riots, antiwar protests, realignments in the country's major political parties, transformations in the economy that resulted in fewer jobs for low-skilled workers, and the perception of rising crime rates convinced many Americans that a historically unprecedented crime wave threatened to completely unravel the very social fabric that held the nation together.

Scholar Jerome Miller summarized crime rates in the 1960s when he noted, "The decade from 1963 to 1973 saw reported murders double from 4.5 per 100,000 to 9.07. Assault rose from 91.4 to 193.6, Robbery from 61.5 to 177.9, and Theft from 1,128.5 to 2,431.6."[43] Based on the perception of skyrocketing crime rates, journalist Charles Silberman described the fear that gripped many Americans in the wake of these increases when he wrote, "Since the early 1960s, the United States has been in the grip of a crime wave of epic proportions. According to the Federal Bureau of Investigation's *Uniform Crime Reports*, the chance of being the victim of a major violent crime such as murder, rape, robbery, or aggravated assault nearly tripled between 1960 and 1976; so did the probability of being the victim of a serious property crime, such as burglary, purse-snatching, or auto theft."[44] Not only has the frequency of crime changed, Silberman argued, but the nature of the crimes themselves transformed. In the past, he wrote, criminals engaged in premeditated crime where they specifically targeted individual victims. By the 1970s, however, murder, rape, and robbery happened at random, suggesting that everyone is always a potential victim. Silberman was also concerned by the "turn toward viciousness, as well as violence" that accompanied the new generation of crime, suggesting that 1970s' criminals were more depraved and callous.[45]

Politicians saw the rising crime rates a decade before Silberman analyzed them and they capitalized on crime to advance their political agendas. Notably, Barry Goldwater made "law and order" a central piece of his 1964 presidential campaign where he linked the epidemic of crime to liberal campaigns like the war on poverty, and by default, to New Deal Keynesianism.[46] Instead of helping America's "have nots," the war on poverty, he argued in racially coded language, inspired a new generation of lazy Americans more prone to commit crime than to commit themselves to an honest day's work. Goldwater's message resonated with the evolving Republican Party, and despite his electoral defeat, Goldwater's message survived. Journalist Christian Parenti noted the impact of Goldwater's candidacy when he wrote, "Goldwater lost to Johnson, but the Goldwater message won."[47] Several years later, Richard Nixon resuscitated Goldwater's message when he bemoaned the sharp rise of crime. In explicitly racial language, Nixon linked rising crime rates to the civil rights movement, suggesting the latter caused the former.[48]

Goldwater and Nixon's comments were but two pieces of the larger and growing political movement that positioned "tough on crime" as mainstream issues in conservative politics. The development of federal agencies and legislation such as the Law Enforcement Assistance Administration, the Office of Law Enforcement Assistance, and the Omnibus Crime Control and Safe Streets Act of 1968 similarly placed crime as a federal legislative and administrative concern.

Part and parcel of the tough-on-crime movement was the additional desire to remove rehabilitative programs from prison, both as a deterrence against criminal behavior and because interested parties increasingly doubted that the incarcerated can become better citizens. Prominent political scientist James Q. Wilson suggested the latter when he condemned as naïve and perhaps even dangerous the larger idea that offenders can fundamentally change their basic character in prison. He wrote, "It requires not merely optimistic but heroic assumptions about the nature of man to lead one to suppose that a person, finally sentenced after (in most cases) many brushes with the law, and having devoted a good part of his youth and young adulthood to misbehavior of every sort, should, by either the solemnity of prison or the skillfulness of a counselor, come to see the error of his ways and to experience a transformation of his character."[49] The implication was clear: once a criminal, always a criminal.

That same year, three criminologists published their now-famous "Nothing works" essay where they argued that all rehabilitative efforts have failed to reduce prison recidivism and criminal behavior.[50] The so-called Martinson study provided academic capital and validation to the growing call for more punitive criminal justice policies. Collectively, scholars such as Wilson and Martinson helped persuade more Americans to add the rehabilitative ideal or the progressive prison philosophy to the list of failed liberal social experiments. Emboldened by these studies—and by shifting cultural, political, economic, and religious trends more broadly—correctional departments began to curtail rehabilitative programs.

In summary, in the 1960s and '70s a growing portion of Americans embraced the tough-on-crime movement as academics like Martinson questioned the underlying philosophies that supported progressive or rehabilitative prisons.[51] Academic analysis fed the tough-on-crime movement as more Americans were ready to incarcerate more offenders in more prisons where they would serve harder time. This movement impacted America's criminal justice system in the 1970s, where the nation's incarcerated population increased by 74 percent. This stark increase, however, pales in comparison to the increase that occurred in the following decade.

The New Christian Right Embraces "Tough on Crime"

One group in particular embraced the punitive turn in American corrections in the 1960s and 70s: the Christians who constitute what scholars often term the New Christian Right (NCR). The NCR consists of conservative Christians who primarily identify as evangelicals and fundamentalists, along with Christians with similar theologies who do not embrace either term.[52] The NCR was (and is) a diverse group, but it consists primarily of white Protestants who favor Christian nationalism, who are skeptical of the government and of government regulation, who advocate for what they call Bible-based social and cultural norms, and who embrace capitalism as God's preferred economy.[53]

Scholars have long noted the compatibility of the NCR and tough-on-crime criminal justice policies, although they disagree on the root cause. Some argue that conservative Christian theology (with its emphasis on depravity and human corruption) predisposes conservative Christians to embrace these policies, while others argue that their support for tough-on-crime criminal justice policies are the lingering results of Christian racism that influenced conservative Christianity after World War II. Michael Tonry, professor of criminal law, voiced the former position when he wrote, "Many [evangelical Protestants] see crucial criminal justice issues in terms of moral right and moral wrong and are likewise closed to the possibility of compromise. If criminals and drug users are immoral, well, then they deserve neither empathy nor compassion. They have sinned, and they should be severely punished for it. That's that."[54] James Whitman expressed a similar sentiment when he wrote, "It is clear that American harshness has something to do with the strength of its religious tradition, and especially its Christian tradition."[55]

Historian Aaron Griffith argued the punitive turn in conservative Christianity was not inevitable or endemic to Christianity.[56] Griffith noted that conservative Christians were interested in crime in the wake of World War II when ministers like Billy Graham identified crime not only as a social problem but as a religious problem as well. The solution to crime and delinquency, Graham argued, lie in religious, not state, intervention. "Jesus Christ is the only control," Graham preached in 1957.[57] "He alone can help you live a clean life." Like other Protestant ministers in the 1950s, Graham taught that widespread revivals and mass conversions would cure crime and criminality. In the 1960s, however, Graham and other influential ministers began to advocate for a different solution to the nation's crime problem. The FBI's Uniform Crime Reports documented rising crime rates in the 1960s as ministers like Graham associated crime with the inner cities and with black Americans.

Historian Khalil Gibran Muhammad addressed the history of the association of blackness with criminality when he argued that in the wake of the Civil War, white Americans viewed newly freed black Americans as predisposed to commit crimes.[58] White Americans believed that class and education could explain white criminality, but black criminality, they wagered, was the result of something more internal—the result of character or moral defects inherent in blackness. When crime rates rose in the 1960s, white Americans like Graham equated the surge in crime with black inner cities, which he routinely characterized—in highly racialized language— as cesspools of crime. "[O]ur city streets have been turned into jungles of terror, mugging, rape, and death," he preached from a pulpit in North Carolina.[59] Graham repeated this message across the country, and when he wanted to survey one of these "jungles" and its black residents, he flew over Watts in a helicopter, clad in a bulletproof vest.

Graham was not alone in his characterization of urban, black America as a threat to white Christianity. A fundraising brochure from a Christian missionary organization repeated this characterization when it stated, "Almost 200,000 people live in squalor, deprivation and perpetual hopelessness in a one square mile area of East Harlem in New York. . . . Most of them are Puerto Rican or Negro. The majority have never lived outside the ghetto, never seen a normal middle class [sic] home or the grass and trees of an American suburb. Most have never known traditional family life. They are untouched by the influence of Christianity. Their plight is typical of youngsters in the ghettos of every major American city."[60] This brochure, like Graham, racialized crime as it juxtaposed black criminality with white rural or suburban Christianity.

Concurrent with the racialization of crime, some ministers increasingly enlisted the government's help to fight crime through tougher criminal justice policies. Jesus, it seemed, would no longer suffice. Graham himself embraced this new approach to fighting crime when he specifically advocated for Congress to enact "tough new laws" that would punish criminals with longer and more punitive prison sentences.[61] Conservative Christians throughout the country followed Graham's lead as ministers preached from pulpits across the nation for tougher criminal justice laws.

In summary, by the 1970s conservative Christians joined other critics who were skeptical of prison's ability to rehabilitate and who also believed that punitive prison sentences could deter crime and criminality. They did not abandon their belief that Jesus could prevent crime in the long term, but they also believed that the government should intervene immediately to remove criminals from society, secure the streets, and detain criminals in prisons. Many of them also shared a contempt of government-run social services and skepticism of the government's ability to solve social, political, and economic problems, preferring a comparably smaller government. In hindsight, this alliance between conservative Christians and critics of rehabilitative correctional policies helped pave the foundation for the criminal justice reforms that would follow.

"Tough on Crime" in the 1980s

The NCR shared tough-on-crime criminal justice policies with the evolving Republican Party, which dominated American politics in the 1980s beginning with the election of President Ronald Reagan in 1980. Reagan's major political agendas are largely evident in the speech he delivered on November 13, 1979, when he announced his candidacy. In this speech, Reagan offered a narrative of American decline and he outlined an optimistic assessment of America's future, provided that the nation embraces the economic philosophy that would later be termed "Reaganomics." In hindsight, not only did this speech outline many of the ideas that would come to define Reagan's presidency, but it also articulated the philosophical and political framework that would later justify Florida's faith- and character-based correctional institutions (FCBIs).

Reagan argued that the United States was experiencing a crisis and that he would consider his election "as proof that the people of the United States have decided to set a new agenda" to solve this crisis.[62] Reagan bemoaned that this crisis involved a deteriorating economy caused largely by a government that was too big for its own good. "The people have not created this disaster in our economy," he told the crowd. "The federal government has. It has overspent, overestimated, and over regulated." Reagan promised to boost the economy by cutting taxes, by reducing regulations, by limiting the government, and by empowering what his supporters would call the private sphere that existed outside government. In short, Reagan articulated the basic framework for what is often called neoliberal economics. Though economists like Milton Friedman and Friedrich Hayek began to develop the intellectual and economic basis for neoliberalism decades earlier, it became ingrained in the United States during Reagan's administration.

Reagan also envisioned a bright American future based on a federal government that recognized its limits and that deferred to the time-honored "institutions which are custodians of the very values upon which civilization is founded—religion, education, and above all, family." As an extension of these priorities, he promised to reduce the federal government's role in welfare programs,[63] suggesting instead that local governments and communities should care for the needy. "There should be a planned, orderly transfer of such functions to states and communities," Reagan stated, "and a transfer with them of the sources of taxation to pay for them." This reallocation of government priorities would also reduce wasteful spending, he argued, as it pried social services from the hands of bloated government bureaucracies.

Reagan's candidacy speech is also important because it highlighted what became an important aspect of his presidency: the union between the Republican Party and politically active conservative Christians, or the NCR. Scholars have long noted that the NCR found in candidate Reagan a politician who was sympathetic to the religio-political philosophy they developed and cultivated over the preceding decades. Beset by their repeated defeats in the so-called culture wars and by a government hostile to their collective interests, members of the NCR advocated for a new breed of politically active conservative Christians who would harness the government's power to restore the spiritual (i.e., Protestant) foundation upon which, as Reagan suggested, "civilization is founded."

Reagan was no stranger either to politics or to the NCR, but even the conservative Christians who were not familiar with Reagan when he delivered his candidacy speech soon found themselves sympathetic to his agenda when, toward the end of his speech, he made a few statements that piqued their interests. America, Reagan said, "hungers for a spiritual revival." Its problems were not just economic and political, Reagan argued, but America also suffered a self-induced malady resulting from a religious deficiency. Reagan promised that he would provide a remedy.

Reagan also channeled Christian sensibilities when he quoted the famous seventeenth-century Puritan John Winthrop. America, Reagan concluded, "shall be as a city upon a hill. The eyes of all people are upon us so that if we shall deal falsely with our God in this work we have undertaken and so cause Him to withdraw His present help from us, we shall be made a story and byword throughout the world." This sentiment resonated with Christians who embraced the idea that America's fate was linked inseparably to its relationship with God.

Reagan solidified the support of the NCR the following year when he told a crowd of 15,000 evangelicals at the Reunion Arena in Dallas, Texas, "I know you can't endorse me because this is a non-partisan crowd, but . . . I want you to know that I endorse you."[64] In other words, Reagan assured his Christian supporters that he shared their interests and agendas—a message that reverberated throughout the NCR. Decades later, historian Steven Miller described this quote as "perhaps the most famous lines of the Age of Evangelicalism."[65]

Perhaps more than any other speech, Reagan's speech at the Reunion Arena cemented the evolving union not only between the NCR and the Republican Party but also between conservative Christianity and neoliberal politics. Historians Kevin Kruse and Darren Dochuk have noted the long and comfortable relationship between corporate politics and the NCR, but the Reagan administration witnessed and helped usher in a new and explicit alliance between the NCR and neoliberal economics.[66] Scholar David Harvey described as much when he criticized the "unholy alliance" of conservative Christians and pro-business economics that galvanized under candidate Reagan to create a new Republican Party centered on a shared contempt of big government liberalism and the Keynesian welfare state.[67] The smaller government that Reagan proposed would potentially benefit the NCR and big business, as it would create an economic and cultural vacuum that business and NCR activists were eager to fill.

Reagan also united these diverse parties as he articulated a theory of individuality and citizenship that appealed to both the NCR and big business. Political scientist William Connolly described their shared ideals as the "evangelical-capitalist resonance machine," meaning the common ethos that united business and the NCR. Channeling the prosperity gospel that emerged in the late 1800s, this ethos positioned capitalism as the guarantor not only of economic freedom but of spiritual independence as well.[68] These *"affinities of spirituality"*[69] equated governmental regulation—be it limits on business or legislation that opposed Christian nationalism—with slavery in opposition to God's preferred form of socioeconomic relations, and it viewed welfare reforms as unnecessary state expenses that not only wasted tax dollars but also similarly incentivized Americans to rely on the government instead of God and the market. As Bethany Moreton wrote, the alliance between "laissez-faire champions of the free market unevenly yoked to a broad base of evangelical activists . . . was crafted in corporate-funded think tanks and conservative economics departments."[70] The resulting ethos appealed to businesses and to the NCR as it posited individual initiative and entrepreneurialism as the sources of economic and religious liberty. It also sacralized labor both in the market and in religion, as laboring in the market prepared the citizen for the religious struggle that would please God and potentially result in eternal salvation. Linda Kintz summarized how this ethos potentially bound "a large portion of the capitalist class to white and middle-class workers by mixing family, gender, religious, and economic themes together."[71] This ethos also enabled Reagan's color-blind approach to sociopolitical issues and criminal justice policies that appealed to white Christian Americans and that fueled the "war on drugs" and mass incarceration, as it downplayed the role of institutional and structural oppression.[72]

Having solidified this powerful political union, Reagan turned his vision into legislation. President Reagan cut corporate and personal taxes; he reduced estate taxes; and he passed multiple bills that deregulated banking, interstate commerce, and various other businesses and industries. Reagan also fulfilled his promise to defund much of the social safety net as he slashed funding for drug treatment, drug prevention, mental health, and educational programs to a fraction of their previous funding levels.[73] While he supported legislation that favored businesses and while he reformed social services, Reagan also supported the criminal justice policies that fueled mass incarceration.

Scholars have written at length on criminal justice policies during the so-called Reagan Revolution, and while a detailed analysis of the minutiae of Reagan's criminal justice policies is not germane to this project, important elements of Reagan's criminal justice policies are worth reviewing.

Prior to the criminal justice reforms of the 1980s, states and local governments were the primary authors and administrators of criminal justice laws. That changed drastically under the Reagan administration, which passed a series of far-reaching criminal justice laws that federalized criminal justice policies, created more punitive criminal justice policies, and nurtured "tough on crime" in the process. In other words, Reagan, the champion of small government, created enormous federal criminal justice machinery unprecedented in American history.

To justify this expansion, Reagan resuscitated the idea of the "war on drugs," a phrase Nixon popularized during his administration. As scholars have noted, Americans in the early years of Reagan's administration did not share Reagan's preoccupation with drugs and drug users. In fact, less than 2 percent of Americans viewed drug use as the country's major issue.[74] Reagan, however, made the war on drugs a centerpiece of his national agenda as he framed the alleged crime epidemic as an extension of the Manichean battle between good and evil, with drug-using criminals on one side and white, law-abiding Christian Americans on the other.

He repeatedly articulated this message in multiple speeches including his speech at the annual convention of the National Association of Evangelicals. Echoing the sentiment he articulated in his candidacy speech, Reagan again argued that America's success is tethered to its relationship with God and to its ability to avoid sin. Drug abuse, he suggested, ranked high on the list of sins. Nancy Reagan repeated these ideas when she said, "Life can be great, but not when you can't see it. So, open your eyes to life: to see it in the vivid colors that God gave us as a precious gift to His children, to enjoy life to the fullest, and to make it count. Say yes to your life. And when it comes to drugs and alcohol just say no."[75] President Reagan repeated this message in numerous speeches as it became a central element in his war on drugs.

Reagan's attempt to mobilize Americans' passions to fight his war on drugs was remarkably successful, and after two years of concentrated and disciplined messaging, Congress passed the first of several wide-sweeping criminal justice policies—the Comprehensive Crime Control Act (CCCA) of 1984—which Reagan immediately signed into law the day after it passed in the Senate. Simply put, the CCCA was the most extensive federal criminal justice law in American history. In a passage that bears citing at length, Christian Parenti summarized the bill when he wrote, "The act created federal preventive detention so that judges could deny bail to defendants, established mandatory minimum sentences and a 'sentencing commission' to devise strict sentencing guidelines, eliminated federal parole, and toughened mandatory minimum sentences for use of firearms in the commission of federal crimes. It also increased the maximum fines leveled in drug cases, scaled back the insanity defense, . . . boosted the penalties for political hostage taking and other acts of 'terrorism,' and . . . made it a federal crime to misuse credit cards or computers."[76] The law also included new asset forfeiture provisions, which increased the government's ability to seize assets from accused drug dealers. In short, the war on drugs provided the political capital for the CCCA, but as the above passage suggests, it impacted more than drug users. Additionally, the CCCA created a host of criminal justice policies that would immediately result in more criminals prosecuted for more crimes who would serve longer prison sentences.

While Reagan and the Republican Congress passed federal legislation, they simultaneously nurtured the tough-on-crime culture that had its strongest impact at the local level. As law professor and criminologist John Pfaff described, local criminal justice policies, often at the county level, account for the majority of criminal prosecutions and convictions. According to Pfaff, "Although it is true that prisons are run by the states, and that state criminal codes define the conduct that can result in prison time, the number of people in those prisons is effectively determined at the county level."[77] Pfaff argues that scholars often overstate the impact of federal laws like legislation associated with the War on Drugs. Perhaps because it is beyond the scope of his project, however, Pfaff largely ignores the political pressure that nurtures "tough on crime." This pressure manifests most potently at the local level, but the federal government and politicians like Reagan nurtured it at the national level.

The impact of Reagan-era criminal justice policies is evident in America's skyrocketing population of incarcerated men and women. Consider that during the 1980 presidential election, U.S. prisons incarcerated 329,122 people, or 140 men and women per 100,000 Americans.[78] Ten years later, however, the incarcerated population increased 134 percent to a total of 441,442 people, or 293 men and women per 100,000 Americans (a 111 percent increase).[79] As these statistics suggest, the so-called Reagan Revolution simultaneously created the highest per capita incarcerated population in U.S. history, and it positioned the United States as a country with increasingly punitive criminal justice laws and policies. Research has repeatedly demonstrated that members of the NCR were statistically more likely to support these policies.[80]

President Reagan's criminal justice, economic, and political reforms were an example of a larger and growing ideology that Americans increasingly embraced over the next several decades. This cycle included several core components: America's success hinges on its relationship to God, crime and drug use are evidence and the results of sin, government programming feeds rather than hinders these problems, and the private sector (particularly religion) is uniquely suited to correct and prevent sin and criminality. These ideas became an important element of conservative politics as conservatives repeatedly criminalized more behaviors and punished these new "criminals" with longer and more punitive prison sentences, and these ideas became more politically salient as liberals increasingly adopted them in the 1990s.[81]

"Tough on Crime" in the 1990s

As historian Michael Flamm noted, liberals in the 1980s and early 1990s had trouble articulating a clear, coherent, and politically viable vision on crime.[82] That began to change in the run up to the 1992 presidential campaign, particularly after the Democrats' presidential candidate, William Jefferson Clinton, embraced "tough on crime" as a constituent element of larger transformations in the Democratic Party.[83] Clinton discussed these changes when he claimed to represent a "new Democrat" and a new Democratic Party, one that wanted to make a new covenant with America. "Make no mistake," Clinton said, "this new covenant means change, change in my party, change in our leadership, change in our country, change in the lives of every American."[84] Specifically, this new covenant acknowledged the limits of the welfare state, it took a tougher stance on crime, and it marshaled the government's power to expand and enhance neoliberal markets. Americans supported Clinton's agenda, and he defeated his Republican rival to become the forty-second president of the United States.

Political scientist Melinda Cooper described how Clinton's "new covenant" resonated with neoliberal theories on a range of issues including poverty management and the role of the state, centered on downsizing the government.[85] Clinton repeatedly described as much, particularly in the 1996 State of the Union speech, where he announced the obituary for big government. "We know big government does not have all the answers," Clinton told the nation.[86] "We know there's not a program for every problem. We have worked to give the American people a smaller, less bureaucratic government in Washington. And we have to give the American people one that lives within its means. The era of big government is over."

Clinton claimed to shrink the government; however, scholars persuasively argued that the changes that occurred in the Clinton administration resembled those of his recent predecessors, as Clinton did not reduce the government as much as he transformed it.[87] This is particularly evident in economic reforms, where Clinton downplayed the state's role as curator of the economy as he supported legislation like the North American Free Trade Agreement. This is also evident in Clinton's signature welfare reform, which did not eliminate welfare as much as reallocate it to faith-based organizations (FBOs) and other seemingly private organizations.

Clinton also transformed and even enlarged the criminal justice system as a result of the Violent Crime Control and Law Enforcement Act. Scholars repeatedly argued that Democrats' interest in "law and order" predate the Clinton administration, but Clinton's crime bill codified into law some of these policies and ideas.[88] Some of the bill's major provisions included tougher criminal sanctions, $9.7 billion in funding for prison construction, funding for 100,000 new police officers, and federal funding for crime prevention programs. It also expanded the category of crimes that could result in capital punishment, and it instituted a "zero-tolerance" policy at the federal level, which instructed law enforcement agents to prosecute all offenders without exception.[89] In short, Clinton's crime bill meant that a larger police force would patrol American streets, where they would arrest more criminals who would serve longer prison sentences. The bill also impacted the day-to-day lives of men and women inside prisons, as it eliminated their ability to get Pell Grants while incarcerated and it also prevented them from lifting weights in prison. In his State of the Union address in 1994, President Clinton not only urged Congress to pass the crime bill but also declared his support for a federal "three-strikes" law that would result in life sentences for repeat offenders.[90] With leaders of both major political parties supporting tough-on-crime policies, Clinton's crime bill, the largest anticrime bill in American history, became law on September 13, 1994.

Despite these sweeping changes, many Americans believed Clinton's crime bill did not do enough to combat crime. Republicans wanted to recapture the tough-on-crime vote, but with Democrats making a move to the right on crime, conservatives explored new strategies to separate themselves from the "new Democrats." As evidenced by the Republicans' policies in the 1994 midterm congressional elections, their new strategy included several policies related to criminal justice. They advocated for a more punitive approach that included longer prison sentences, they vowed to defund or otherwise eliminate prevention programs, and they doubled down on Reagan's theories of crime and criminality.

For decades, Republicans argued that criminality resulted from individual moral failings, not from environmental causes such as racism or poverty; however, the "lack of morality/religion" trope returned as a cornerstone of Republican rhetoric in the 1990s. Moral people do not commit crimes, they reasoned, and since religion is the source of morals, a religious response to crime is not only reasonable but proper.[91] The roots of this new strategy lie in the decades leading up to the 1994 election, but they coalesced into policy during the Clinton administration.

The Heritage Foundation, an influential conservative think tank founded in 1973, was a primary proponent of the attempt to reframe criminality as an essentially moral or religious issue, and it published or sponsored a series of influential reports that argued its case. Many of these reports linked moral depravity with failed liberal policies in general, but they often singled out Johnson's Great Society as the most egregious culprit. The Great Society was doomed to fail, they argued, because it taught people to rely on secular government instead of relying on God and family, the time-tested pillars of American society. The remedy for the Great Society involved an abandonment of liberal policies, tougher anticrime laws, and a larger public role for religion. As William P. Barr, former attorney general under President George H. W. Bush and future attorney general under President Donald Trump, argued in one of these reports, "I think the best hope for genuine community renewal lies in fostering the rebirth of those traditional institutions which emerge from the communities themselves and are the best institutions for the moral formation of children—the family and the church and community groups."[92] A number of other Heritage Foundation reports reiterated similar arguments.[93]

The Heritage Foundation was not the only organization encouraging a more public engagement with religion as the solution to America's alleged epidemic of crime. Led by Ralph Reed, the Christian Coalition of America placed this issue at the center of its political activism as it called for a significant change in American politics and religion.[94] The Christian Coalition summarized its vision and legislative agenda in its Contract with the American Family, which the coalition released at a press conference in Washington, D.C. Speaker of the House of Representatives Newt Gingrich and other members of congress attended the event.[95]

The Christian Coalition's Contract with the American Family echoed many of the themes outlined in the Heritage Foundation's literature as it highlighted the rampant immorality and criminality that resulted from liberal policies. Reed summarized this position when he stated, "The Great Society was not a bold new step, but a failed experiment in social engineering on a massive scale."[96] The solution, he argued, lies at the local level. "We must replace the pity of bureaucrats with the generosity of churches and synagogues."[97] In other words, the government should defer to the religious institutions one finds in the Judeo-Christian model of American religiosity, as they are better equipped to provide Americans with the religious morality that breeds prosocial behaviors. The Christian Coalition carried this message throughout America in what Reed referred to as "one of the largest grass-roots [sic] campaigns in our nation's history."[98]

Led by organizations such as the Heritage Foundation and the Christian Coalition, the "Replace the government with religion in the larger fight against crime" movement spread to become part and parcel of Republican Party politics. The examples of this trend are numerous. James Q. Wilson, for example, articulated this idea in his "Two Nations" speech, where he used racially coded language to assert that America has devolved into two separate nations. He described these two nations when he wrote, "In one nation, a child, raised by two parents, acquires an education, a job, a spouse, and a home kept separate from crime and disorder by distance, fences, or guards. In the other nation, a child is raised by an unwed girl, lives in a neighborhood filled with many sexual men but few committed fathers, and finds gang life to be necessary for self-protection and valuable for self-advancement."[99] After an extended lament on the decline and decay that exist in the second nation, he suggested that a return to traditional, family-centered values offers the best fix for the two-nation divide. He offered five suggestions to help those Americans trapped in poverty and criminality. Suggestions one through four address unwed mothers, adoption, daycare, and parents who are married. Option five, however, was perhaps the most important. "*Fifth, restoring the force of religion.* Religion," he wrote, "independent of social class, reduces deviance. . . . Hundreds of churches and synagogues across the country already try to produce better people out of discarded humans."[100] He concluded, "Religiosity and decency are correlated: in time we may learn that the former causes the latter."[101]

Individually and collectively, these theories positioned religion as a cure for rising incarceration rates. Republican leaders had already embraced this ideology and its attendant theology in the 1994 congressional election when Republicans Newt Gingrich and Richard Armey helped draft public policies based on these ideas. They called their proposed legislation the Contract with America. This relatively short document outlined basic policies signatories vowed to implement if Republicans became the majority party in both houses of Congress, including the U.S. House of Representatives, which the Democrats had controlled for forty years. Congressional candidates throughout the United States signed the contract and ran on its policies, as did hundreds or even thousands of candidates at the local and state levels. Most simply put, the Contract with America expanded on many of the policies associated with the Reagan administration as it called for a reaffirmation of American values such as individual responsibility, smaller government, family values, free-market economic policies, tough anticrime legislation, and respect for religion-based citizenship.

Reflecting a commitment to the latter, the contract promised to increase opportunities for faith-based social service providers. The contract also promised to create more tough-on-crime policies that would increase prison populations. Once incarcerated, religion would help "fix" or "correct" these criminals. Specifically, signatories vowed to implement ten bills reflecting these principles within the first hundred days of office. Americans responded favorably to the Contract with America, resulting in a major shift of power that placed the Republican Party as the majority party in both congressional houses for the first time since 1954. The legislation that they proposed impacted both criminal justice policies and FBOs, with welfare reform specifically addressing the latter.

The authors and signatories of the Contract with America embraced the idea that liberal welfare policies were primary catalysts behind rising crime rates, and they made welfare reform an important part of the Contract with America. In 1996, the new Congress passed a welfare reform bill titled the Personal Responsibility and Work Opportunity Act, which President Clinton subsequently signed into law. The Personal Responsibility and Work Opportunity Act is an important bill not only because it constituted the largest welfare reform bill in decades but also because the bill's Charitable Choice provisions required the federal government to partner with local organizations and FBOs to provide social services.[102] In this regard, Charitable Choice expanded the existing scope of partnerships between the government and FBOs, which while significant, was not in and of itself particularly groundbreaking. Several additional provisions, however, did fundamentally influence the terms of these new relationships.

Prior to Charitable Choice, religious organizations receiving federal funds were generally required to separate their secular activities from their religious activities, usually in "neutral" settings such as community centers or in other settings outside the church where the recipient of the church's services would not be exposed to sectarian images and symbols. Charitable Choice, however, allowed the FBO to administer social services in religious or "sectarian" settings where the FBO retained "control over the definition, development, practice, and expression of its religious beliefs."[103] Charitable Choice also extended to FBOs religious exemptions that allowed religious organizations to discriminate in their hiring practices. The provisions then provided the foundation for a new level of partnerships between FBOs and various branches of the government. In the process it contributed significantly to the larger trend toward deregulation as it closed highly regulated government programs and reallocated government funds to the alternatively regulated sphere of state-sanctioned socialization in FBOs. "Competition" characterized this new market as these provisions welcomed FBOs and welfare recipients to the marketplace of American consumerism. Not only did Charitable Choice frame FBOs as participants in a newly empowered market of state-funded social services, but it also theorized welfare recipients as consumers able to exercise their authority in this new market.

With welfare reform in place, Republicans also fulfilled their promise to pass more punitive criminal justice laws. Shortly after the election, Republicans quickly introduced the first of seven bills designed to rewrite Clinton's crime bill. One of these bills, the Taking Back Our Streets Act, promised to make "punishments severe enough to deter criminals from committing crimes."[104] As Michael Ross wrote, Republicans hoped that the proposed anticrime legislation would "grab[] back an issue that [Republicans] believed Democrats had stolen from them last year."[105] The new legislation promised to eliminate most of the crime-prevention programs that were part of Clinton's bill, it authorized over $10 billion for prison construction at the state level, it mandated longer prison sentences for a variety of crimes, it established mandatory minimum sentences for various crimes, and it included truth-in-sentencing provisions that reduced one's ability to shorten his or her prison sentence and to qualify for parole.[106] The Taking Back Our Streets Act became law and had an immediate impact on criminal justice systems throughout the United States as states and the federal government struggled to admit, process, and detain the waves of incarceration that soon followed.

"Tough on Crime" in Florida

America's evolving criminal justice policies impacted some states more than others, particularly the state of Florida, which from 1980 to 1990 saw its incarcerated population increase 217 percent, resulting in chronic over-population.[107] "Tough on crime" not only impacted Florida's prisons and its incarcerated population but also impacted Florida's prison administrators, including Secretary Wainwright, who found himself a casualty of the new, punitive culture. For decades, Wainwright advocated for what he called progressive prisons based on his larger belief in the state's ability to help convicted felons reform their lives. Wainwright's optimism fell out of vogue in the 1980s as the qualities that made him an asset for several decades rendered him a liability in the new tough-on-crime era.

In 1980, a reporter wrote, "A convict once shot Louie L. Wainwright, and there's no telling how many politicians have wanted his scalp."[108] Clearly, Wainwright had his share of critics, but in the 1980s, his critics grew in number as they became more vocal, and more importantly, more politically connected. His critics alleged that Wainwright was indifferent to violence, that he exploited the DOC for personal gain, and that he had an affair with a female employee. At one point, his detractors accused him of plagiarizing his master's thesis.[109] Wainwright's biggest liability, however, lay in the perception that he was soft on crime and that he coddled criminals in "Wainwright's condominiums for the convicted."[110] By the mid-1980s, Wainwright was more of a liability than an asset. In hindsight, it is clear that his days as head of Florida's DOC were numbered. The question was not *if* he would leave, but *when*. And when he left, what would become of the progressive prisons he helped create? History soon answered both of these questions.

In December 1986, Wainwright learned that he had reached the end of his twenty-four-year term as head of Florida's DOC when Florida's governor Bob Martinez asked for Wainwright's resignation. Martinez was a rising star in the Republican Party (and future director of the Office of National Drug Control Policy—that is, the so-called drug czar—under President George H. W. Bush), and he believed that Wainwright's progressive prison philosophy conflicted with the growing tough-on-crime climate.[111] Wainwright's philosophy also conflicted with the growing idea that the government should cut taxes and curtail its involvement in welfare programs, especially for people who abuse welfare or who do not demonstrate sufficient need. The incarcerated, many believed, fell firmly in the category of citizens who do not deserve the government's help.

When Martinez tapped Richard L. Dugger as Wainwright's replacement, he promoted a career DOC employee whose tough-on-crime attitude reflected the public's growing desire for punitive prisons. Dugger publicly articulated his carceral philosophy just a few months after he became DOC secretary when he spoke to the Florida Council on Crime and Delinquency. Dugger outlined his goals for the DOC when he stressed "the importance of discipline, staff responsibility and accountability, and chain of command."[112] Rehabilitation did not make the list. Dugger also acknowledged the public's desire for tough-on-crime and "Lock 'em up" policies, and he assured the public, "I am not opposed to that approach. In fact, I support a tough stance on crime."[113]

The historical records suggest that Secretary Dugger oversaw changes in prison culture that effectively implemented the tough-on-crime policies inside Florida's prisons. For its part, Florida's state legislature supported this process as it reduced funding on rehabilitative, vocational, and recreational programs. As a result of these changes, in a few short years, punitive prisons replaced Florida's progressive prisons. These prisons became the norm for roughly a decade until a new wave of prison reformers sought to reintroduce rehabilitative correctional programs via faith-based correctional facilities.

The tough-on-crime movement grew in force in Florida, particularly after the 1996 election, when Florida Republicans became the majority in both houses of the state legislature for the first time since Reconstruction.[114] As a result of this sudden shift to the right, the *Almanac of American Politics* described Florida as "the most Republican of the 10 largest states,"[115] and the new Republican legislators were the primary catalyst behind a series of bills that impacted criminal justice policies in Florida and the incarcerated population in Florida's DOC.

From 1993 to 2001, Florida's state legislature passed several major laws that drastically altered sentencing laws and criminal justice policies. The Safe Streets Act of 1994 was one such law, followed by a series of bills introduced during the fiscal year 1994–95, which a DOC legislative liaison referred to as "a year for criminal justice and crime issues."[116] From 1994 to 1995 alone, the DOC tracked over 500 bills that potentially impacted corrections in Florida.[117] According to one report, four bills in particular resulted in longer sentencing policies, although smaller bills also addressed

Florida's criminal justice system more broadly.[118] Collectively, these bills made it harder for the incarcerated to reduce their prison sentences via good behavior, and they required offenders who committed crimes after October 1, 1995, to serve at least 85 percent of their sentences.

Another law, Senate Bill 172 (the Crime Control Bill of 1995), eliminated a judge's ability to use discretion in sentencing and instead mandated minimum prison sentences for certain crimes. With the passage of Senate Bill 168, Florida also became the fifth state to pass a three-strikes law creating a new class of criminals called "violent career criminals."[119] The law defined these criminals as "persons convicted three or more times of any forcible felony, aggravated stalking, aggravated child abuse, other sexual crimes, escape, and certain weapons crimes."[120] In addition to the three-strikes provision, the law also included "mandatory life sentences for those convicted of a life felony or a first degree felony, 30 to 40 years for a second degree felony, and 10 to 15 years for a third degree felony." The aforementioned laws resulted in longer prison sentences, while other laws impacted life inside the prison. For example, one bill allowed the courts to restrict privileges, including, but not limited to, canteen purchases, telephone access, outdoor exercise, and library access.[121] As a result of this legislation, men and women in Florida's criminal justice system were doing longer and potentially harder time for a wider variety of crimes with fewer options to appeal or reduce their sentences.

The sum total of federal and state laws significantly impacted Florida's criminal justice system as it admitted thousands of people and saw the DOC's budget increase exponentially. When Wainwright left the DOC in 1987—119 years after the state of Florida opened its first prison—Florida's DOC housed 32,764 people, it supervised 80,441 men and women in community supervision, and it cost the state $355,204,977 to run its residential facilities.[122] Ten years later, however, the population had almost doubled as the DOC incarcerated 64,713 people, it monitored 142,911 on community supervision, and the annual budget exploded to $1,643,223,982.[123]

As Florida's DOC approached the end of the twentieth century, it faced a growing prison population and operating costs that increased annually by hundreds of millions of dollars. With no end in sight to this unprecedented expansion, the DOC's executive administrators were willing to consider new and innovative approaches to reduce recidivism and to ease the financial burden on Florida's taxpayers. The Florida state legislators who helped bring mass incarceration to Florida would have to support any new programs, but as their records demonstrated, they frowned upon state-run re-habilitation and crime prevention programs. More so, they believed that governmental programs were a primary cause of the criminality they rigorously punished, as they believed that the government discouraged both accountability and morality. They did, however, trust their religion, and they were prepared to create new partnerships between religion and state to fight their imagined crime waves.

2 Corrections as Business and the Business of Faith

. . . .

Few people have been more consistently involved with Florida's faith-based correctional institutions than Hugh MacMillan. Hugh worked as an employee in the Department of Corrections (DOC) in the 1990s, where he helped create Florida's first faith-based dorm, he was a DOC consultant for subsequent faith-based correctional institutions in Florida, he later worked with Horizon Communities (a nonprofit created to mobilize private resources for the benefit of Florida's faith-based correctional institutions), and then for the past several years he volunteered multiple days each week at Wakulla Correctional Institution (CI). I interacted with Hugh numerous times over the course of my research, and when we sat down for a formal interview, we met at a local restaurant where, at his request, we could discuss faith-based prisons over beer.

During our interview, we discussed the history of Florida's faith-based correctional facilities and the DOC more broadly, his role in the facilities, and his personal philosophy that motivated him to help create the first faith-based dorm.[1] According to Hugh, he primarily wanted to change carceral culture. Everything else flowed from that central point. He wanted the incarcerated to take ownership of their environment, to support each other as they confront their troubled pasts, to encourage each other's rehabilitative efforts, and to leave prison with the practical life skills that many people acquire as children. His explanation surprised me, as none of it explicitly referenced religion or faith. "Given your goals," I asked him, "why the emphasis on faith? Why create faith-based facilities?" That, apparently, was the wrong question to ask.

Hugh cocked his head, furrowed his brow, and looked at me as if I had asked the most absurd question imaginable. "Why religion?" he shot back. "It might be as simple as, why order a second beer? It seems like a good idea." That, of course, was not the end of the discussion. Hugh then described how religious socialization is the most stable and consistent source of support for the incarcerated. He argued that any meaningful change *had* to empower religious volunteers and religiosity more broadly. "The only sustainable support [for the incarcerated] is from the faith community," he said. *"You'd be crazy to interrupt that! You wouldn't want to!"* Hugh's reaction was habitual. It never crossed his mind that significant carceral reform would not include a more robust partnership between religion and government centered on religious volunteers and their free labor.

Recall that Hugh entered the DOC years after the transition that occurred in the 1980s and 1990s, when Florida's DOC eliminated or curtailed many of the rehabilitative and recreational programs. Prior to this transition, incarcerated men and women had access to a host of comprehensive rehabilitative programs—religion was but one piece. When the DOC hired Hugh in the late 1990s, however, that equilibrium was confined to the DOC's past. Religious socialization thrived in the new DOC as it filled much of the void that emerged in the transition's wake. The DOC's memory is short as it moves from one crisis to the next, so the culture that supported religiosity and religious volunteers seemed natural to people like Hugh. In the words of Pierre Bourdieu, this culture permeates correctional *doxa*, meaning that the prioritization of religious volunteers and their pro bono labor is "beyond question."[2]

This chapter follows the administrative and legal processes that created Florida's first faith-based dorm. It then follows the DOC as it expanded this dorm into the world's largest faith-based correctional facilities program. Broadly speaking, this chapter has two important goals. First, it highlights the institutionalization of a culture that assumes religious volunteers will provide comprehensive socialization, that assumes that religious volunteers are uniquely suited to provide comprehensive socialization, and that is skeptical of professionals with academic training or state certifications (like licensed psychologists or social workers). This culture is not entirely skeptical of credentialing; rather, it redefines common definitions of credentials as it positions personal religiosity as the ultimate credential, surpassing any state-sanctioned or academic certifications or training protocols.[3] The culture that supports this logic permeates the DOC, but it extends beyond the DOC into the halls of Florida's state government and into the minds of reformers like Hugh.

Second, this chapter documents the neoliberal epistemology that identifies religion as an element of the private and that prioritizes both religion and the alleged private.[4] Scholars have repeatedly argued that privatization is one of the central tenets of neoliberal thought, based on the assumption that the government should defer to private, market-based solutions for a host of America's problems ranging from the economic to the sociocultural. Ronald Reagan articulated his contempt for the government when he famously said, "The nine most terrifying words in the English language are: I'm from the government, and I'm here to help."[5] Americans find freedom, Reagan argued, when they reject the government and embrace the private. The architects of Florida's faith-based correctional institutions replicated this logic as they laid the legal and political framework for Florida's first faith-based dorm, where they associated religion with the imagined private.[6]

The association of religion with the private is a relatively recent concept that emerged concurrently with the development of liberalism.[7] This association is legislated in the United States in the First Amendment to the U.S. Constitution, which prevents the government from establishing religion.[8] Winnifred Sullivan noted the impact of the First Amendment when she wrote, "Disestablishment has resulted in a privatization and individualization of religion."[9] More accurately, however, disestablishment resulted in the *perception* of privatization, as the category of religion is not a fixed or stable category; rather, to quote Joan Wallach Scott, religion is a "discursive operation of power whose generative effects need to be examined critically in their historical contexts."[10] In other words, the category of religion is a multivalent signifier that, despite having no inherent meaning or substance, is profoundly consequential due to the category's immense sociocultural, political, and legal capital. The legal disestablishment of religion in the United States impacts perceptions and discourses of religion as it helps construct religion as an element of the imagined private. Instead of relying on direct state support for clergy, for the maintenance of churches, and for ensuring church attendance, Americans imagine religion as a personal decision outside the government.

This imagining obscures the relationship between what we commonly label religion and government, as history is replete with examples that would contradict the association of religion and private. Christian history itself demonstrates that in Christian societies, Christianity was a prerequisite for participation in political, social, and even economic life. Additionally, in the United States, Christian symbols and discourse routinely appear on money, on flags, in schools, in courts, and on monuments. As the Supreme Court noted repeatedly, the government accommodated what we commonly call religion (primarily Protestant Christianity) from the nation's founding even as it forbade federal religious establishment. Religion is also implicated in the imagined public as Christians repeatedly argue that their Christianity is the source of their political, sociocultural, and even economic values.

The movement to divert government funds to faith-based organizations (FBOs) itself undermines the association of religion and the private, premised, as it is, on government's cooperation with religion. The government also exercises judicial and political control over both the category of religion and the religions themselves (that is, the courts routinely determine what, for legal purposes, counts as religion, and various branches of the government pass laws that empower or constrict what it considers religion). Far from existing as separate entities, the relationship between the imagined public and what is commonly deemed religion is one of entanglement and engagement. In short, the problem is not that religion is entangled with politics; rather, we fool ourselves by thinking that what we commonly call religion can fully separate from politics.

Neoliberal ideology—and by extension, the movement to empower state-funded FBOs—ignores this entanglement as it reinforces the imagined binary between the public and private. It casts a narrow net to corral and prioritize the imagined private, and it embraces religion or faith as a component thereof. As a result, faith-based reforms like faith-based correctional facilities not only are compatible with neoliberal thought but are extensions of neoliberal thought and praxis. In Foucauldian terms, the imagined distinction between the private and the public functions as a form of governmentality, simultaneously disciplining people for the neoliberal economy and mobilizing them to act upon the imagined distinction.[11]

The Corporatization of Corrections in Florida

In 1990, Florida's electorate briefly signaled a move away from tough-on-crime politics when it elected Democrat Lawton Chiles as Florida's forty-first governor. As is common, the new governor surveyed the major departments within Florida's state government to ensure that like-minded administrators staffed the major branches. The DOC's Secretary Dugger apparently did not make the cut, as Governor Chiles quickly replaced him with a seasoned DOC employee named Harry K. Singletary Jr. Years later, Secretary Singletary would help spearhead the movement to create Florida's first faith-based dorm.

By all accounts, Singletary was a charismatic and tall African American with a reputation within the department as a competent administrator and motivational speaker.[12] On Friday, April 12, 1991, Governor Chiles held a news conference to announce that he selected Singletary as the new head of Florida's DOC. "In selecting Harry," the governor said, "we combed Florida and the rest of the country for someone who could help us to craft and implement a vision of crime fighting that goes beyond the rhetoric of prison building to the very causes of crime."[13] Governor Chiles said that Singletary was the right man for the job because he understood that the DOC has the dual responsibilities both to incarcerate convicts and "to return inmates who are released back into our communities in better shape than when they were locked up." In other words, Chiles hired Singletary because of their shared support for rehabilitative programs and programming. For the next eight years, Secretary Singletary struggled to reconcile the two principles of detention and rehabilitation within an environment increasingly hostile to the latter.

While many people in the DOC knew and respected Singletary, he officially introduced himself to the DOC's 20,000 employees when he delivered his first "Secretary's Message" in the monthly DOC employee newsletter, where he outlined many of the policies that would dominate his administration. Chief among these, Singletary wanted to reorient DOC employees away from his predecessor's tough-on-crime policies. He wrote, "Offenders will be subject to firm, fair, and consistent discipline. Inmates are sentenced to the Department as punishment, not for punishment. We must take individuals whose lives are out of control and interject the appropriate corrective discipline. This must be accomplished in a humane, fair, consistent and lawful manner, so they are either retained or returned to our communities with self-control and able to function in our society."[14] Singletary sided with the former secretary Wainwright more than Dugger insofar as he believed that incarcerated men and women in Florida's prisons could use their time productively to better prepare themselves for reentry and for productive lives outside the prisons. His obstacles, however, were numerous, and tended to include budgetary limitations and ideological resistance imposed by state legislators and their tough-on-crime constituents, particularly after the state elections in the mid-1990s when Florida's state government took a sharp turn to the political right.

Regarding the former, less than a year after he became DOC secretary, a financial crisis hit both the DOC and the state of Florida. Florida's state constitution requires Florida's state government to produce a balanced budget. This became a problem in 1991 when Florida's tax revenue did not support its budget, so the state legislature convened a special session in December 1991 where it reduced state spending by $622 million.[15] The DOC lost $46.6 million, with an additional $2 million in cuts the following

February. As a result of this loss (just over 5 percent of the annual operating funds for the 1991–92 fiscal year),[16] for perhaps the first time in DOC history, the department found itself with prison beds that it was unable to fill. It had the inmates, but the DOC did not have the funds to move them into the new prison beds or to staff the facilities that would house them.[17] As Singletary learned firsthand that his job description included navigating through dire economic crises, he channeled the corporate world and neoliberal thought as he began to speak of a "new DOC,"[18] one that theorized corrections as a business run on market principles.

Since its inception in 1868, the administrators of Florida's correctional department theorized the department as a branch of government only subject to market trends and commodification insofar as the market impacted the tax revenues that funded corrections. Prison administrators experimented with various revenue streams, but they rarely theorized corrections itself as a business or an agency that should operate entirely on business principles. This began to change in the late 1900s within the larger context of the neoliberal reforms that enlarged the economy's domain, that eroded barriers that previously limited capitalist commodification, and that opened the government to market epistemologies.[19] These changes not only redefined the nation's sense of itself and its purpose but impacted corrections as well.

Secretary Singletary channeled these trends when he argued that the DOC was in essence a large corporation, with "chief executive officer (CEO)" Singletary at the helm.[20] Singletary referred to the DOC as a "billion dollar corporation," and he designated the phrase "Corrections as a Business" as the theme of the DOC's Annual Report for fiscal year 1992–93.[21] As part of the new "Corrections as a Business" model, the DOC tried to reduce operating expenses wherever possible. Whether the DOC saved money by contracting with private prisons, by charging the incarcerated for more goods and services, by contracting with a specific toothpaste vendor,[22] or by reducing the cost of ground beef by supplementing it with soy,[23] the DOC tried to save every dollar it could. Long gone was the era when former secretary Wainwright asked the state legislature for millions of dollars as he proudly itemized the goods and services that the DOC provided incarcerated men and women. In its place emerged a correctional department that tried to trim every financial corner while still meeting its legal obligations to provide the incarcerated with basic needs.

Singletary argued that the DOC's Chaplaincy Services Office was a valuable partner in the "Corrections as a Business" approach to prison administration. For Singletary, an expanded Chaplaincy Services Office was both "constitutionally guaranteed and legislatively mandated,"[24] but it also resonated with his "Corrections as a Business" model. In the era of tight prison budgets and skyrocketing inmate populations, Chaplaincy Services helped relieve the state's financial problems primarily by administering the hoard of volunteers that entered Florida's prisons daily, bringing not only volunteer labor but a host of tangible goods and services including books, electronic equipment, food, and study material for the courses they taught in every prison. Volunteers also helped improve morale in the prisons as they taught the incarcerated to accept their prison sentences as punishment for their sin-induced criminal behavior, to obey the prison's rules, to study, and to learn prosocial behaviors. In the DOC's annual report for the fiscal year 1992–93, Singletary summarized the chaplaincy program's financial benefits when he wrote, "Chaplaincy Services was cost-effective by enhancing institutional security and morale. Thousands of inmates were counseled or attend programs, maintaining a proactive legal posture in dealing with religious requests, using community resources for donated materials and programs, and helping prepare inmates for reentry. For example, 7,781 participated in religious pre-release counseling. These practices place Chaplaincy Services in the center of reducing both daily operational and recidivism costs."[25] In short, Singletary believed that the Chaplaincy Services Office provided a variety of benefits to the financially beleaguered "billion dollar corporation" that was Florida's DOC.

The decision to elevate the status and jurisdiction of the Chaplaincy Services Office coincided with the retirement of the head chaplain and with the hiring of his replacement, Tyrone Boyd.[26] Chaplain Boyd settled into the DOC with a secretary-approved mandate to expand the Chaplaincy Services Office. Singletary specifically encouraged Boyd and his team to create more community outreach programs with the larger goal of increasing religious volunteer labor. For prison chaplains, their larger communities centered on their religious identities, so they naturally looked to their churches and larger networks based on religious affiliations. The DOC used to partner with local colleges, research institutions, and various other agencies and organizations willing to help the DOC and Florida's convicts. These partnerships dwindled over the years, leaving religion to fill the gap.

In sum, Governor Chiles hired Singletary as the new DOC secretary because he agreed with Singletary's correctional philosophy that included both detention and rehabilitation. Singletary quickly learned that he had to achieve these two goals within the larger context of rising inmate populations, complicated budgetary issues, and a larger cultural environment that wanted the incarcerated to have uncomfortable experiences behind bars. Status quo approaches to prison reform and prison administration were unable to reconcile these competing factors, but motivated by his experiences with the Chaplaincy Services Office, Singletary believed he might have found at least a partial solution in faith-based reforms.

Florida's DOC Finds Faith

In 1997, Secretary Singletary reminded DOC employees that Thomas Edison once said, "Genius is one percent inspiration and 99 percent perspiration."[27] To help DOC employees reach their full potential, he wrote, "I am challenging each of you to perspire often and regularly. Go forth and sweat." This was a rather timely motivational statement, as the DOC staff already perspired often and regularly as they worked feverishly to keep up with their rapidly growing incarcerated populations.

Secretary Singletary continued to build prisons and prison beds, but he believed that "building prisons alone will never solve Florida's dilemma."[28] The solution, he believed, consisted of preventing criminal behavior in the first place and in providing the incarcerated with the tools to stay out of prison once they served their sentences. Singletary wanted to encourage both prevention and rehabilitation, but few politicians could publicly utter these words if they wanted to win elections.[29] Despite dropping crime rates, the United States' per capita inmate population was now one of the highest in human history, and Wainwright's progressive prisons were a relic of the DOC's past. Floridians were increasingly skeptical of the government's ability to solve much of anything, much less the problem of crime. Singletary, however, wanted something to change. He wanted something new, something innovative, something that would satisfy the public's demands for justice, and above all, something that would not increase the DOC's budget. Religion, he wagered, might provide a partial answer to the DOC's many problems.

Singletary was willing to explore an expanded faith-based approach to fighting crime, and he found a potential partner in Kairos Prison Ministry's (KPM) Cursillo program. KPM started in Florida in the 1970s as a Protestant or ecumenical organization based on the Catholic Cursillo movement.[30] The Cursillo movement began in the 1940s in Spain after World War II when Catholic laity gathered to help each other recover from war-related traumas. Their weekend-long meetings (Cursillos) consisted of several-day "short courses" in Christianity where participants learned how to practically apply Christian theology to heal themselves and their communities. The Cursillo movement spread beyond Spain and eventually to Florida, where several people took the Cursillo movement into Florida's prisons for three-day "short courses" in Christianity. To facilitate this, they created KPM, and in 1972, KPM held its first Cursillo in one of Florida's prisons.[31] KPM continued to offer Cursillos every year in multiple prisons. Singletary wanted to learn more about this program, and more specifically about its impact on recidivism and institutional behavior, so in 1995 he asked his chaplaincy team to produce a report that addressed these issues.[32]

Chaplains wear many hats, so to speak, as ministerial duties account for but a fraction of their professional responsibilities. Chaplains also recruit and train volunteers, they monitor religious programs, and they help administer the prison itself. Chaplaincy training prepares the chaplains for much of this work. It does not, however, teach chaplains to perform quantitative data analysis and to account for controls or variables that might explain any benefits that accompany any regime of rehabilitation, including faith-based reforms like KPM's Cursillos.[33] Some of these controls include age, nature of crime, and length of prison sentence, to name but a few. Either Singletary was not aware of these concerns or he chose to ignore them as he broke with the standard protocol of asking the DOC's Bureau of Research and Data Analysis to conduct this research. Instead, Singletary enlisted the help of chaplains, the very people who would benefit from a report that spoke positively of KPM's Cursillos. The chaplains' report did just that as it documented a causal relationship between KPM's Cursillos and the behavior of the incarcerated. The chaplains' findings impressed Singletary, who continued to explore the possibility of expanding the Kairos program through a more direct partnership between religion and government.

There were, however, two potential problems with this expanded partnership. The first potential problem resulted from the legal requirements that regulate such partnerships. The second potential problem consisted of the state legislators who wrote and supported the legislation that effectively removed many of the rehabilitative options. Singletary reasoned that these legislators might support faith-based rehabilitation, as it embodied the values outlined in the Contract with America and the policies on which Republicans campaigned. Faith-based programming might not negate the tough-on-crime mentality as much as it might provide the incarcerated with the necessary moral foundation that many believed was the prerequisite for law-abiding behavior. Additionally, as local religious volunteers constituted the bulk of the labor force, it would not significantly increase the DOC's budget.

Singletary's hunch was correct, and state legislators found a type of rehabilitation they were able to support both ideologically and financially. In 1997, the Florida state legislature expressed its support when it passed Florida Statute 944.803. This statute provided an important step in the process that resulted in Florida's first faith-based correctional dormitory.[34]

Statute 944.803 stands in stark contrast to the bulk of the legislation related to crime, incarceration, and criminal justice issues more broadly in the 1990s, as after several years of tough-on-crime legislation that resulted in longer and "harder" prison sentences, the authors of Statute 944.803 wanted to help the incarcerated adjust to prison and then return them to society as productive citizens. Why the sudden change? The answer lies in the statute itself, which stated, "The Legislature finds and declares that faith-based programs offered in state and private correctional institutions and facilities have the potential to facilitate inmate institutional adjustment, help inmates assume personal responsibility, and reduce recidivism."[35] Many of the politicians in Florida's state legislature campaigned on the idea that religion or faith is a solution to social problems, and Statute 944.803 codified this idea into law. This statute also provided a legislative mandate for Singletary's preexisting goal to expand the Chaplaincy Services Office.

Statute 944.803 instructed the DOC to increase the number of religious volunteers; to develop additional relationships with "churches, synagogues, mosques, and other faith-based institutions; to assist inmates in their release back into the community";[36] to fund an "adequate number of chaplains" and support staff;[37] and perhaps most importantly, to "conduct an in-depth study to measure the effectiveness of faith-based programs in both public and private correctional institutions and facilities."[38] Statute 944.803 instructed the authors of the study to include policy recommendations and to submit their findings by January 1, 1998. The question remained, which branch of the DOC would conduct this study? The DOC's Bureau of Research and Data Analysis seemed a logical choice, as it routinely measures and reports on DOC data. This particular report, however, addressed religious issues, so the DOC again turned to its resident experts on religion—the Chaplaincy Services Office.

The DOC's Chaplaincy Services Office conducted the requisite research, which it published in December 1997 in a report titled *A Report of Faith-Based*

Programs in Correctional Facilities.[39] At a modest fourteen pages, this relatively short report reaffirmed the underlying philosophy in Florida Statute 944.803, as it concluded that religion, or what it termed "the faith factor," is uniquely important in the carceral environment.[40] Religion "works" in the carceral environment, the report argued, because it helps discipline the incarcerated and because it substitutes symbols of freedom for actual freedom. In short, "the faith factor" works because it makes the incarcerated more manageable.

The remainder of the report outlined the many services the chaplaincy performed for the DOC; it summarized religious diversity; it listed the major FBOs that already partnered with the DOC; and it summarized the existing residential and nonresidential faith-based programs operating in Brazil, England, and the United States. In accordance with Statute 944.803, it also included statistics addressing the relationship between faith-based programs, recidivism, and disciplinary reports, where the chaplains tasked with measuring the impact of faith-based programs found that incarcerated people who participated in faith-based programs had a lower rate of disciplinary reports and lower recidivism rates than incarcerated people who did not participate.[41]

Having demonstrated to their satisfaction that faith-based programs improve behavior and reduce recidivism, the chaplains made specific policy recommendations based on their findings. First, the Chaplaincy Services Office requested that the state legislature provide administrative staff to support Chaplaincy Services at each institution. The authors also asked the state legislature to create new faith-based partnerships both inside and outside the prison. Specifically, they stated, "In an effort to transform lives and break the expensive recidivism cycle, Florida should consider initiating one or more pilot faith-based residential programs. To support transition [back into the community after prison, Florida should] implement two or more moral affirmation transition centers that support inmates as they re-enter communities."[42] In other words, the authors of this report asked the state to create at least one residential faith-based correctional dormitory and at least two faith-based reentry centers. Less than two years later, the former request came to fruition.

While Florida's DOC fulfilled its obligations under Statute 944.803, Florida state legislators preemptively prepared an additional report to similarly lobby for a residential faith-based dorm. In January 1998, just one month after the DOC published *A Report of Faith-Based Programs in Correctional Facilities*, the Committee on Corrections in Florida's House of

Representatives released its own report. Representative Allen Trovillion, the chair of the Committee on Corrections, similarly believed in the transformative power of faith and in its ability to fight crime, and he wanted to leverage the Committee on Corrections' authority to help the DOC create a faith-based dormitory.[43] The report that his office produced, *Faith Based Programs in Florida Prisons*, consisted of several parts. It referenced several academic studies that documented the prosocial benefits of faith-based programming, it summarized various faith-based programs in Florida's DOC and beyond, and it addressed potential legal issues that might result from the pending partnership between religion and state. In the latter section, the report highlighted the various Supreme Court decisions that allow for partnerships between religion and state provided that partnerships have a secular benefit.

To this end, the report's authors highlighted the secular benefits that would result from the proposed faith-based dorm. They suggested, "If the state decides to implement an innovative faith-based program, the state should ensure that there is a secular goal that can be implemented in a religiously neutral manner."[44] They reiterated this point when they stated, "If such a program were implemented, the state should only be interested in the secular objectives that will be accomplished and must remain neutral as to religion. Therefore, the state should not be responsible for development or implementation of any religious content, and the criteria by which secondary religious goals will be achieved should not be within state control. Possible secular objectives include: lowering the incarceration cost per inmate, lowering the recidivism rate, and lowering the long term state expense."[45] It is important to note that in all three specified goals, the word "secular" functions as a signifier for economic benefits. The report also suggested that the incarcerated must volunteer to participate in the program and the program should be religiously neutral and not favor any particular religious group. If the state accommodated these recommendations, the report argued, the new dorm should pass constitutional scrutiny.

In the fourth and final section of *Faith Based Programs in Florida's Prisons*, the authors addressed an issue that they were all too familiar with— the issue of funding. The Committee on Corrections knew that new prison programs require additional startup costs and ongoing administrative expenses. After years of objecting to unnecessary DOC expenditures, the Committee on Corrections recommended an allocation of over $1.6 million for fifty-five secretarial positions for prison chaplains and over $204,000 to fund two pilot residential programs: one based on the KPM model and one based on the InnerChange Freedom Initiative's (IFI) model—the model, that is, that the state of Texas previously created in one of its prisons.[46] Backed by this congressional report, by the recommendations in the DOC's *A Report of Faith-Based Programs in Correctional Facilities,* and by a new head chaplain—Chaplain Alex Taylor—hired specifically with the understanding that he would create multiple faith-based correctional dormitories, the DOC went to work to create its first faith-based dorm.

While the DOC and state legislature worked together to create the administrative and political support for Florida's first faith-based dorm, they received additional support from their new state governor, Governor Jeb Bush. State governors play large roles in their state's correctional departments, where they routinely hire and fire senior administrators to create administrative teams that reflect their positions on crime, criminality, and carceral philosophy more broadly. When a majority of Florida's citizens elected John Ellis "Jeb" Bush as their new governor in 1998, it potentially elected a politician who would oppose the pending faith-based dorm. Based on conversations with many of the major architects of said dorm, however, none of them shared this concern, as Bush campaigned on the larger social and political platform that argued both for tough-on-crime politics and for "faith-based solutions" to social problems. In many ways, the Contract with America provided a template for Bush's campaign.

Channeling the major themes that dominated the Republican Party in the final years of the twentieth century, Bush advocated for a larger role for America's faith communities, particularly as they related to social service providers. Bush campaigned on this issue, and as governor, Bush repeatedly supported legislation premised on this philosophy, and he supported the DOC in its efforts to create and expand Florida's faith-based correctional facilities program.[47]

Bush also positioned himself as the tough-on-crime candidate, and as governor, he fulfilled his campaign promises when he supported or introduced a series of bills and policies designed to incarcerate more offenders for longer periods of time, including a law that came out of the Governor's Office, titled 10–20-Life.[48] This law required a minimum prison sentence of ten years for an offender convicted of committing or attempting to commit a felony crime while armed with a gun, a minimum prison sentence of twenty years if the offender fired the gun, and a mandatory life sentence if the offender killed or hurt someone. The law 10–20-Life was perhaps Governor Bush's most significant criminal justice policy.

To implement his tough-on-crime policies inside the DOC, immediately after his inauguration ceremony on January 5, 1999, Bush appointed Michael Moore as the new secretary of the DOC.[49] Secretary Moore had spent his career in corrections, first as a correctional officer in Texas and then as head of the corrections department in South Carolina.[50] Bush said that he chose Moore not only because Moore was an effective administrator but also because Moore shared Bush's desire to incarcerate more people who would serve harder time.[51] As history soon demonstrated, Bush and Moore succeeded on both fronts.

The impact of "tough on crime" during Governor Bush's administration is evident in the following statistics. Governor Bush inherited a DOC with over 27,000 employees, a budget quickly approaching $2 billion, 68,599 incarcerated people, and a DOC that supervised over 200,000 people either incarcerated or under DOC supervision.[52] When Governor Bush left office just eight years later, the number of DOC employees remained relatively stable, but the annual budget burst well past $2 billion annually, the incarcerated population increased to almost 93,000, and over 246,000 Floridians were either incarcerated or under supervisory control.[53] Some of those people would serve time in Florida's faith-based correctional facilities.

Florida's Faith-Based Dorms

As Florida's DOC entered 1999, it had many of the requisite pieces in place for the pending faith-based correctional dorm. These pieces included a sympathetic state legislature, a DOC secretary who supported the project, a team of experienced administrators at Kairos Horizon (a new organization that would administer the faith-based dorm), money from both the private sector and government to supplement the state's expenses, and a series of Supreme Court decisions and congressional legislation that arguably created a constitutional foundation for the project. The big day finally occurred in November 1999, when Florida's DOC officially admitted sixty-four men into its first faith-based correctional dormitory at Tomoka Correction Institution, a prison outside Daytona Beach.[54]

Less than a month after the DOC opened the faith-based dorm at Tomoka, it already planned to open five more faith-based dorms within the next five years.[55] While the DOC proceeded with its plan for expansion, the Florida state legislature devised its own plan. This plan developed during the 2000 legislative session when Senator John McKay introduced Senate

Bill 1266 (SB 1266) creating the Task Force on Victims of Self-Inflicted Crimes within the Executive Office of the Governor (later renamed the Task Force on Self-Inflicted Crimes).[56] This bill set in motion a string of events that soon resulted in the single largest expansion of faith-based correctional facilities in U.S. history. The production of SB 1266 replicated a familiar pattern where chaplains, religious Floridians, and supporters of faith-based programming provided the rationale for the bill and wrote the bill itself.

The fifteen-member task force (which included no academics or trained criminologists) released a report titled *Task Force on Self-Inflicted Crimes: Final Report Submitted to the Governor, the Senate President, and the Speaker of the House*, which concluded unanimously that drug addicts need a "spiritual awakening" to overcome their addictions.[57] The task force also recommended that the state increase the penalty from a misdemeanor to a felony for certain convicted prostitutes, which would create longer prison sentences and trigger additional requirements as a result of felony convictions. The task force also suggested that drug treatment programs include a work component and that schools and other government agencies more rigorously look for "drug-abuse indications" in young offenders.[58] The task force also suggested that in juvenile and dependency cases, the state should require the child's or the dependent's parents to participate in Drug Court programs when applicable.

Finally, in their eleventh proposal, the task force wrote,

> The Task Force strongly recommends that the Legislature amend Section 397.333, Florida Statutes, to require the appointment of at least two persons who are engaged in faith-based organizations devoted to breaking the cycle of drug addiction and prostitution. The Task Force further recommends the Legislature to enhance the state's consideration and use of faith-based organizations for substance-abuse recovery programs. Faith-based organizations are truly "armies of compassion" devoted to changing individuals' hearts, and lives. In addition, such organizations can offer more cost-effective substance-abuse treatment through the use of volunteers and other cost-savings measures.[59]

Collectively, if the state adopted these recommendations, it would replicate a familiar pattern where it would simultaneously broaden the category of crime, increase the criminal sanctions for a broader category of crimes, and present faith as a cure for these criminal behaviors.

After the Task Force on Self-Inflicted Crimes released its report, two staff members in Florida state Senate's Criminal Justice Committee wrote a new bill based on the task force's recommendations, a bill entitled An Act Relating to Criminal Rehabilitation, or, the Criminal Rehabilitation Act (CRA).[60] The CRA turned the Task Force on Self-Inflicted Crimes' recommendations into policy, but it drew inspiration—and verbiage—from a task force in Texas.

To understand how a task force in Texas inspired the staff members in the Florida state Senate's Criminal Justice Committee, consider that when George W. Bush ran in the mid-1990s for governor of the state of Texas, his platform advocated both for tough-on-crime criminal justice laws and for faith-based reforms. After the election, Bush made faith-based reform a central part of his administration. He embraced the idea that the government is more often the cause of America's problems than its cure, and he vowed to empower FBOs to provide the spiritual fiber that government is fundamentally incapable of providing. Bush described this philosophy when he stated, "Government can hand out money, but it cannot put hope in our hearts or a sense of purpose in our lives. It cannot bring us peace of mind. It cannot fill the spiritual well from which we draw strength day to day. Only faith can do that."[61] Bush wanted to expand opportunities for FBOs to administer government-funded social services, so on May 2, 1996, he signed an executive order to help facilitate this.[62]

The executive order created the Governor's Task Force of Faith-Based Programs, which served as an advisory group to the governor. This task force was charged with examining existing faith-based programs in Texas and with identifying ways the state can encourage and maximize the effectiveness of partnerships between faith-based programs and the state of Texas.[63] This task force would consist of sixteen people, including "members of religious organizations, persons affiliated with faith-based programs, and community volunteers."[64] In other words, it did not include scholars or professionals such as trained criminologists, psychologists, and social workers.

After Governor Bush signed this executive order, the task force assembled, held four meetings, and heard testimonies from "hundreds of Texans."[65] In December 1996, the task force published its recommendations in a seventy-two-page report titled *Faith in Action . . . A New Vision for Church-State Cooperation in Texas.*[66]

More than simply fulfilling their obligations pursuant to Governor Bush's executive order, the authors of *Faith in Action* created a document that reflected their religio-political ideology. *Faith in Action* simultaneously indicted the welfare system and proposed a theory of governance predicated on religious subjectivity. *Faith in Action* also recommended specific legislation that created unique guidelines for FBOs to receive government subsidies free from the policies that typically regulate government-funded social services and socialization. The authors of *Faith in Action* also criticized paid professionals as they touted the benefits of Christian volunteers, who they argued have a biblical mandate to help solve social problems.[67] Christian social activism not only is required, they argued, but is more effective than governmental solutions. Specifically, the report stated, "By any objective measure, one-on-one private and religious charities . . . are often more effective, efficient and compassionate than government programs at shaping and reclaiming lives. Why? They're free to assert the essential connection between responsibility and human dignity by requiring changed behavior in return for help. Their approach is personal, not bureaucratic. Their service is not primarily a function of professional background, but of individual commitment. They inject an element of moral challenge and spiritual renewal that government programs cannot duplicate."[68] Based on these conclusions, the task force recommended that the Texas criminal justice system expand partnerships with FBOs, and it specifically recommended that the state of Texas create faith-based rehabilitation centers and prisons. As scholar Jonathan Burnside noted, *Faith in Action* "paved the way" for the state of Texas to open its first faith-based dorm.[69]

When the staff members of the Florida state Senate's Criminal Justice Committee sat down to draft Florida's CRA, they consulted *Faith in Action*, which, along with the recommendations from the Task Force on Self-Inflicted Crimes, provided a template for Florida's CRA. Mirroring similar points made in *Faith in Action*, the CRA legislates a theory of governance that transcends the traditional binary of religion and politics. Specifically, this theory juxtaposes "government" and "private" (with "religion" or "faith" as a core and constitutive component of the latter) and then legislates the superiority of the private. Borrowing almost verbatim from *Faith in Action*, the authors of the CRA wrote, "WHEREAS, research has proven that 'one-on-one' private and faith-based programming is often more effective than government programs in shaping and reclaiming lives because they are free to assert the essential connection between responsibility and human dignity; their approach is personal, not bureaucratic; their service is not primarily a function of professional background, but of individual commitment; and they inject an element of moral challenge and spiritual renewal that government cannot duplicate."[70]

The authors of the CRA developed a binary where responsibility, human dignity, individual commitment, morals, and spiritual renewal are associated with "religion" and "the private," while bureaucracy and professional training are associated with the pejorative category "government." In this paradigm, a person's religiosity would be his credentials, his faith would provide his expertise, and his commitment to God would be evidence of his effectiveness. Based on this assumption, the CRA suggested that the government defer to the private, as it alone can address and rectify the nation's problems.

In short, the CRA legislated the assumption that the private (which includes religion) is uniquely capable of instilling the proper morals, ethics, and spiritual fortitude that are the foundation of American society. Building off this assumption, the CRA stated that Florida "should not and cannot bear the sole burden of treating and helping those suffering from addictions and self-injurious behaviors," and it instructed the state to partner with FBOs and their "armies of compassion" who are most suited to instill the types of inner, moral reform that would transform criminals and reduce recidivism.[71]

Specifically, the bill created a new Statewide Drug Policy Advisory Council staffed by the attorney general or his or her appointee and the heads of eight departments in Florida's state government. The advisory council also included eleven members from the public, two of whom "must have professional or occupational expertise in faith-based substance-abuse-treatment services."[72] The bill also instructed the DOC to place chaplains in community correctional centers, and it instructed the DOC to increase the number of prison chaplains from its current roster of 105 with the explicit goal of encouraging volunteer participation and increasing the relationships between religion and the prison system. Additionally, the bill instructed the state to partner with private organizations that would house ex-offenders in 400 new "transition-housing beds."[73] Private organizations without a faith component would build and administer half of these beds, but faith-based groups would administer the other half. Finally, the DOC already planned to create five more faith-based dorms, but the CRA increased that number to six. To achieve all these goals, the bill allocated over $5 million to the DOC budget for the 2001–02 fiscal year. The bill became law when Governor Bush signed it on the last day of the month.[74]

The DOC subsequently fulfilled its obligations under the CRA as it created a total of seven faith-based dorms by May 2002.[75] Florida's DOC continued to create more faith-based dorms to its current total of thirty-two.

Some senior administrators would like to see a faith-based dorm in every prison, and at the rate the program is expanding, that does not appear an unrealistic expectation.[76]

Faith-Based Prisons

The decision to appoint Secretary Moore would prove to be one of Governor Bush's more controversial decisions, as Secretary Moore was never a popular secretary. Quite the contrary. In the course of my research, I interacted with many people who worked with Moore to create Florida's first faith-based dorm, and when I asked about Moore, my respondents typically asked if we could continue our discussion "off the record," as they were about to say things they would rather not have quoted and attributed to them. Over the course of my research, Moore's colleagues described him as incompetent, vulgar, stupid, the worse secretary anyone could ever have, arrogant, a control freak, an asshole, and a son of a bitch. Why the near universal condemnation?

When Governor Bush hired Moore, he hired an outsider, someone who had not come up through the ranks in Florida's DOC and someone who had not earned the respect of his peers in the DOC and in the other branches of the government that work with the DOC. Moore had no favors to call in; he had no cultural, social, or political capital that he could leverage; he had no "go to" people inside the system he ran; and his management style alienated many of his peers and employees. In short, he was an outsider trying to reform one of the largest branches of Florida's state government who alienated many people in the DOC and beyond. After four rather tumultuous and controversial years as head of Florida's DOC, Secretary Moore announced his resignation on December 4, 2002, saying only that he wished to "pursue other areas of interest."[77]

Determined not to make the same mistake he made when he hired Moore, Governor Bush looked inside the DOC for Moore's replacement, where he found James "Jimmy" Crosby Jr. In Crosby, Bush found a "good ol' boy," a career DOC employee, and an experienced politician who commanded the respect of many people inside the DOC and throughout the state of Florida.[78] Crosby would bring his own problems—problems that would shake the DOC to its core—but those problems took several years to surface. In the meantime, Crosby made the decision that secured his legacy as an innovator in American corrections, as Crosby oversaw the conversion of Lawtey Correctional Institution (CI) into the nation's first faith-based prison.

According to Crosby, the history of Florida's first faith-based prison dates back to December 2002, when he received the phone call for which he had waited for his entire professional career.[79] On the other end of the line was Florida governor Jeb Bush calling to offer Crosby the position of secretary of Florida's DOC. Should he accept the job, Secretary Crosby would lead the nation's third-largest correctional department, he would oversee almost 24,000 employees, and he would administer an annual budget rapidly approaching $2 billion.[80] As Crosby recalls the conversation, he knew his answer the moment Governor Bush offered the position. He accepted on the spot.

The DOC secretary is considered one of the governor's cabinet positions, and like all other members of the governor's cabinet, Secretary Crosby and Governor Bush had a yearly meeting where Crosby outlined his goals and priorities for the coming year. It was during his first annual meeting that Crosby proposed the idea that would cement his legacy as an innovator in the larger history of America's prisons. Several states, including Florida, already created and operated faith-based correctional dormitories, where the state isolates religious offenders and encourages religiosity with the stated goal of reducing recidivism. No correctional department, however, had taken the bold step that Crosby was about to suggest. Crosby proposed that the DOC should transform an entire prison into America's first faith-based prison.

As Crosby recalls, Bush initially balked at the idea, but Crosby persisted. The faith-based prison made sense, Crosby argued, because it resonated with Governor Bush's desire to empower faith-based social service providers. It made sense because it reflected the larger political trends that were increasingly sympathetic to more robust partnerships between religion and state. It made sense because it reflected the "corrections as business" mindset that Singletary helped usher into the DOC in the late 1990s. The faith-based prison adhered to this culture, as it would not significantly increase the DOC's already-bloated budget, since religious volunteers would teach the bulk of the religious programs. It also made sense because it would cement Bush's legacy as a leader and an innovator willing to embrace cutting-edge crime-fighting tactics in an era where a politician's position on the war on crime could make or break this person's political career.

The two debated back and forth until Bush acquiesced and approved the project—the state of Florida would own and operate America's first faith-based prison. Crosby was soon distracted by other responsibilities, however, and the project fell to the bottom of Crosby's priority list until Bush called Crosby several months later and suggested the two take communion together at the new faith-based prison on Christmas Eve. As discussed later in this book, that phone call kick-started a transformation that required the attention and collaborated effort of many DOC administrators for the next couple months as Florida's DOC transformed an entire prison into the faith-based facility.

The big day occurred on Christmas Eve 2003, and Florida's DOC shocked the correctional world and beyond when it dedicated Lawtey Correctional Institution as the nation's first faith-based prison. The dedication ceremony began at noon and lasted well into the night, and those who attended the ceremony speak of it as a monumental event that included an overwhelming amount of pomp and circumstance. Governor Bush and his wife, Secretary Crosby, Head Chaplain Alex Taylor, and various politicians and DOC senior administrators attended this event, as did reporters from newspapers and television stations from the United States and beyond.[81] As Lawtey CI's chaplain William Wright recalled, "It was one of those things where you just get out of the way and let things happen because you know it's bigger than you."[82]

The ceremony began in the prison's chapel at noon, where Catholic bishop Victor Galeone administered Mass to Bush and to the other Catholics in attendance.[83] Following Mass, everyone convened outside the chapel under a large tent that draped the prison's courtyard where Governor Bush gave a dedication speech. Bush told the incarcerated, their families, and other attendees who had gathered for this historic change in American carceral practices, "I can't think of a better place to reflect on the awesome love of our lord Jesus than to be here at Lawtey Correctional. God bless you."[84] He continued, "This is not just fluffy policy, this is serious policy. For the people who are skeptical about this initiative, I am proud that Florida is the home to the first faith-based prison in the United States."[85] Secretary Crosby made a similar statement when he said, "We've developed a cocoon, a place where [the incarcerated] can practice their faith and not have the severe negative pressures and interactions that naturally take place in some of our institutions. . . . It gives them an environment to give them a chance."[86]

The festivities lasted the remainder of the day, often resembling an evangelical revival more than a traditional state-sanctioned dedication ceremony. A local minister delivered a Protestant benediction, followed soon by a gospel singer who sang an impassioned version of "His Eye Is on the Sparrow" while many of the attendees danced and shouted "Amen!" and

"Sing it!"[87] After the dedication-turned-worship-service, Florida state leg-islators talked to the prison administrators and the incarcerated. Perhaps never before had the governor and his wife mingled so freely with con-victed felons, but such was the spirit of trust and safety that accompanied the faith-based prison.

After the successful conversion at Lawtey, Crosby continued to support and nurture Florida's growing faith-based correctional facilities program before his untimely departure from the DOC less than three years later. Crosby's thirty-plus-year tenure with the DOC ended abruptly on Friday, February 10, 2006, when Governor Bush once again called Crosby on his cell phone, this time to ask for Crosby's resignation. Unbeknownst to Crosby, federal investigators were currently raiding Crosby's office and seizing DOC files related to alleged kickbacks that Crosby received from a DOC vendor in exchange for lucrative contracts. In the months that followed, a host of allegations emerged placing Crosby at the center of a larger crimi-nal underworld that allegedly operated out of the secretary's office. By various accounts, Crosby and his colleagues facilitated steroid abuse, they were involved in grand theft, they had a role in a sexual assault, they hired a minor league baseball player as a ringer for a DOC softball team, and they routinely held drunken orgies on prison grounds after softball games.[88] One former warden even accused Crosby of running a "fiefdom" that heavily favored DOC employees from Crosby's hometown and the surrounding area.[89] Crosby adamantly denied all but one of the charges.

In July 2006, Crosby was indicted and pleaded guilty to taking roughly $130,000 in illegal payments, and in April the following year, a federal judge sentenced Crosby to eight years in a federal prison, to three years of probation, and ordered Crosby to pay $30,000 in restitution.[90] Crosby left prison in October 2012 after the courts reduced his prison sentence to five and a half years.[91] Before he went to prison, however, Crosby made an ar-rangement with the Jacksonville Theological Seminary that allowed him to study theology inside the prison. Crosby completed his doctorate while he was incarcerated and was subsequently ordained.

I interviewed Rev. Dr. Crosby in 2014, when I asked him to reflect on the history of Florida's faith-based correctional facilities program. "What mo-tivated you," I asked him, "to create the first faith-based prison?" I already knew the answer—or at least I thought I did. I expected to hear that he cre-ated the prison because he believes in the transformative power of faith. I expected to hear that he created the prison because he wanted to encourage inmate religiosity. I expected to hear that he created the prison because he wanted to create a space for God to work miracles. Wrong, wrong, and wrong.

By Crosby's own account, the faith-based prison was a ruse, a distraction, or perhaps even a decoy that would allow him to achieve his ultimate goal of reintroducing rehabilitative programming into Florida's comparably punitive prisons. In short, Crosby created the faith-based prison to leverage the political capital that accompanies the term "faith." To understand Crosby's logic and motives, consider that Crosby came of age (professionally) in the 1970s when Florida's prisons had numerous rehabilitative programs for the state's convicted felons. The combination of tough-on-crime politics in the 1980s and '90s, soaring inmate populations, skepticism in the government's ability to reduce recidivism, and a budget that refused to prioritize rehabilitative programming effectively removed many of the programs once common during Crosby's earlier years. Florida's tough-on-crime politicians wanted the incarcerated to do "hard time," but Crosby wanted to re-create the old prisons where the incarcerated used their time in prison to better themselves, to prepare for reentry, and to stay out of prison for good. Crosby knew he had to build a political consensus to reintroduce a more comprehensive program of state-sanctioned inmate rehabilitation, but Crosby, an otherwise partisan conservative Christian, feared that tough-on-crime Christian Republicans would object to any such plans or proposals. The consummate politician, Crosby asked himself, "How can I get a constituency to support me?"[92] Crosby believed that he had to "trigger social Christian conservatives to move away from monolithic, chain gang . . . thinking" and instead support rehabilitative programs and programming. He found his answer in the category of "faith."

When asked to reflect on the factors that motivated him to propose the first faith-based prison, Crosby responded, "I thought it would be *the* way to get programs back in prison and to bring Republicans on board." In other words, he wagered that the emphasis on privatized "faith" would reorient his colleagues, constituents, and potential allies who would otherwise balk at any attempts to reform Florida's prisons or to expand the government's role in rehabilitative programming. The question remained, however, would this "rebranding" allow Crosby to create a rehabilitative prison?

Not only did Crosby's idea work, but Florida's Republican legislators and Christian communities enthusiastically endorsed the proposal. Both of these groups supported the tough-on-crime policies that removed the rehabilitative programs that Crosby wanted to reinstate, but they supported these programs in the allegedly private faith-based context.

Character Matters

In May 2004, the DOC expanded its faith-based prison program when it converted Hillsborough Correctional Institution (CI) into the first faith-based prison for women.[93] It subsequently closed Hillsborough CI early in 2012, leaving the incarcerated women without a faith-based prison.[94] Due to vocal outcry by the incarcerated and volunteers, a year and half later the DOC transformed Hernando Correctional Institution into a faith-based prison for women.[95]

The DOC expanded its faith-based correctional facilities program for men when it converted Wakulla Correctional Institution and Wakulla Annex into its third faith-based prison. Wakulla CI is technically a separate prison from Wakulla Annex; however, the two prisons share a fence and have the same warden. When the DOC converted Wakulla CI and Wakulla Annex, it arguably converted two prisons, but since both prisons share senior administrators, they are often grouped together. The conversion of Wakulla was particularly important for two reasons. First, DOC administrators decided to make the prison the flagship institution for its growing faith-based correctional facilities program. Crosby originally wanted to convert Marion Correctional Institution near Gainesville, Florida, but Rev. Allison DeFoor persuaded him to convert Wakulla instead. DeFoor intended for the next faith-based prison to serve as a model for subsequent reform both in Florida and throughout the country (if not the world), and he believed that Wakulla would be the ideal location, as it was closer to the state's capital where he and other proponents of faith-based corrections could shuttle state legislators and other visiting dignitaries to view the prison. DeFoor soon won the day, and Wakulla became the world's largest faith-based facility.

The conversion of Wakulla was also important because it coincided with a larger transformation of Florida's growing faith-based correctional institutions program designed to ensure its legality. As discussed earlier, the DOC's lawyers and state's legislators wagered that faith-based correctional institutions were legal, but they were reluctant to test their theory in court. They waited for organizations like the American Civil Liberties Union (ACLU) and Americans United for the Separation of Church and State (AU) to challenge the program's legality. Much to their surprise, however, these lawsuits never appeared. Instead, both organizations issued tacit or qualified approvals. Elizabeth Alexander, director of the ACLU's National Prison Project, expressed conditional support for faith-based prisons when she suggested that they help provide *some* form of state-approved rehabilitation, which has all but disappeared from prisons as state budgets cut or eliminated other rehabilitative options.[96] Similarly, AU's executive director Barry Lynn originally called Lawtey a "terrible program,"[97] but AU stated, "Religious programs run by volunteers are acceptable, but all faiths (and equivalent secular philosophies) should be given equal access to the facility."[98] DOC administrators feared that either of these groups (or anyone, for that matter) might eventually challenge the program's legality, and a development in Iowa stoked their fears.

As the DOC laid the administrative framework for the conversion of Wakulla, proponents of Florida's growing faith-based correctional facilities program monitored a court case involving a faith-based dorm that the state of Iowa owned, but that subcontracted the administration to the IFI. In 2002, AU filed a lawsuit against the IFI after an incarcerated man contacted AU alleging that the IFI discriminated against him because he did not share the IFI's theological views.[99] Where the IFI argued that the dorm was a nondenominational dorm open to all inmates regardless of their religious beliefs, some participants began to complain not only that the dorm was a religious dorm but that it was pervasively sectarian, with evangelical Christianity the default—or in legal terms, the established—religion. The court would ultimately side with AU, although that decision came months after Florida's DOC completed the conversion of its third faith-based prison.[100]

The ongoing litigation surrounding the IFI program in Iowa, however, reminded the DOC that its entire project rested on constitutionally shaky ground. The court in Iowa would not release its decision until 2006, but the trial itself motivated the DOC to take an additional step to safeguard the faith-based prison program from constitutional challenges. A simple change, they surmised, would suffice. Senior administrators believed that they could assuage potential legal challenges by highlighting the program's secular benefits and by making a concerted effort to ensure that the new faith-based prison would accommodate all of the incarcerated regardless of their faith or lack thereof.

To signify more inclusive and pluralist faith-based correctional facilities, in 2005 the DOC changed the name of its faith-based correctional facilities program to the "faith- and character-based institutions" program (FCBIs), where "character" is thought to be synonymous with "secular." The DOC was reluctant to include the word "secular" in the name, as it might dissuade the religious volunteers from participating, as many volunteers equate secularity with atheism or Satanism. "Character," the DOC reasoned, was a more neutral term that would satisfy the legal requirements to be neutral between religion and secularity without offending the volunteers who drove the program. Based on conversations with program administrators, volunteers, and the incarcerated, the addition of the character component was mostly cosmetic and did not impact the programming, which already included courses and programming that some might identify as secular or character-based programming. Regardless, in November 2005, Wakulla CI opened as the state's (and the world's) largest faith-based prison, or more precisely, the largest FCBI.[101]

· · · · · ·

Increasingly convinced of the legality of the FCBI program, Florida's DOC subsequently expanded its FCBI program to its current total of three FCBI prisons and thirty-two FCBI dorms. Prison administrators now contend that FCBIs are not faith-based facilities as much as they are rehabilitative facilities that include and encourage faith-based rehabilitation as but one component of the larger attempts to change behaviors and mindsets. Almost 100,000 people are currently incarcerated in Florida's prisons, and there does not appear to be any significant effort to change the carceral culture for the bulk of them. The majority of these people will serve long sentences in punitive prisons, and most will return to society with the same levels of education and skill sets they possessed when they were incarcerated. The few voices who advocate for widespread reform often meet deaf ears.

Incarcerated people in FCBIs, however, inhabit different spaces. These spaces are flush with programming where they learn financial skills, anger management skills, and parenting skills, to name but a few of the common programs in FCBIs. This more comprehensive programming exists in this allegedly privatized sphere where religious proponents are the facilities' architects, advocates, administrators, and proponents. By recalibrating these state-run facilities as private and by theorizing them as comparably disentangled from the state, FCBIs are designed to be different than the rest of the state's prisons. Remove the label "faith," and that recalibration disappears.

What is the actual content of the rehabilitative programs in FCBIs? What messages, theologies, and ideas circulate in these FCBIs? Equally important, what notions of subjects and citizenship emerge in these spaces? The next several chapters answer these questions.

Policing Participation, Manufacturing
Pluralistic Rehabilitative Space

· ·

When Secretary Jimmy Crosby decided to create the first faith-based
prison, he knew he faced a series of obstacles.[1] Chief among them were the
legal concerns associated with creating an entire faith-based facility. He
lived in a nation that upheld the separation of church and state as one of its
founding-era values, and the idea of a state-run faith-based prison seemingly contradicted that ideal. As a former politician and chief administrator of one of the world's largest correctional departments, however, Crosby
knew firsthand that there were exceptions to the proverbial rule. The DOC
spent annually over a million dollars on prison chaplains, these chaplains
held weekly worship services in every prison, the chaplains routinely
prayed at prison dedications and at graduation ceremonies, almost every
prison opened its gates daily to accommodate religious volunteers, the
DOC had a legal obligation to accommodate religiosity (often at the DOC's
expense), and the DOC already operated several faith-based dorms. Crosby
was not aware of the details of the legal framework that made all this possible, but his fellow state employees were.

To address the legal concerns head-on, Crosby organized a meeting with
a state attorney who listed a string of Supreme Court decisions and legal
precedents that provided guidelines for various partnerships between religion and state. The faith-based prison tested the boundaries of these precedents and statutes, the attorney suggested, but the attorney believed that
the faith-based prison should pass constitutional scrutiny if it implemented
several policies. Specifically, participants should volunteer to live in the
prison, they should not receive special benefits from living in the facility,
the prison should include both religious and secular programming, the
state could not directly fund religious education, volunteers should teach
most of the religious classes and programs, volunteers should not proselytize to everyone they encountered in the facility, and the prison should admit all of the incarcerated regardless of their religious beliefs or lack thereof.

In other words, the prison could not be a Christian prison that only offered Christian programs and programming; rather, it should be a reli-

giously pluralistic facility that accommodated everyone, including atheists. Christian programming could be the dominant form of programming—and Crosby imagined it would be, as the majority of the participants would be Christians—but it could not *be* the program. To accommodate this principle, senior administrators developed the following litmus test to serve as the standard by which they administered the prison: If an atheist could do time in the faith-based prison without feeling pressured or coerced, the facility should pass constitutional scrutiny.

According to Crosby, he walked away from this meeting simultaneously feeling empowered and constricted. He felt empowered by the legal framework that might make his novel correctional facility possible, but that same framework included significant restrictions as the emphasis on faith-based corrections triggered alternative criteria for recipients of social services in the era of the faith-based initiative. Crosby could accommodate these criteria, but it would take some work.

Crosby and his team first had to identify a prison they could convert into a faith-based facility. They settled on Lawtey Correctional Institution (CI). Lawtey CI made sense for a variety of reasons—it already had a strong volunteer base, it was close to several large cities that could provide additional volunteers, and it had ample classrooms for the rehabilitative programs and programming that would provide the backbone of the prison's rehabilitative mission.[2] The facility itself, Crosby reasoned, was close to perfect.

The prison also presented potential problems, however. Every participant in the faith-based prison—including administrative staff, correctional officers, the incarcerated, and the volunteers—had to support both rehabilitative programming and religious pluralism. Neither were organic; rather, Crosby and other senior administrators had to engineer them from the ground up. To various degrees, many of the people who worked at, lived in, and volunteered at Lawtey CI objected to religious pluralism, rehabilitative prisons, or both. Crosby and his team had to create a regime of rehabilitation that would encourage personal growth and a regime of pluralism that would satisfy constitutional concerns.

Crosby first addressed these concerns with Lawtey CI's warden, who assured Crosby that he could support both pluralism and rehabilitation. The prison's chaplain, however, presented a problem. The chaplain at Lawtey CI was a passionate and conservative Protestant who allegedly chastised and intimidated the incarcerated religious minorities and the volunteers who entered the prison's gates to help them. He believed that all of these religious minorities would spend eternity in the fiery pits of hell, and he rarely hesitated to tell them as much. Fearing that the chaplain would not be a good fit for the pluralist prison, Crosby transferred the chaplain to a different facility. In his absence, Crosby recruited Chaplain William Wright, a fairly new chaplain who, though a devout and conservative Baptist, fared much better in a pluralist environment. Wright accepted the position and transferred to Lawtey CI to help convert it into a faith-based prison.

With the addition of Chaplain Wright, Crosby and the warden identified other administrators who would support the new faith-based prison. The next step consisted of finding the right correctional officers. This presented additional problems, as correctional officers are notoriously hostile to the incarcerated in general and few of them would support the prison's new emphasis on respect, civil behavior, rehabilitation, and religious pluralism. The DOC did not require or even create specific training for correctional officers who work in the faith-based facility, but in lieu of training, Warden White and his team identified the correctional officers most likely to support the prison's new mission, and they retained them at Lawtey CI. Correctional officers deemed a bad fit were transferred to other facilities as Warden White worked with administrators from several prisons near Lawtey CI to identify "softer" correctional staff who would support Lawtey's regimes of rehabilitation and religious pluralism. The DOC then transferred these officers to Lawtey CI.

With the administrative and correctional staff in place, senior administrators set their sights on the intended beneficiaries of their faith-based, rehabilitative puzzle—the incarcerated. Florida's DOC already possessed basic guidelines for participation in faith-based dorms, and they applied many of these guidelines to the incarcerated men who would live in the new faith-based prison. Generally speaking, participants needed relatively clean disciplinary reports, they had to be literate, they had to complete a workbook demonstrating interest in and dedication to faith-based programming, and they had to be involved in rehabilitative programming.[3] The DOC extended these guidelines to the new faith-based prison. Twenty-seven percent of the incarcerated men at Lawtey CI met the admission standards and voiced their desire to stay; however, the admission criteria also excluded a large portion of the men already incarcerated at Lawtey CI.[4] The DOC simply transferred them to other prisons, creating space for additional people who met the admission criteria. The DOC identified these men and transferred them to Lawtey CI, and by Christmas Eve 2003, the DOC assembled roughly eight hundred participants ready to serve in the nation's first faith-based prison.

Having secured the administrative team and the incarcerated population, Crosby and his team had to address one of their biggest obstacles—the volunteers. Volunteers are an indispensable element in Florida's faith-based correctional facilities program, but they are also predominantly evangelical or fundamentalist Christians who have little to no respect for religious pluralism (or even Catholic Christianity). Crosby saw a potential problem, as these conservative Christians would constitute the majority of the volunteers, and they had to agree to accommodate people who were not Christians. To facilitate this, Crosby told Chaplain Wright to tell all volunteers that they could not speak disparagingly of other religions, nor could they roam the prison halls condemning non-Protestants to hell. These instructions, Crosby reasoned, would help identify the volunteers who would "fit" the new pluralist prison, and it would also isolate and exclude the volunteers who would threaten the facility's legality. The chaplain complied, and with these policies in place, Crosby believed that he had fulfilled the state attorney's recommendations. Lawtey CI was ready to become America's first faith-based prison.

This anecdote reveals a larger process that occurs every time Florida's DOC creates a faith- and character-based institution (FCBI). Whether it converts an FCBI dorm or prison, the DOC has to identify the various parties who qualify for the program. These parties include prison administrators, correctional officers, chaplains, volunteers, and the incarcerated. This process disrupts status quo policies and procedures in Florida's prisons, but then again, supporters of faith-based correctional programs argue that this disruption is precisely the point. The combination of legal requirements that legislate pluralism and the practical considerations that stem from the facilities' emphasis on rehabilitation combine to reprioritize correctional goals, rules, and procedures. Participants who meet these new guidelines are allowed to participate, and those who do not are excluded. In other words, pluralism is not a natural or universally inclusive space. As prison administrators learned, they have to engineer every aspect of it.

This chapter documents this engineering as it examines in detail the regimes of pluralism and rehabilitation that exist in Florida's FCBIs, paying particular attention to the massive and concerted effort required to create these spaces and to their necessary acts of exclusion. Drawing from critical theory, this chapter takes issue with liberal pluralists who argue that intolerance and exclusion are unfortunate by-products of illiberal impulses.[5] Instead, this chapter suggests that systems of regulation and the means of punishing transgressors are necessary preconditions for stable societies, and it applies this insight to the regimes of pluralism that exist in FCBIs. The proponents of FCBIs argue that these facilities create inclusive spaces that welcome any and all interested parties. This chapter contends, however, that FCBIs are not only necessarily exclusionary but perhaps the most tightly regulated government-funded spaces in Florida. Not only do administrators of FCBIs more consistently enforce all the DOC's rules, but the chaplains and volunteers worship a God whom they believe has strict moral and ethical guidelines. The Venn diagram of state laws, federal laws, and the moral prescriptions of the average chaplains and volunteers overlaps significantly, thereby empowering these administrators who introduce comprehensive regimes of discipline and punishment that resonate with their moral prescriptions. In other words, the administrators, chaplains, and volunteers find freedom under God, but their God has high and strict expectations. Since they are the FCBIs' primary administrators, their God's expectations become the state's expectations.

Finally, this chapter explores the central paradox that lies at the heart of neoliberalism in the United States. As discussed in the introduction, proponents of neoliberalism targeted Keynesian economics and the comparably larger federal government that supported it.[6] While neoliberalism's sympathizers call for deregulation, for a smaller government, and for free-market economies, however, they harness the power of the government at multiple levels (from the federal to the local) to help manufacture the economy and to help marshal cultures that support neoliberalism.[7] This results in alternative regimes of regulation, not in deregulation per se. This chapter explores these dynamics in FCBIs where federal legislation influences FCBIs, but where local, neoliberal regimes of governance provide FCBI administrators with the ability to police participation in state-sanctioned socialization and to reprogram the state's priorities. This seemingly fulfills neoliberalism's mandate to redirect or to reconfigure the government in service of perpetuating neoliberal culture.

Correctional Officers

In the early 1800s, prison reformer Thomas Eddy argued that correctional staff tend to be negative influences on the incarcerated. "Prisoners," he wrote, "are made desperate by the profaneness, violent hasty tempers, inhumanity, and ill usage of their keepers."[8] In other words, correctional staff can encourage untoward behaviors, particularly when they engage in behaviors that contradict the facilities' emphasis on rehabilitation. Eddy highlighted a perennial grievance that frustrated prison reformers as they consistently bemoan correctional officers' negative influence on prisoners. To reform prisons, Eddy argued, prisons first need to reform correctional staff.

The state of Florida similarly struggled with this problem as the various versions of Florida's penal system often tried in vain to find long-term, educated, and committed employees who treat Florida's incarcerated populations with respect. The problems began in Florida's first prison in 1868, which one critic described as "horror's den."[9] "The story of this regime," he continued, "is one of almost unrelieved barbarity."[10] According to this critic, the staff routinely disciplined, beat, and even tortured the incarcerated, and the staff's preferred forms of discipline consisted of "stringing [the incarcerated] up by the thumbs, 'sweating,' and 'watering.'"[11] "Sweating" was a form of discipline similar in all but name to the "nigger boxes" slave masters previously used to punish slaves, where a slave was confined in a small box with little ventilation or light.[12] On a hot and humid Florida afternoon, the temperature in these boxes could be lethal. The practice of "watering," on the other hand, is akin to waterboarding. According to the critic who described these practices, incarcerated men who received these punishments died "quite frequently" and their remains were buried in shallow ditches where animals routinely made meals of their corpses.[13]

From the first prison to the present, the administrators of Florida's prisons struggled to recruit and retain qualified correctional staff who treated the incarcerated with respect. These problems dogged the administrators of Florida's convict lease system (which began operating in 1877), burdened the administers of Florida's prisons after the state closed its convict lease system in the 1920s, presented a problem for Secretary Wainwright throughout his tenure as head of Florida's correctional department, and beleaguered subsequent secretaries. In short, every director of every manifestation of Florida's DOC struggled to find devoted and stable correctional staff who treated Florida's incarcerated population with respect or compassion. As evidenced by a series of high-profile examples, many correctional officers continue to abuse the incarcerated, and some correctional officers are implicated in the deaths of the incarcerated.

Every year, several hundred people die in Florida's prisons. Most die of natural causes, but several involve suspicious circumstances, and correctional officers are often implicated.[14] As a case in point, in September 2014, an incarcerated woman in Lowell CI with just seven months left in prison wrote a letter to a family member where she claimed that a correctional officer named "Sgt. Q." had threatened her life. Ten days later, the woman was found dead in protective custody. Suspecting foul play, her family hired an attorney who ordered an autopsy, which according to the attorney, revealed that she "suffered blunt-force trauma to her abdomen consistent with being punched and kicked in the stomach."[15] Her death is one of nearly two hundred state prison death investigations the DOC turned over to the Florida Department of Law Enforcement.

In an unrelated story, a fifty-year-old incarcerated man named Darren Rainey died in Dade CI in June 2012 after correctional officers handcuffed Rainey in a scalding hot shower and left him there for hours.[16] Rainey was a mentally ill man who defecated in his cell, and the officers allegedly punished Rainey by leaving him in the hot shower where he essentially boiled to death as the skin melted off his body. The next morning, another man tasked with cleaning the shower found chunks of Rainey's skin.[17] According to many of the block's residents, hot showers were a common form of punishment at Dade CI.

Another story implicates two racist correctional officers charged with plotting the murder of a black man after he left prison.[18] The men were charged with conspiracy to commit murder after an FBI informant infiltrated a local branch of the Ku Klux Klan and allegedly confirmed that the correctional officers wanted someone to kill the ex-convict. The FBI then staged the man's death as part of its investigation and arrested both correctional officers after they allegedly expressed their satisfaction with the murder.

Stories like these routinely make headlines, reminding Floridians that correctional officers who physically abuse and even allegedly kill Florida's incarcerated population staff Florida's prisons. What do not make the headlines are the numerous times correctional officers abuse the incarcerated. According to almost every incarcerated person I interviewed, this happens on a daily basis in most of Florida's conventional prisons. These abuses include frequent insults directed at the incarcerated, passive-aggressive threats intended to intimidate them, and even mild forms of violence correctional officers inflict on the incarcerated.

The DOC's senior and executive administrators generally agree that the more abusive correctional officers should not work inside the FCBIs where they will disrupt the facilities' regimes of rehabilitation.[19] Researcher

Nancy LaVigne and her colleagues noted as much when they wrote, "Respondents report that correctional officers who adhere to a strictly traditional approach that focuses solely on security are neither well prepared nor well suited to work in an FCBI environment, given its heavy emphasis on mutual respect between correctional staff and inmates."[20] Accordingly, the DOC takes additional measures to ensure that every correctional officer working inside an FCBI supports the institution's mission of faith-based rehabilitation.

Correctional officers are important agents in FCBIs' rehabilitative regime. In addition to securing the facilities, correctional officers also organize and monitor "call-outs" when large groups of incarcerated people move about in the prison.[21] The incarcerated repeatedly contend that grumpy or foul-tempered correctional officers will delay or interfere with call-outs for no other reason than to annoy or retaliate against them. One man described a call-out where a correctional officer was upset with a single person who lived in a larger cellblock, so the officer kept the entire cellblock on lockdown during an important call-out. In this particular instance, the men in this block had to sit on their bunks with no reading material for over two hours. The administrators of FCBIs contend that correctional officers like this cannot work in FCBIs, as FCBIs are predicated on the assumption that correctional officers will facilitate instead of inhibit movement for the sake of rehabilitative programming.

To ensure that the "right" correctional officers work in FCBIs, the administrators of each facility developed screening protocols and processes that weed out correctional staff who will undermine the faith-based regimes of rehabilitation. According to Chaplain Steve Fox, head chaplain at Wakulla CI, the administrators at Wakulla used to "handpick the COs [correctional officers] to ensure that they were men and women of faith."[22] Today, however, they drop the emphasis on faith and instead focus on the correctional staff's overall attitude. Similarly, Susan Davis, assistant warden at Lawtey CI, said that correctional officers in the FCBI prisons have to be "softer," meaning that while they do not necessarily have to be "people of faith," they do have to support the rehabilitative programming, and they also have to be sensitive to the rehabilitative culture they attempt to create.[23] Major Brown, a "white shirt" at Gulf Coast CI, echoed this sentiment. ("Whites" or "white shirts" are correctional administrators who have obtained the position of lieutenant or above. The "browns" or "brown shirts" are the junior correctional officers who monitor the incarcerated.) Gulf Coast CI is a conventional prison that has an FCBI dorm, and Major Brown interacts with all the correctional officers whom he supervises at Gulf Coast CI, where he identifies the officers who "have a positive attitude" and who tolerate religious pluralism.[24] He reassigns these officers to work in the FCBI dorm, where they are more likely to support the incarcerated and their faith-based rehabilitative efforts, leaving the correctional officers with less-than-positive attitudes to work in the conventional prisons, where their interactions with residents in FCBIs are kept to a minimum.

Correctional officers are also important because they interact with the hundreds of volunteers who daily enter FCBIs. These interactions begin when volunteers first enter the prison, where correctional officers will search volunteers. Everyone entering the prison has to remove all clothing except pants, socks, and shirts. They then walk through a metal detector where the correctional officers inspect everything they bring in with them and where they are subject to random pat-downs. Volunteers also typically have to pass through two secured areas that require correctional officers in secured guard stations to activate electronic locks that open the doors. This process can be frustrating, as you can see the correctional officers in the guard booths and you can watch them talking while you wait in a small room for someone to reach over and push the button that activates the release mechanism. Volunteers routinely complain about the intake process, particularly religious minorities like River, a Wiccan who volunteered to help the Wiccans at Wakulla CI, who contends that members of minority religions are singled out for additional scrutiny.[25]

River said that he often sees the correctional officers efficiently process the Christian volunteers and then detain him for much longer. He said that the correctional officers barely open the Christians' Bibles to search for contraband, but they rigorously scrutinize every page of his religious literature. River contends that the situation is better in FCBIs than in the conventional prisons where he volunteers, but FCBI administrators strive to eliminate these disruptions in FCBIs.

Incarcerated Wiccans in FCBIs similarly complain that correctional officers harass them more than they do any other group, as Wiccans contend that correctional staff closely monitor their weekly study sessions and routinely interrupt them. Consider the Wiccan study group at Wakulla CI, where a small group of roughly twenty Wiccans meet in a classroom inside the chapel once a week to read tarot cards, cast runes, discuss books they are reading, and manipulate energy. According to the Wiccans, the Christian correctional officers became so intrusive that the Wiccans turned to the only source of help at their disposal—the supernatural. Before they celebrate their sacred holidays, one of the Wiccans places a handkerchief with sacred symbols on the floor directly behind the classroom's door, which connects the chapel's main hallway to the classroom. They then recite a sacred prayer that summons an ancient demon named Astaroth. The symbols on the handkerchief trap Astaroth, who emits supernatural Christian repellent through the door and into the hallway, causing all Christian correctional staff to ignore the Wiccans. The Christians are unaware that Astaroth is there, but, according to the Wiccans, Astaroth's power is such that his presence makes the Christians uncomfortable so they instinctively avoid the classroom. The Wiccans contend that Astaroth helps protect them by keeping abusive and intrusive correctional staff away from their meetings.

This summary of correctional officers highlights the extent to which the prison administrators in Florida's DOC recognize that they have a problem with their correctional officers, and they go out of their way to correct this problem in FCBIs. Correctional officers in FCBIs are more lenient, more tolerant, less likely to inflict verbal or physical abuse, and more willing to tolerate minority religions. Not all correctional officers in Florida's DOC embrace this mindset, and they are consolidated in the conventional prisons. As a result, the DOC is potentially making conventional prisons worse, as they are increasingly run by punitive correctional staff. This "remaking" of conventional prisons is an important but overlooked aspect of the larger transformations that accompany faith-based correctional reforms.

Chaplains

It is hard to overstate the prison chaplains' roles in FCBIs, where they are the primary administrators in all of the FCBI prisons and in most of the FCBI dorms.[26] The wardens, assistant wardens, classification officers, and correctional officers all work together to administer the facilities, but chaplains are more intimately involved in the FCBIs. They are directly involved with every class and program as they recruit, supervise, and train volunteers and inmate facilitators (as discussed elsewhere in greater detail, inmate facilitators are incarcerated authority figures in FCBIs); schedule and coordinate classes and programs; approve new courses; monitor the incarcerated and their progress; and recommend people for expulsion.

Chaplains are also physically closer to the incarcerated, as the chaplains' offices are located in the chapels where the bulk of the FCBI programming often occurs.

Because of their various duties, they typically do very little ministering. In this regard, they resemble prison chaplains in conventional prisons. As the Pew Research Center recently documented, prison chaplains spend the bulk of their days processing paperwork, returning phone calls and emails, and monitoring the incarcerated chapel clerks and inmate facilitators.[27] Prison chaplains in FCBIs are no exception. Quite the contrary: they spend a large portion of their days processing paperwork, and the chaplains are less than enthusiastic about this aspect of their job.[28] When I asked Chaplain William Wright from Lawtey CI if he laments the administrative work, he responded assertively, "Oh God, yes! And I dislike it immensely. We drown in data entry. It's not that it's beneath me, but I don't have the time to do what I want to do."[29]

To understand the sheer volume of paperwork the chaplains process on a daily basis, keep in mind that written requests are the primary form of communication between the incarcerated and the DOC. If someone wants to enroll in a course, he submits a written request. If he wants to change his schedule, he submits a written request. When he wants the DOC to make any special accommodation, he requests that in writing. If he has a grievance, he expresses his grievance in writing. If he has a special religious diet, he requests his special diet in writing. On any given day, one person can potentially make multiple requests, and the chaplain has to enter every request into the DOC's database. As a result, chaplains receive stacks of requests on a daily basis, and they spend hours simply inputting these requests into computers. Additionally, they coordinate special meals on holy days, help formulate new policies, and coordinate all the special events inside the chapel such as graduations and special meetings (revivals, guest lectures, etc.). The sheer volume of administrative duties can be overwhelming. According to Chaplain Steve Fox, chaplains spend 90 percent of their time doing administrative work such as data entry.

When they are not performing administrative duties, the chaplains occasionally get to do what they love, which is teach and preach. Every chaplain and every facility is different, but most chaplains teach one class and preach on Sunday, where they lead what is commonly labeled the interdenominational (i.e., Protestant) service. These services are vastly different from prison to prison, as the evangelical chaplains preach from evangelical perspectives and the fundamentalist chaplains preach from fundamentalist perspectives. Perhaps the only factor that unites their interdenominational services is that they are distinctly Protestant. This is important, as beneath their denominational differences, the conservative Protestant chaplains have comparably similar understandings of "true religion," and they project their biases onto all other religions. Essential and important actors in the FCBIs, the chaplains simultaneously are subject to and reinforce the restrictions that regulate participation in the FCBIs.

The incarcerated tend to arrange into a hierarchy the various people they encounter in prisons, based largely on the degree to which the people discipline or help them. The chaplains typically fall in the middle of this hierarchy, somewhere between the prison administrators they blame for many of the problems inside the facilities, and the volunteers, whom the incarcerated respect more than anyone working inside the facilities. With the possible exception of the DOC psychologists, the prison chaplain is the only DOC employee allowed to show compassion and affection. That alone makes incarcerated people sympathetic to the chaplain; however, the chaplain might disagree with an incarcerated person, might discipline someone, or might seemingly discriminate against a member of a religious minority. This reminds the incarcerated that the chaplain is a DOC administrator tasked with their detention and punishment. Chaplains, then, occupy a unique place in FCBIs, where they are DOC employees tasked with policing the rehabilitative environment they help nurture and create. The DOC's administrators try to identify the chaplains who can successfully balance these responsibilities and restrictions.

Whether the chaplain works in an FCBI dorm or prison, the expectations are similar. These chaplains understand that they are primarily administrators, they know that they have to tolerate religious pluralism, and they also agree not to proselytize unless someone asks a direct question that allows the chaplain to answer with an affirmation of his faith. Chaplain David Smith described this when he said, "As a believer, whether I'm in this seat [as a chaplain] or in Walmart or in a grocery store, my job is to embrace that opportunity to share my faith."[30] As chaplain, however, he recognizes there are limits to his ability to proselytize. "I don't care if [the inmate is] a Christian, a Muslim, a Jew, a Buddhist, an atheist, or a Satanist. It doesn't matter to me. Because in my *profession*, my job is to help that inmate discover and develop as a result of his faith."

Chaplain Smith suggested that he cautiously tolerates pluralism, but other chaplains embrace it enthusiastically, as it places them in direct and potentially intimate contact with people who are not Christians. Consider that in conventional prisons, chaplains are overwhelmingly Protestant and incarcerated people who are not Protestant typically try to avoid these chaplains. In FCBIs, however, most of the incarcerated people have to talk to the chaplain, who helps monitor their progress. They might also find themselves in a class that the chaplain teaches, or they will interact casually with the chaplain between classes. All of these interactions potentially create opportunities for proselytization, provided the opportunity presents itself.

Chaplain Smith, for example, said that when someone in the prison asks him a question that allows him to reference his faith, he does not hesitate to take advantage of that opportunity. "If an inmate asks how I cope with my day," he said, "the door is open [for proselytization]."[31] Chaplain George Lajueness in the FCBI prison at Wakulla Annex reiterated this idea when he said, "Listen, the inmate's First Amendment freedoms are also mine. I also have religious freedom, and while it is limited here in the prison, I still use it when I can." Every chaplain I encountered articulated some version of this sentiment.

Head Chaplain Alex Taylor himself expressed a version of this when he said, "Our Constitution guarantees that everyone has an opportunity to practice his or her faith. I've found that if I am fair to people of different faiths, they become more receptive to mine. When we start with fairness in our dealings with different faiths that actually opens doors to ministry."[32] In other words, religious pluralism creates missionary opportunities, provided the chaplain can tolerate the boundaries that accompany pluralism. The problem for the DOC is that not every chaplain understands these boundaries, nor is every chaplain sympathetic to the regimes of pluralism in FCBIs.[33]

Religious pluralism in FCBIs occasionally creates problems in the personal lives of the conservative Christian chaplains. Chaplain Lajueness discussed how his participation in FCBIs precipitated a conflict in his church, where some members basically accused him of conspiring with Satan to introduce or encourage non-Christian religions. Lajueness's version of Christianity leaves limited space for interreligious ecumenicism, as it teaches a strict dualism where everything empowers either God or Satan. By accommodating the religious pluralism that might empower the latter under the guise of toleration, some members of Lajueness's church accused him of being an unwitting agent of the devil. Lajueness felt vindicated after he reminded his critics that their own church has Christian yoga, which itself is arguably an appropriation of heretical religion. Another FCBI chaplain explained a similar problem in an off-the-record conversation where he described how his personal minister convened a meeting with the church deacons to address the chaplain's involvement in religiously pluralistic FCBIs. The church was concerned that the chaplain encouraged false religions, but they ultimately approved of the chaplain's involvement after he explained how the pluralist setting allows him to engage in stealth proselytization. The increased missionary field, he argued persuasively, adequately offsets the religious pluralism and the limits it imposes.

Some chaplains, however, refuse to accept these limits on their religious freedom, including the right to proselytize to any non-Christian whenever they deem it appropriate. If a chaplain insists on proselytizing at his discretion or if the chaplain demonstrates hostility toward religious pluralism, the DOC will not allow the chaplain to work in an FCBI. If the chaplain is employed at a prison when it is converted into an FCBI, the DOC transfers the chaplain to a conventional prison. The DOC has to exclude many chaplains from FCBIs, as they spend the bulk of their days in the prisons' chapels, the hub of religious pluralism, where the DOC regulates the chaplains' behaviors.[34] DOC executive administrators search for the chaplains who agree to work under these conditions, and they transfer those chaplains to FCBIs.

From a certain perspective, the pluralist FCBIs do not require much theological compromise from the conservative Protestant chaplains who thrive in these facilities as they exercise unparalleled influence in FCBI programs and programming. From this perspective, they reclaim far more than they compromise in the pluralist setting. Not all chaplains agree with this narrative, nor are they willing to tolerate religious pluralism, so they are not allowed to work in the FCBIs. For them, any compromise that displaces the focus on Christ is too great a sacrifice. Pluralism of any stripe is itself the enemy. From their perspectives, the chaplains who administer the pluralist dorms or prisons are themselves the problem.[35] They are the enemy, and someday soon these pluralist chaplains will stand at the feet of Jesus, where they will answer for every soul they helped steer directly into hell.

The Incarcerated

Reverend John Spicer stood at the pulpit in Wakulla CI's chapel for the beginning of his weekly Discipleship class. Per usual, he engaged the men in some rather mundane or lighthearted banter before he opened his Bible and started teaching. "Good morning, students," he began. "So, how the hell how are you?" After several people responded, Spicer signaled a change in tone when he shared that he had spent the last several days deep in prayer and mourning as the Baltimore Ravens recently defeated his beloved Pittsburg Steelers. One of the men replied that the Ravens were his favorite team ("Naw, Reverend, them's my boys!"), prompting Spicer to jokingly threaten to expel the man from the room, as "we don't tolerate heresy in this class!" Everyone identified the threat as a joke, but Spicer unknowingly addressed a larger issue that is part and parcel an important element of FCBIs—the issue of inmate qualification, inclusion, and expulsion in the FCBI program.

The proponents and administrators of Florida's FCBIs routinely boast about the diversity of the incarcerated population in FCBIs. "That's the beauty of FCBIs," one chaplain told me in passing. "We welcome everyone and they leave better people. Christians, Jews, Muslims, even Wiccans. You name 'em, we take 'em." Several studies seemingly support this assertion. One such study documented this religious diversity when it reported, "Nearly seven out of ten inmates (68 percent) in the three [FCBI prisons] . . . identify as Christian non-Roman-Catholic, one in ten (9 percent) identify as Roman Catholic, and an additional one in ten identify as belonging to Muslim (4 percent), Jewish (1 percent), or other religious faiths (5 percent) such as Wiccan and Rastafarian. 13 percent of FCBI inmates identify as having no religious orientation or have an unspecified religious affiliation."[36]

Florida's DOC offered a more detailed summary of the religious pluralism in FCBIs where it concluded that people from over 110 different faith groups participate in the program. Over three-quarters of the participants are Christian (most of these faith groups are various Protestant denominations), 4 percent are Muslims, and 1 percent are Jewish. Roughly 6 percent are members of various other religions such as Wiccans, Odinists, Hebrew Israelites, Buddhists, Native Americans, and Rastafarians, and over 11 percent do not select or identify with any religious affiliation.[37] This latter group is not composed of atheists, as very few atheists are incarcerated in FCBIs. Instead, this 11 percent predominantly consists of people who for various reasons choose not to identify with any religion listed on the DOC's list of religions. When queried, most readily admit that they worship Jesus. The larger point is that interested parties quickly identify this religious pluralism as evidence of the program's inclusivity. This inclusivity, however, is not without boundaries. Some of these boundaries are strict and offer people no opportunities to contest or dispute them, while others are malleable and vary from facility to facility.

The factors that regulate participation in FCBIs begin in the classification centers, where people first learn about FCBIs. When people are transferred to the DOC, they are temporarily incarcerated in a classification center. Classification centers serve several purposes. Incarceration can be a shock, particularly to people who are incarcerated for the first time. Classification centers help acclimate these people to Florida's DOC, where they learn DOC protocols, rules, and procedures. Classification staff members also evaluate or assess people before transferring them to the appropriate prison. Someone who needs vocational skills, for example, will transfer to a prison that includes more options for vocational programming, or an elderly person will be transferred to a prison that caters to the elderly. People learn about the FCBIs during the classification process, where they can immediately express interest in the program and, assuming they meet the qualification criteria, add their names to the waitlist. If they do not express interest at classification centers, they can later express interest at any point in their sentences. Classification officers at individual conventional prisons even remind the incarcerated several times a year that they can potentially participate in the FCBI program. Regardless of when someone expresses interest in the program, the DOC evaluates each person to ensure that the person meets the program's eligibility requirements.

According to DOC guidelines, to be eligible for an FCBI, the prospective participant must meet the following eligibility requirements: "1. S/he must have received no disciplinary reports that resulted in disciplinary confinement during the previously ninety (90) days; 2. S/he must be in general population housing status; 3. S/he must not be in work-release, reception, or transit status; and 4. S/he must fall within the parameters of the institutional profile. Factors to be considered include the following: medical grade, custody, youthful offender status (nineteen to twenty-four [19–24] years of age), escape level, length of sentence (e.g., death row, life), close management status, or sex offenses."[38] They must also have to serve at least eighteen months of their sentences. Collectively, these eligibility requirements prevent large groups of people from serving time in FCBIs, including people who are unruly, who are disruptive, or who violate DOC rules and policies. Assuming the prospective participant meets the eligibility requirements, though, the participant is qualified to live in an FCBI. The participant expresses interest in the program either by completing the appropriate paperwork with the classification officer or by completing the standard request form.

Additionally, until January 2014, prospective participants also had to complete a 156-page workbook, appropriately titled *Workbook*.[39] According to Head Chaplain Alex Taylor, the DOC created the workbook to separate people who are interested in earnestly pursuing faith and character-based studies from people who simply want to serve easy time.[40] The workbook required each person to demonstrate a commitment to personal development before the DOC will even consider a transfer into an FCBI.

The workbook introduces people to the topics they will explore in the FCBIs such as life goals, anger management, responsibility, truthfulness, courage, addiction, and faith. Regarding the latter, the chapter titled "Faith Formation" is the largest chapter in the workbook (besides the thirty-day journal at the end of the workbook).[41] In this chapter, each person completes a personal statement of faith, and the workbook includes the Apostles' Creed and the Nicene Creed as examples. After the participant completes the statement of faith, the participant then answers a series of questions designed to help teach the participant that his or her faith should be a core component of prosocial relationships. For example, the workbook asks each person to answer the following questions: *"What does your faith teach you regarding the type of relationship you should have with your parents? According to your faith what type of relationship should you have with your spouse or future spouse? How does your faith teach you what type of parent you should be and how to treat your children? Are other people important according to your faith? If so how are they important? [and] Does your faith expect you to be a good citizen and productive member of society? Why?"*[42] The nation's prisons are filled with people who believe that their religion justifies not only their crimes but also the behaviors, attitudes, and beliefs that offend the regime of rehabilitation that FCBI administrators want to create. These questions allow the chaplains and FCBI administrators to identify the people who believe that their religion justifies behaviors or beliefs the chaplains and administrators deem antisocial or disruptive. If chaplains identified such beliefs in the answers, that person was disqualified from participating in FCBIs.

In January 2014, the DOC eliminated the workbook as a program prerequisite, against the objection of many FCBI administrators. According to Chaplain Taylor, two reasons motivated their decision.[43] First, the DOC occasionally had more beds in FCBIs than eligible prospective participants waitlisted to transfer.[44] The DOC reasoned that the workbook requirement was a significant deterrent, so DOC senior administrators eliminated the workbook requirement to allow more people to transfer on short notice. The DOC also eliminated the workbook requirement because people who were illiterate or who had trouble reading and writing could not qualify for admission into the FCBI program, and they complained that the workbook requirement was a form of institutionalized discrimination. For many years, however, the DOC officially excluded these people from participating in FCBIs. Today, the workbook is no longer a program prerequisite, but incarcerated people in FCBIs can complete it for course credit once they are admitted into an FCBI. During the period when the workbook was a requirement, however, it successfully marginalized and prevented illiterate inmates, who are statistically the group most likely to recidivate, from participating in FCBIs.

According to the DOC, prospective participants who do qualify are placed on a waitlist, and they serve their sentences in a conventional prison until a chaplain or classification officer notifies them that a bed is available in an FCBI. The person is reevaluated to ensure that he or she still qualifies, and assuming that the person does, the DOC transfers the person to an FCBI. According to a DOC report from 2007, that waitlist included 6,353 people, waiting an average of 245 days before transfer into an FCBI.[45] The question remains, however, is the waitlist a hard list where a person is transferred when it is that person's turn, or does the DOC privilege any people on the waitlist? My research suggests the latter.

A report titled *Evaluation of Florida's Faith- and Character-Based Institutions* summarized the DOC's standard answer when it wrote, "When a spot in an FCBI becomes available, the inmate at the top of the list is reviewed for eligibility, and, if eligible, he or she is transferred."[46] The authors of this report acknowledged in a footnote that "conversations with DOC officials indicate that other factors are sometimes taken into consideration, such as the inmate's overall disciplinary history and whether the inmate fills a specific institutional need (carpentry skills, for example)."[47] These "other factors" appear to play a larger role than FCBI administrators suggest, as numerous participants told me that they transferred to FCBIs within weeks or sometimes within days of their initial requests, while other participants waited for extended periods of time. Several incarcerated men at Wakulla CI even said they transferred to the FCBI prison after their classification officers either suggested they transfer because it would look good to a parole board or after the classification officers simply told them that they were being transferred to the Wakulla prison. Such transfers typically occurred within days or maybe weeks at the latest, but definitely nowhere near the average of 245 days. This suggests that some prospective participants receive preferential treatment as they are placed at the top of the list. The fact remains that a senior administrator decides which individuals to place in particular FCBIs, and the data suggest that the waitlist is more likely a priority list where administrators subjectively grant priority to certain people.

Regardless of the admission process, once someone enters an FCBI, that person has to obey the FCBI's unique rules or risk expulsion from the program and transfer back into a conventional prison. Perhaps the first important step in the expulsion process lies in the various strategies and techniques that FCBI administrators, supporters, and sympathetic incarcerated participants use to frame the issue of participation and expulsion. This framing is important because it shifts the burden onto the participant as opposed to the FCBI's extensive rules and regulations. According to Karen Moffett, a former Other Personnel Services (OPS) Chaplain at Lawtey CI, she told new participants in their FCBI orientation, "[In conventional prisons] you're out in the middle of the Atlantic Ocean. We're throwing you a life preserver [in the FCBI], but it's up to *you* to grab it."[48] Daniel Crawford, a classification officer at Lawtey CI, echoed this when he said that they tell newly admitted residents, "You chose to be here, but you can't choose not to participate."[49] In other words, the burden is on the incarcerated to embrace the FCBI's various procedures and rules. The administrators want the incarcerated to internalize and embrace this mindset because, as Warden James Coker from Wakulla CI said, "We enforce *all* the rules here. If you don't follow rules here—if you don't make your bed, clean around your bunk, listen to the correctional officers—what makes you think you can follow rules on the outside?"[50] Obedience to FCBI rules, he suggests, conditions the residents to live crime free lives after prisons.

Not all of the incarcerated embrace this mindset, and those who reject it either voluntarily leave the FCBI or are simply expelled. Other people, however, reject the administrators' framing of FCBI rules, but for various reasons they adhere to the minimum standards because they find some benefit in the program. Peter Fowler, an incarcerated man at Wakulla CI whom I met only once, expressed this idea one afternoon after he flagged me down while I crossed the path from the chapel to the education building. "Hey," he said to me. "You're the guy who's gonna write the book on this place, right?" "Well, that's the plan," I told him. "Here's the deal," he continued. "These guys are feeding you a bunch of shit. This place ain't half what it's cracked up to be, and you need to tell the world *that*."

"Fair enough," I responded, "but why do you still choose to serve your time here?"

Without missing a beat, he replied, "Man, I'm closer to my family here. I get to see my kids more often; I get to see my mom more often. That's it! I've been here a year and I ain't never stepped foot in [the chapel]. I take a few classes in [the educational building], I keep a low profile, and I stay for my family."

While people like Peter may never embrace the FCBIs' mission centered on responsibility and obedience, many incarcerated people appear to embrace it wholeheartedly. One person in an FCBI dorm expressed as much when he said, "Look, we hold [each other] to higher standards. Higher than in [conventional] prison, higher than they've ever had! If they can't follow our standards, it's on them, and they got to go!" Brandon Maher, an inmate facilitator at Wakulla CI, repeated that notion when he said, "Brothers aren't kicked out of the program as much as they remove themselves from it by violating the rules." In other words, both men repeated a sentiment I had heard countless times in various classes, interviews, and informal discussions where the participants agree with FCBI administrators that strict obedience is the key to success in FCBIs and that anything short of strict obedience is solely the individual's fault. The question remains: What exactly are these rules?

Before I can answer that question, I first need to note three important caveats. First, every FCBI has a unique attitude toward participant behavior and codes of conduct. The chaplains, program directors, and inmate facilitators help determine the unique character of each FCBI, so what occurs in one FCBI would never be permitted in another. In one of the FCBI prisons, for example, an inmate facilitator named JD admitted to me, in front of other inmate facilitators, that he steals bleach from the facility and sells it in smaller bottles for $2 per bottle. He has no shortage of customers, he said, as even the incarcerated want clean rooms. This type of behavior would never be acceptable in some FCBIs that have a zero-tolerance policy for any and all contraband. Chaplain Moffett recalled a man who was expelled from an FCBI prison because he manufactured and sold barbeque sauce. He purchased ingredients from the prison's canteen, mixed them together, and then sold them on the prison's underground black market. Prison administrators kicked him out after someone in the FCBI prison "snitched" on him, yet JD openly steals from the facility and participates in the underground market with complete impunity. Each facility stresses the importance of obedience, but people do not uniformly interpret and enforce that directive.

Second, while each FCBI is unique, collectively, FCBI dorms tend to be stricter than FCBI prisons, aided by the structure of the FCBI dorm itself. FCBI dorms typically include seventy-two incarcerated people who live, worship, sleep, study, eat, take classes, and enjoy recreation time together. Participants in FCBI dorms are commonly placed in eight-person "pod families" who are first and foremost accountable to each other. When one family member commits an infraction—any infraction—it potentially disrupts the discipline-based regime of rehabilitation that begins in the pod family, so pod family members rigorously police their fellow family members, both to help the "fallen brother or sister" and to prevent the person's disruptive behaviors from spreading and contaminating the family and potentially the dorm itself. Aaron, an incarcerated man in an FCBI dorm, described as much when he said,

> Look, if I let him [points to his neighbor] slide, I'm not helping him! I'm allowing him to repeat the behaviors that got him here in the first place! By helping him [that is, by telling authority figures when he violates an FCBI policy], I'm gonna help him stay out of prison for good! But I'm not just doing it for him, I'm doing it for me, too. You see, I used to hang out with bad dudes. I know how to be around people who break the rules. I gotta learn, though, how to avoid those people, and one way I avoid them here is by correcting them when they fall. It's in his interest, but it's really in mine.

This person described a sentiment I had heard numerous times in FCBI dorms where the incarcerated contend that they hold each other to high standards.

People who live in FCBI prisons, however, are often (but not always) more lenient. Consider that FCBI prisons incarcerate hundreds of people, and while the majority of them live in dorms, the people interact daily with people who live in other dorms. They may sleep and even study together in the dorms, but outside their dorms they eat, worship, study, and participate in classes with potentially a hundred or more incarcerated people outside their dorms who share neither the intense pod family clique mentality nor the desire to so rigorously police each other's behaviors. This not only creates a more relaxed attitude but helps the participants justify their more relaxed behavior toward certain transgressions. Two inmate facilitators at Wakulla CI summarized this approach.

Noel Gilli said that he does not make a habit of snitching on people who violate minor rules in Wakulla CI. "I'm not gonna snitch on someone doing wrong," he said. "God gave me an opportunity to learn from my mistakes, so maybe God is doing the same for them." Dennis Lonsdale echoed this sentiment when he said, "Listen, if a guy really wants to gain an edge on life, he can do that here. But not all guys know how to *accept* that edge, so we have to give them time [to adjust]." Broadly speaking, these inmate facilitators are willing to tolerate someone who violated some of the FCBI's policies, as they believe that these violators need the type of faith-based programming the FCBI prison offers. Throw the offenders back into conventional prisons, they reckon, and it drastically diminishes the offender's chances of having a genuine conversion experience.

Finally, while each facility has a unique character and while there are differences between FCBI dorms and prisons, each individual facility can change over time in its approach to transgressions. Wakulla CI, for example, experienced a significant change in its infancy as it transformed from a facility with a strict zero-tolerance policy to one that tolerates minor policy violations and disciplinary infractions. An incarcerated man named Tyler Walsh lived at Wakulla CI when it was a conventional prison, and he continues to live there a decade after its conversion to an FCBI. He described the strict environment that emerged in the immediate wake of the conversion when he said, "Back then, it was one strike and you're out! One DR [disciplinary report or infraction] and you're out." Chaplain Steve Fox echoed this sentiment when he said, "It used to be one DR and you were gone. If you get a DR today, you can be placed in disciplinary confinement while you're evaluated, but you won't necessarily be kicked out. That wasn't the case before."

In short, the preceding analysis suggests that each facility takes a unique approach to adjudicating rule violations, yet despite these differences, the facilities do overlap in their treatment of transgressions. That is, beneath their differences, certain similarities exist that create an enforceable hierarchy of values—that is, a hierarchy of normalcy—in all FCBIs. This hierarchy of values is most evident in the FCBI dorms at Tomoka CI, where a manual itemizes the facility's rules, regulations, and punishments for transgressions.

Transgressions typically fall into one of three categories, each with its own disciplinary procedures. The first category of offense refers to "Violations of DOC rules witnessed by Security Staff [that] will be handled per DOC policy."[51] Many violations occur outside the staff's purview or sight, but if a staff member sees or is notified of the infraction, the correctional officer is supposed to follow written disciplinary procedures. The participation manual at Tomoka CI explicitly acknowledges that the officers should follow this protocol; however, for minor offenses, correctional officers occasionally refer the offender to his peer leaders in the FCBI. Several of the correctional officers whom I talked to confirmed that they often allow peer leaders to discipline fellow offenders who violate DOC policies, as it not only reduces correctional officers' paperwork but allows the offender to remain in the program, where the correctional officers believe the offender will more likely experience contrition and reformation. As a case in point, a correctional officer at Gulf Annex CI caught a man smuggling food from the chow hall into the dorm, and instead of formally disciplining the man, the officer turned the offender over to his peers, who coordinated his punishment.

This highlights a second category of offenses that will not necessarily result in program expulsion but are subject to internal disciplinary action inside the FCBI. This punishment is coordinated and approved by the incarcerated in conjunction with the chaplain or facility administrator.[52] Punishable offences include nonparticipation, stealing, disrespect, lying, destruction of property, profanity, talking during count or yelling across dormitory, negative behavior or communication, repeated negative behavior, sowing discord, excessive noise in the TV room, breaking confidentiality, and verbal threats. People who violate these policies are subject to internal discipline, which commonly consists of program probation, additional cleaning duty in the dorm, a 500- or 1,000-word essay (depending on the infraction), restitution (when applicable), public apologies, and additional classes that might benefit the offender. If the violator is unrepentant, is a repeat offender, or is otherwise deemed particularly problematic, he can be expelled from the program. When an offender commits one of these violations, a peer council meets and determines the appropriate penance. At Tomoka CI and some of the other FCBIs, the incarcerated use a Bible-based reconciliation program called Matthew 18.[53]

Matthew 18 is a formal policy based, as the name suggests, on biblical verses from the Gospel of Matthew 18:15–17, which state, "If your brother or sister sins, go and point out their fault, just between the two of you. If they listen to you, you have won them over. But if they will not listen, take one or two others along, so that 'every matter may be established by the testimony of two or three witnesses.' If they still refuse to listen, tell it to the church; and if they refuse to listen even to the church, treat them as you would a pagan or a tax collector." The men attempt to replicate this in the faith-based dorms where an incarcerated person "initiates Matthew

18" with someone who violates one of the rules that do not explicitly result in his removal from the program. The aggrieved or offended party tells the alleged offender that he violated one of the dorm's policies, and he suggests a penance. If all parties do not approve of the proposed terms, they involve their "family leader" and initiate another conversation. There are anywhere from two to four attempts to address and punish the offender before the Grandfather (as discussed later, the Grandfather is an incarcerated man who holds a formal leadership position in many FCBI dorms), chaplain, and facility administrators participate in the conversation. Eventually, either all parties agree to the proposed punishment or, if the offender refuses, the administrators remove the offender from the dorm.

Several of the incarcerated men in the FCBI dorms at Tomoka CI provided an example of Matthew 18 when they shared the story of someone who jumped out of bed one night after curfew and screamed at the other dorm residents, "Y'all's a bunch of pussy motherfuckers!" This was a clear violation of dorm policies, and sensing that something must be wrong with the man, instead of assigning a standard punishment or expelling him from the dorm entirely, several people approached the offender to initiate Matthew 18. Over the next twenty-four hours and several rounds of Matthew 18, the offender confessed that he spoke to his aunt the previous day, who informed him that his mother was no longer going to add money to his prison canteen account. This meant that he would only eat prison-cooked meals for the remainder of his lengthy sentence. This upset the offender, who decided to take out his frustration on his dormmates. As he lay in bed thinking about his future, he became increasingly frustrated with everyone in the dorm, so he stood up and screamed.

Once the other residents heard this explanation, they consoled him and expressed their support for their fellow brother. They forgave him for his transgression, but they agreed that he should write a five-hundred-word apology that he would read to the entire dorm, that he should devote five additional hours to cleaning the dorm, and that he should be on sixty-day probation. The offender agreed to the penance, and according to the men who told me this story, Matthew 18 "worked." Matthew 18, then, is one of the ways incarcerated people police and punish one another in many FCBIs. Those who do not agree to the punishments are expelled.

Program participation similarly falls under the second category of offenses that do not necessarily result in program expulsion but are subject to disciplinary action. It is one of the most important issues, so it deserves special consideration. Participation in rehabilitative classes is the cornerstone of FCBI programming, so people who do not enroll and participate in the minimum number of classes are expelled from the FCBIs. At Lawtey CI, the men have to participate in a minimum of ten classes per month. Prison administrators maintain a list of every resident, classifying them as either compliant or noncompliant. If someone is noncompliant three months in a row or more than three months in a six-month period, he is expelled from the prison. The administrators at Lawtey make an exception for new residents, who have a one-month grace period to enroll in classes. "The first month is on the house," the classification officer said.[54] "After that, it's on the inmates." After the first month, residents are subject to the compliant and noncompliant list. How large is the noncompliant list? When I discussed this issue with the classification officer at Lawtey in May 2014, he said that the previous month, almost 8 percent of the incarcerated were noncompliant, although that statistic included the most recently admitted men who had not been there a full month. Of the residents who had been there longer than a month, 5 percent were noncompliant. As previously discussed, FCBI dorms are typically stricter about resident participation; however, the other FCBI prisons (besides Lawtey, that is) have more lenient policies primarily because of limited classroom space.

Finally, the third category of violation falls under the zero-tolerance category, which barring some extenuating circumstance will result in immediate dismissal from the program. Zero-tolerance violations include "Violence—Physical confrontation; Drugs: Usage/Possession; Tobacco: Usage/Possession; Alcohol: Usage/Possession; Weapons: Usage/Possession; Sexually Acting Out (Includes masturbation); Destruction/Vandalism of PROGRAM Property; [and] Disrespect to Outside or Compound Volunteers."[55] Anyone who commits any of the zero-tolerance violations is expelled immediately from the FCBI dorm. One man summarized this category best when he said, "Look, man, it's not super easy to get kicked out, but it's not hard."

Of the various transgressions listed in this third category, violations of the "Sexually Acting Out" category appear to be the most common. Keep in mind that to be admitted into an FCBI, a prospective resident basically needs a clean disciplinary report, which typically means he is already not involved in violence, drugs, tobacco, alcohol, weapons, or vandalism. In other words, he is "clean."[56] Incarcerated men and women typically do not, however, receive disciplinary reports for masturbation, which is a routine and common aspect of incarceration. In FCBIs, however, all sexual activity, including masturbation, is a zero-tolerance violation and results in expulsion.

Many prisons—both in Florida and beyond—have penalized masturbation, where it is typically classified as "indecent exposure."[57] People have masturbated in prisons for as long as prisons have existed, but masturbation became a more contentious legal issue after 2003's federal Prison Rape Elimination Act (PREA), which addressed sexual assaults in prisons and which penalized a variety of sex acts. A question emerged in wake of PREA: Would PREA eliminate all sexual activity including masturbation?[58] The state of Florida answered in the affirmative, as the incarcerated occasionally face disciplinary action for masturbating in Florida's prisons and jails.[59] PREA provides FCBI administrators with additional leverage to outlaw masturbation in FCBIs. Masturbation, FCBI administrators reckon, not only offends the god of the conservative Christians who administer Florida's FCBIs, but it also violates Florida's legal code. As such, masturbation is a zero-tolerance violation in many FCBIs, and anyone who masturbates risks expulsion from the FCBI program.

Residents in FCBIs are also expelled for engaging in consensual sexual activity, which happens in both female and male FCBIs. According to the people I interviewed in both male and female prisons and dorms, homosexual sex is more common in female than in male prisons. In women's facilities, it is not uncommon for women to be "prison gay, outside straight." Women who engage in same-sex relationships occasionally transfer to an FCBI, and they will be expelled from the dorm if they continue to engage in these relationships. According to the incarcerated women and the chaplain at the FCBI dorm for women at Lowell Annex CI, one or two women are expelled from the seventy-two-person dorm each month for consensual sex (for example, one month there will be no expulsions, but the next month two will be expelled after they are caught having consensual sex).[60] Women are also occasionally expelled for masturbating.

Sexual activity—consensual or otherwise—also occurs in the male facilities. A correctional officer confirmed as much when he described how his fellow correctional officers found a magazine rolled up inside a sock. The sock had blood and what appeared to be fecal matter that surrounded the sock about six inches up. The officers agreed that the sock had been inserted into a prisoner's anus, but they could not determine if it was consensual. In another example, a young female volunteer described how a man was removed from her class after he appeared to be stroking his erect penis over his pants. The offender was most likely expelled from the FCBI, and the person or people who used the magazine-filled sock would also have been expelled if they had been caught in the act.

Outside of the formal regulatory policies, informal policies also regulate residents' behavior and participation in FCBIs. For example, the administrators of the faith-based dorm in Tomoka CI expelled someone because his bunk quite literally smelled like shit. Like an increasing number of the incarcerated in correctional departments throughout the United States, this particular man is developmentally delayed.[61] (The incarcerated refer to such people as "bugs," as in, "They have bugs in their brains.") Prior to the tough-on-crime movement, this man would most likely not be incarcerated; rather, he would live in a hospital or care home for the developmentally delayed. Funding for such programs has decreased significantly over the last several decades, so the developmentally delayed are increasingly incarcerated. This particular man first served time in conventional prisons before he transferred to the faith-based dorm at Tomoka CI, where he lived for a short period of time before he was expelled from the program. Why was his tenure so short?

Instead of cleaning himself with toilet paper after a bowel movement, he wiped himself with a washcloth he kept in a plastic cup at the head of his bunk. Recall that Florida's prisons are not air conditioned, and on hot and humid days, which are the majority of the days in Florida, the slightest offending odor can travel through the dorm. According to the men in the FCBI dorm, either the "bug" had to adjust his routine or he had to go. Due to his mental condition, the former was not a realistic option, so the man, his cup, and his washcloth returned to a conventional prison. While this person's story is unique (I have yet to encounter another person expelled for offensive personal hygiene), it highlights how certain people are occasionally deemed a bad fit for the program and subsequently expelled even when they do not violate one of the formal rules or policies.[62]

Another woman left a female facility after she faced disciplinary action for forming the word "prick" during a Scrabble game. According to the women who described this story, the woman contended that she used the word as a verb (meaning, to poke or pierce) but some of the women in the FCBI dorm believed that she referred to the word as a noun (referencing a phallus). According to the incarcerated women who knew this woman, the offender decided to transfer out of the FCBI, as her peers, she allegedly felt, were looking for reasons to discipline one another.

This summary of life in FCBIs suggests that FCBIs might provide people a place to do easy or safe time, but participants are also subject to the strictest moral, ethical, and behavioral standards in the entire DOC. The application process itself effectively designates large groups as ineligible to participate in the FCBIs, and those who are admitted into the program are similarly subject to expulsion for violating DOC codes, but they are also excluded if they do not complete their programming or if they violate various moral prohibitions. In other words, they are expelled from the FCBIs if they offend the morality of the conservative Christians who are the facilities' primary administrators. As a result of these policies, on any given month, roughly 5 to 7 percent of the residents in FCBIs leave the program.[63] In a particularly high month, that figure reaches 10 percent. According to Classification Officer Crawford, the incarcerated leave the FCBIs for one of three reasons: they self-terminate, they do not participate, or they are expelled for rule violations.[64] The people who leave the program, Crawford said, are divided almost evenly between the three categories. These people are transferred back into conventional prisons, which opens additional beds for new participants in FCBIs. This process repeats itself every month in every FCBI.

Volunteers

From the first prison in Chattahoochee in 1868 to the present, a steady stream of religious volunteers has consistently reminded Florida's prison administrators that they will always be reliable partners, as they provide valuable services for the DOC; particularly, they provide volunteer labor to a correctional department that is drastically underfunded. Former secretary Michael Crews summarized the importance of volunteer labor when he said, "Without the volunteers, we'd really be in trouble. They provide such a service for us, and it's a service with no cost. . . . Without the volunteers and community partnerships, we'll never get to where we need to be."[65]

Every prison benefits from volunteer labor, and volunteer labor is more common in FCBIs (compared with conventional prisons), where they provide the bulk of the religious programming and where they mobilize financial resources from their communities primarily for the benefit of incarcerated Christians. It is not an overstatement to refer to volunteers as the heart or the lifeline of the FCBI program. The only potential problem from the DOC's perspective is that the overwhelming majority of the volunteers are conservative Protestants (according to one chaplain, 98 to 99 percent of the volunteers "come from a Christian background," and it is not a stretch to think that for him "Christian" means conservative Protestant)[66] who bring into the FCBIs their aversion to religious pluralism, their disdain for any governmental regulation that limits their ability to proselytize, and their desire to preach the gospel on their terms free from governmental regulation or oversight.

According to many involved in prison administration, this is particularly true for the evangelical and fundamentalist volunteers. Ike Griffin, one of the architects and senior administrators of Florida's first faith-based dorm, described this problem specifically as it relates to evangelicals. According to Griffin, evangelicals "are diametrically opposed to federal law regarding proselytization, and that makes them a risk for ongoing programs."[67] Griffin continued,

> The evangelicals give us more problems than any . . . group. They're the ones who say, "Well, you know, we all speak to God and we think that we hear the one true God, and we all think that God speaks to us a little more clearly than to anyone else, and therefore, you don't tell me what God is telling us to do." And that's fair, and [prison administrators] can't operate without those people. What we have to do, is to tell them in this instance, the court system has told us that we will not have access if we proselytize. You can't have a dorm program without the state having to spend at least some taxpayer money, some public funds on it. You can't segregate a portion of the population without spending some public funds. Spending public funds means that you cannot proselytize. So, let's think about that for a moment. If you can proceed without proselytizing, we want you. If you can't do that, we want you to go do whatever you want to, but don't do it with us, because you'll get us into problems; into trouble.[68]

As Griffin described, FCBIs are government-run institutions and are subject to First Amendment jurisprudence and other federal and local legislation that regulates their actions. The Supreme Court has never specifically addressed the legality of FCBIs, so the executive administrators in Florida are forced to interpret the courts' previous legal decisions to identify constitutionally permissible behaviors for all volunteers in the FCBIs.[69] Based on these decisions, the administrators determined that volunteers have to adhere to very clear and specific rules. They are allowed to invite the incarcerated to their services and programs, but they are not allowed to proselytize at will. They are allowed to preach their personal theologies and their interpretations of religious texts, but they are not allowed to promote violence or to encourage the incarcerated to break any DOC rules, nor can they overtly condemn specific religions.

Depending largely on the prison administrators and chaplains, FCBIs also either exclude or marginalize Christian volunteers who engage in a variety of practices common in evangelical and fundamentalist services. FCBI administrators typically forbid dancing in the spirit, faith healings, and being slain in the spirit (where someone suddenly falls to or lays down on the ground) as they involve some degree of human-on-human contact. People can shake hands in FCBIs, but not much more. Even hugging is not permitted, much less any act that involves a potentially violent embrace such as an aggressive or assertive laying on of hands. According to Warden Barry Reddish from Lawtey CI, the laying on of hands and faith healing are potentially problematic, as the minister or church leader might suddenly grab someone.[70] This might startle the person or hurt the person, or the person might interpret it as a threat and retaliate. Similarly, someone who is slain in the spirit might collapse to the floor and hit his head on a bench or some other hard substance. For these reasons, Lawtey CI regulates this activity. Other facilities do not aggressively regulate these activities, particularly in FCBIs, where the chaplain is more sympathetic to these behaviors. For people like the chaplain at Lawtey CI, faith healing, the laying on of hands, and being slain in the spirit are common and perhaps even essential forms of worship, and they not only tolerate but encourage these behaviors. The administrators and chaplains who are critical or suspicious of these behaviors forbid them in the FCBIs they administer. Many volunteers are able to accommodate these requests and prohibitions, but many of the volunteers refuse to allow any state agency to regulate their religious rhetoric and behavior, so the DOC does not allow them, in theory, to volunteer in FCBIs.

In summary, volunteers are essential components of the FCBIs, without whom the DOC would potentially abandon the entire program and convert all the FCBIs into conventional correctional facilities. In theory, FCBI administrators could recruit volunteers from local colleges or the surrounding communities in general, including the religious organizations and churches that populate every community in Florida. Instead, chaplains recruit primarily from their networks of like-minded Christians and from the Christians who treat prisons as missionary fields, meaning that the majority of the volunteers are similarly conservative Protestants. These volunteers are typically skeptical of the government and its attempts to regulate the performance of their Christianity, but like all parties involved in FCBIs, volunteers have to accept restrictions imposed both by federal laws and by the chaplains and prison administrators who administer individual FCBIs.

What results are patchwork regimes of authority that, while influenced by federal laws and legislation, are interpreted and implemented at the local level. Federal legislation fuels this reallocation of authority as it provides what it designates religion with the right to participate in social services free from many of the regulations that accompany state-sanctioned socialization in other government-run and administered spaces. Prison administrators have additional authority, as American courts typically defer to prison administrators, whom the courts believe are most equipped to administer prisons. Collectively, the combination of faith-based reform and the relative autonomy granted to prison administrators coalesce in FCBIs to create local and alternatively regulated spheres of state-sanctioned socialization that impacts all participants from administrators, to volunteers, to the incarcerated people who are the intended beneficiaries of FCBIs.

4 Rehabilitation

• •

On any given morning, chapel clerks and inmate facilitators (incarcerated people who teach rehabilitative classes) arrive in the chapel at Wakulla CI between 7:00 and 7:30 A.M., where they prepare the chapel for the various meetings and services that will soon begin. The chapel contains a large room used for worship and meetings, an overflow room that can either enlarge the main room or be divided by a partition that makes it a separate room, several smaller classrooms, a library, the chaplain's office, a room for correctional staff, and two restrooms (one for the incarcerated and one for volunteers). These rooms will soon fill as the men meet for the first round of classes they will attend that day.

On Tuesdays, for example, roughly fifteen men file into Classroom B at 8:00 A.M., where they participate in their weekly Beyond Anger class. Two inmate facilitators teach this class. One is a Christian and the other a Muslim, but they work together as inmate facilitators based on their shared commitment to help the students rely on their religions to overcome the anger that played some role in the crimes that resulted in their incarceration.

Two additional groups will shortly enter the chapel. One will head to the overflow room for their weekly Advanced Yoga class while the other group enters the main room for their weekly Christian Discipleship class. Many people pass the chaplain's office, where the chaplain can usually be seen sitting in front of his computer every morning responding to emails and processing paperwork. The chaplain takes a break at 10:00 A.M. to step outside the chapel and supervise the Native Americans who conduct a brief service where they burn incense and honor their ancestors, traditions, and god(s).

All of these men will soon disperse and return to their work assignments, to their dorms, or to lunch, but many will return to the chapel around 1:30 P.M. for the Hebrew Israelites' study group, New Testament Survey class, and Beginner Yoga. They will leave the chapel after these classes, although another round of incarcerated people will enter around 5:00 P.M. for evening classes, which on Tuesdays include a self-help class called Quest and the Vital Truth Bible Study class.

As this summary suggests, the chapel is a busy place as people meet daily for several rounds of classes. The educational building that sits across a walkway is equally busy, where more people meet for various classes ranging from GED study groups to business development classes to self-help groups like Toastmasters. Many people will also voluntarily meet in their dorms, where they will study class materials, read religious material, or debate the issues they discussed earlier that day.

This diversity of classes is the intended result of faith- and character-based correctional institutions' (FCBIs) senior administrators, who typically believe that religion alone is a necessary but insufficient form of rehabilitation. Based on this belief, and on the constitutional concerns that require them to offer religious and secular programming, every FCBI is religiously pluralistic and contains classes intended to span the religion-secular spectrum.

This chapter introduces readers to the dominant regime of rehabilitation that exists in all FCBIs, including FCBI dorms and prisons for both women and men. It not only summarizes the structure of FCBI programming but also explores the classes' content, the dominant ideas that are repeated in classes, and the models of self and subjectivity that FCBIs nurture and naturalize. The history of prison reform demonstrates that prison reformers disagree about the essential contents of their respective rehabilitative regimes, all of which reflect the reformers' assumptions about citizenship and subjectivity. FCBIs' proponents and administrators are no different, as they create state-sanctioned spaces based on subjective models of the self and society that privilege the imagined private, with religion and markets constituting the core components. Both the structure of FCBI programming and the classes' content articulate and naturalize a theory of subjectivity predicated either on mastering or on accepting the confines of the neoliberal economy and the imagined private.

Methodologically, this chapter draws heavily from Michel Foucault, who argued that neoliberalism reprograms or replaces liberalism and liberal values as society and socializing agents absorb and reflect neoliberal epistemologies.[1] Building off this insight, sociologist Antonio Negri argued that neoliberalism works to produce neoliberal subjects who internalize neoliberal tropes and ideologies, which become organizing principles for all areas of life beyond the economy.[2] This chapter argues that FCBIs are extensions of this reprogramming, as when the material addressed in FCBIs does not overtly address the economy or economic language, ideas that replicate neoliberal values provide the core of FCBI programming.

FCBI Culture

An incarcerated man named David Mollett told me that each prison has its own personality. He would know, as he has spent the last thirty-five years in prison. During that time, Florida's DOC transferred him to multiple prisons where David experienced firsthand that each prison is somewhat unique. There are fifty-one correctional departments in the country, and prison administrators in each department run their departments more or less autonomously. Federal laws require that all prisons provide certain basics, but federal laws are only one factor that influences prison life at the local level. Wardens, junior administrators, correctional officers, chaplains, and even the prison itself influence prison life and carceral cultures, resulting in hundreds of different correctional cultures in the country. This presents a challenge for ethnographers and for anyone interested in documenting carceral cultures, as generalizations are often difficult to support.

Carceral cultures in FCBIs are no different. The state of Florida currently operates thirty-five FCBIs, and while I did not research in all of them, ethnographic research confirmed that each FCBI has, to quote David, its own personality, as the local administrators, volunteers, and even the incarcerated influence the culture in the individual FCBIs. Behind this diversity, however, lies a common regime of rehabilitation that exists to various degrees in all FCBIs. Several factors contribute to this regime.

First and foremost, the architects and administrators of FCBIs agree that rehabilitation is their primary goal. All of their efforts stem from this central point. To create rehabilitative environments, they have to invert the dominant prison culture. In his now classic book, *The Prison Community*, Donald Clemmer described how the overall structure of the prison combines with the social relationships that develop inside prisons to routinely result in what Clemmer termed "prisonization," that is, the process by which the incarcerated acquire behaviors inside prisons that impede their ability to successfully reenter society.[3] This important insight might be a novel idea to the casual observer, but scholars and other interested parties have long noted that prisons are breeding grounds for the antisocial behaviors that any regime of rehabilitation has to address and attempt to correct. David Skarbek similarly addressed this issue when he described how the incarcerated create alternative forms of governance in American prisons that include underground economies and informal disciplinary mechanisms that, once learned, might similarly prevent the person from successfully desisting.[4] These alternative forms of governance thrive in direct opposition to the prisons' formal rules and procedures, as their parallel economies and disciplinary mechanisms are often premised on disobedience to carceral authority.[5] Collectively, these insights suggest that instead of creating carceral spaces suitable to rehabilitation, prisons have a tendency to encourage the behaviors and mindsets that often motivate criminal and antisocial behaviors. This is the carceral culture that proponents of FCBIs want to reform.

Supreme Court decisions and First Amendment jurisprudence are also factors that influence the common regime of rehabilitation that exists in FCBIs. The architects and administrators of FCBIs are keenly aware that FCBIs exist on the boundaries of legally permissible partnerships between religion and state, and Florida's DOC created and subsequently modified FCBIs to adhere to its lawyers' interpretation of First Amendment jurisprudence and relevant legislation. For this reason, the administrators of FCBIs contend that their facilities are open to everyone regardless of their religion or lack thereof. The DOC contends that inmates from dozens of faith groups are incarcerated in FCBIs, although conservative Protestants are the overwhelming majority. A market mentality drives participation in FCBIs, and incarcerated people from all religions compete in this market, but if the majority of the consumers are conservative Protestants then that group constitutes the majority.

In addition to developing pluralistic spaces, the DOC's lawyers believe that FCBIs must include both religious and secular programming. As the next section shows, this legal mandate overlaps with the broader idea common among even the staunchest supporters of FCBIs that religion or faith is a necessary but insufficient component of rehabilitation.

Faith Alone?

According to Chaplain Alex Taylor (head chaplain of Florida's DOC from 1999 to 2016), when Florida's DOC hired him as head chaplain, senior prison administrators gave him "two directives—to standardize chaplaincy ministry across the state and to introduce faith-based residential programs."[6] Chaplain Taylor fulfilled his duties as he presided over the largest expansion of faith-based correctional institutions in history.

Chaplain Taylor was one of the first people I interviewed for this project, where I asked him the first of two questions I asked every person I interviewed: "Can religion alone reduce recidivism?" Based on his personal beliefs and his professional experience, it surprised me when he immediately replied, "No." He jokingly continued, "If everybody had like an Elijah fiery chariot experience; if we had that? Maybe." In other words, if every incarcerated person had a direct encounter with God, religion alone might reduce recidivism. Short of that, however, incarcerated men and women need additional forms of rehabilitation. He continued, "Learn John 3:16 and this'll be the answer to all your problems, right? It doesn't work. You're still going to have to learn a skill." In other words, capitalism does not recognize "faith" as a form of currency. A person needs to earn a living.

Taylor was by no means the only chaplain to voice this idea. A Pew study from 2012 suggests that prison chaplains throughout the United States overwhelmingly agree that faith-based reforms should include a combination of secular, vocational, and educational reform. Forty percent of prison chaplains believe that religious programming is not even the best method of treatment.[7] Almost every person I interviewed—senior administrators, junior administrators, chaplains, correctional officers, and the incarcerated themselves—echoed this sentiment as Christian proponents of faith-based correctional reforms tend to agree that faith is a necessary but insufficient foundation for successful desistance.[8]

Other senior administrators in Florida such as Ike Griffin, the former president of Kairos Horizon and one of the primary architects of Florida's first faith-based dorm, agreed with Taylor. When I asked Griffin if religion alone can reduce recidivism, he replied, "Religion? No, not religion alone. Religion can start more fights than pacify things in a contentious environment, and prison is a contentious environment."[9] Griffin elaborated that faith-based correctional programs need additional forms of rehabilitation if the incarcerated are going to avoid future criminal behavior.

Dale White—the Florida State Reentry representative for Celebrate Recovery (a self-proclaimed Christ-based twelve-step program), mentor in the Florida DOC's mentoring program, founder of Harvest House (a Christian reentry home), and seasoned volunteer at several prisons including Wakulla CI—offered a similar theory of rehabilitation when he said, "I believe in treating the whole individual. Whether we're in the prisons or at Harvest House, faith is nice, but when the doors close, if you don't have any personal skills, chances are less than average you'll stay out of prison."[10] Faith, he argued, is not only an important but an essential part of rehabilitation. "Without faith," he said, "their chance [of staying out of prison] is less than average. If I had to lose one component, [faith] would be the last I'd want to lose."

Academic proponents of faith-based correctional facilities similarly agree that religion is important but insufficient. Byron Johnson, for example—the most vocal and prolific academic proponent of faith-based correctional reforms—similarly voiced this idea. "Let me be clear," he wrote, "simply relying only on faith-based prison programs to reform prisoners and reduce crime would be a misguided policy recommendation."[11] Collectively, these examples suggest that a large majority of the proponents of faith-based correctional reform agree that religion alone will not reduce recidivism rates.

Of all the people I interviewed, only Allison DeFoor suggested that religion alone prevents or reduces recidivism.[12] Even then, he argued that faith alone reduces recidivism because it provides the incarcerated with the moral and ethical components that make them seek work and education. Faith "works," DeFoor argued, because it motivates people to develop the other necessary components associated with successful desistence.

Scholars interested in faith-based correctional reform have long noted that faith-based correctional programs typically include what most would consider both religious and secular programming, although they disagree on which programs belong in each category.[13] The irony, according to one study, is that FCBIs contain less educational and vocational programming than Florida's conventional prisons.[14] The emphasis on religion or faith arguably displaces the secular programming that many agree is not only important but essential. Consider, for example, that collectively, the three FCBI prisons only offer four vocational programs—Environmental Services and Software Essentials at Wakulla, Drafting Architectural at Lawtey, and Web Development at Hernando. Additionally, some of Florida's conventional prisons partner with various parties to offer in-prison college educational courses. To my knowledge, none of the FCBIs have any such partnerships, although individuals in FCBIs can enroll in remote study courses and programs at their expense.[15] Critics of FCBIs might highlight the virtual dearth of vocational and educational programming at FCBIs as evidence of their limitations. The proponents of FCBIs, however, have a ready response.

They would remind their critics that incarcerated people, ideally, serve only a portion of their prison sentences in FCBIs. Instead, most people who participate in the FCBI program serve a maximum of three years in FCBIs until they graduate from the program and are transferred to a conventional prison, are expelled, or leave voluntarily. FCBIs resemble colleges insofar as participants receive "credits" for each class or program they complete, and they have to complete 1,220 credits of programming to graduate from an FCBI. Assuming a "full-time" course of study, incarcerated people in FCBI dorms complete the programming in eighteen months while participants in FCBI prisons complete the program in three years. The difference in length is not the result of more extensive programming in FCBI prisons; rather, people in FCBI prisons typically have work assignments, but people in FCBI dorms typically do not. Instead, the incarcerated in FCBI dorms spend the bulk of their time immersed in FCBI programming, which allows them to complete the program in half the time. After they complete the program and graduate, the vast majority of the participants typically transfer back into conventional prisons.

Proponents of FCBIs argue that incarcerated people who need vocational or educational programming can receive that programming in Florida's conventional prisons, either before or after they serve time in an FCBI. They would argue that FCBIs are important precisely because they provide the religious foundation that helps the incarcerated *apply* the educational, vocational, secular, or character-based skills they acquire both in conventional prisons and in FCBIs. In other words, they would argue that FCBIs supplement rather than replace nonreligious programming. This argument assumes that these vocational and educational programs exist in Florida's conventional prisons, which are few and are between.

In short, proponents of FCBIs believe that faith is necessary but insufficient, and they attempt to supplement faith-based programming with secular or character-based programming as well. This supplementing raises two important points. First, due to the faith-based environment and the unique history of FCBIs, every class includes what most could classify as a faith component, with theologies associated with conservative Christianity the default form of socialization in FCBIs. Second, the content of the additional classes is particularly important, as these classes teach neoliberal tropes and neoliberal theories of subjectivity, citizenship, and society in general.[16]

Domains/Modules

From Florida's first faith-based dorm to the present, Florida's faith-based correctional facilities have always included character-development classes. To highlight the character-development component in FCBIs, Chaplain Steve Fox from Wakulla CI attempted to standardize FCBI programming when he organized the various classes, workshops, seminars, and worship services into seven "domains" or areas of study. In 2017 the DOC substituted the term "domain" with "module," but the name change did not impact the organizational structure, which still includes the following seven domains or modules: Attitude, Community Functioning, Marital/Family, Healthy Choices, Mentoring, Reentry, and Faith. The DOC subsequently adopted this approach when it required all FCBIs to follow Fox's domain model.

To implement the domain approach to rehabilitation, the DOC created the Florida Department of Corrections Faith and Character–Based Completion Worksheet, which resembles a college graduation checklist.[17] It lists the seven domains, and beneath each domain it itemizes the required classes and the optional classes, leaving space for approved electives that satisfy the domain's requirements. When someone completes the requisite class, the person places an "X" or a check mark in the box next to the class title. All participants in the FCBI program receive a Completion Worksheet when they enter an FCBI, although the chaplains keep the worksheets in their files. This worksheet helps the participants track their progress and stay on track to complete the program in the allotted time. Chaplains repeatedly stress that the worksheet contains rough guidelines as opposed to strict rules, meaning that the curriculum is comparably flexible. What follows is a summary of each domain, including a brief introduction to the required and elective courses. This summary also introduces major themes and ideas the incarcerated learn in each domain.

Attitude Domain

"Sins are like puppies and babies," said inmate Lucas Ingraham. "They're cute when they're small, you have to clean up after them, but they can grow to be rabid monsters if you don't discipline them." Lucas was one of six men seated in a circle during the weekly Bridge Builders meeting. According to Pat Cornell, the volunteer who teaches this class at Wakulla CI, Bridge Builders is a Christ-based twelve-step recovery program designed to treat not only substance and alcohol abuse but "any sin that controls your life—eating, porn, sex, masturbation, gambling, homosexuality, and things like that." Bridge Builders is one of the more common classes in FCBIs.

That day's lesson addressed character defects focusing on gluttony, lust, anger, pride, and envy. The men quickly agreed that sin is the ultimate cause of these defects, hence Lucas's comments about sin. A problem soon emerged, however, as evidenced by the subsequent conversation.

"You know, you're right," another man named Brian replied to Lucas.

My sins started as small and grew over time. I used to live with my grandma. I think I committed my first sin at age five when she gave me money for something at the store. I spent the change on candy and lied to her and told her I lost it. I started cheating at cards at age eight, started shoplifting, and committed my first federal crime at [age] fourteen when I broke into an air force building. I didn't do time for that crime, but I later had sex with minors, and I'll be lucky if I don't die before I get out of here.

An incarcerated man named Jackson replied, "You ever think about how things would be different if you didn't have your background?" Jackson had recently transferred to Wakulla CI and was not versed in dominant FCBI culture related to issues like crime, sin, and incarceration. Unbeknownst to him, he was moments from an introductory encounter with these ideas.

Jackson continued to talk to Lucas, although the entire group was listening. "Like you, I wasn't raised in a godly household. My mom was an addict and my father left us when I was one or two, so my aunt raised me. She worked several jobs so I grew up on the streets in a town that was racist as all get out. I know it was sin that got me here, but I mean, did we have a chance? We have different backgrounds, you and me, but coming from where we did, being dealt the hand we were dealt . . ." Jackson's comment caused Reggie, the group facilitator, to interrupt him.

I hear you, brother, but I have to be honest with you. Racism isn't in the Bible, sin is. Bad parenting isn't in the Bible, sin is. Having a hard life isn't in the Bible, sin is. Most of us in this room lived some version of the same story, but so did millions of people who didn't commit the crimes we committed. So did all these people who had it worse than us but didn't commit the crimes we committed. God wants us to know we and we alone are responsible for our sins. You can't explain it away with "racism" or "I had a hard time as a kid," you feel me? If you're sinning, that's not on [points to Lucas] your grandma. If you're sinning, that's not on [points to Jackson] your auntie. That's on you! We can't blame anybody else for our sins. Bridge Builders is about taking responsibility for our actions, and it starts by owning the sins that got us where we're at.

In this exchange, Jackson learned that residents in FCBIs cannot explain or excuse their crimes because of any structural disadvantage or institutional oppression. Instead, they learn that sin and sin alone is the source of most of their problems.

The incarcerated also learn that Satan and even God are responsible for some of their problems. Satan causes problems in our lives because he constantly tries to tempt us and to punish the faithful. In fact, the men learn that the more they obey God's commands, the more obstacles they can expect from Satan. In other words, turmoil is evidence of righteousness. God also occasionally allows people to suffer as he tests their faith, but they learn to trust, first, that God will not test them with more than they can handle, and second, that God always tests them for a reason. In short, the men learn that if they fail, if they sin, if they commit a crime, or if they are incarcerated, their propensity to sin is the ultimate cause.

Assuming Lucas remains in the program, every day for the next three years he will hear a version of this message. If he internalizes it, he will leave the FCBI attributing all of his problems to a combination of Satan, God, and sin. He will look to God to right every wrong in his life, and he will view extended periods of suffering as evidence of his spiritual shortcomings. Not all of the incarcerated residents in FCBIs embrace these ideas, but those who do not know better than to criticize these ideas, as they will risk being transferred out of the FCBI for sowing discord.

Proponents of FCBIs support this comprehensive reprogramming because it reflects their theological commitments, but they also contend that their no-excuses approach to social and economic life motivates the participants to take complete responsibility for their lives and to rely only on God and the community of the faithful for support. These empowered men will ideally become independent and successful agents of God, and if they fail, personal and religious shortcomings are ultimately to blame. Bridge Builders is but one of the many places where Lucas will hear this message.

Lucas, like perhaps every other man in the room, is taking Bridge Builders because it is one of the more common and respected twelve-step programs offered in FCBIs. Bridge Builders is not a required or optional course in any of the domains, but it will count as an elective class for Lucas to help him earn the requisite forty-five credits he will need to complete the Attitude domain. Required classes in this domain include Journal, Personal Faith Statement, and Portfolio Development (Life Goals). Religious Education, Character Training, and Seminar 1 (Goals, Motivation) are the optional classes, although other electives can also help satisfy the requirements for the Attitude domain.

"What'd I get out of my Kairos weekend?" rhetorically asked inmate Scott Ayd in response to another man's query. "Brother, I got, brothers! And sisters! I got community outta Kairos! I got family outta Kairos! I got people, ya know what I'm sayin'? I had my street people when I ran the streets, but they wasn't good people. In Kairos I didn't get good people, I got the best people!"

The Kairos Cursillo is a three-day "short course" in Christianity designed to repair damaged lives based on Christian values. Cursillos are often termed "Fourth-Day Christianity," referring to the idea that three-day Cursillos prepare Christians for the fourth day, that is, the day after the Cursillo, and every day thereafter. In this paradigm, every day after the Cursillo is the fourth day.

As scholar of religion Kristy Nabhan-Warren described in *The Cursillo Movement in America*, "Since the late 1950s, millions of American Catholics and Protestants and Christians around the world have participated in a seventy-two-hour Cursillo weekend course, or one of its many spinoffs. Catholic and Protestant graduates of the weekend Cursillo claim to be new individuals, refreshed and renewed. Cursillistas seek to demonstrate their new identities by living a life they believe Christ would want them to live. They share a desire to become part of a community of committed Christians who are, in their world, the 'hands and feet of Christ.'"[18] Kairos is just one of the organizations that offer Cursillo weekends in the United States, but it is the primary organization that holds Cursillos in American prisons, including Florida's conventional prisons and FCBIs, where the Kairos weekend helps fulfill the graduation requirements for the Community Functioning domain.

The Kairos weekend typically begins months before the event itself. Preparations include meal prep, baking cookies (made from a specific recipe that lists "prayer" as "the key ingredient"),[19] coordinating musicians, gathering musical instruments, gathering handwritten "agape letters" of support and love prepared by the members of the sponsoring organization and their extended Christian networks, and materials for other activities that will occupy the participants during every waking minute of their seventy-two-hour course.

Not all of the incarcerated love the Kairos weekend (one incarcerated woman privately referred to it as a cult), but those who do enjoy it speak of it as a once-in-a-lifetime, life-changing event. According to Ike Griffin, former executive director of Kairos Prison Ministry, the goal of the Kairos Cursillo is to create a therapeutic environment for three full days.[20] To facilitate that, Kairos reserves a large room, hall, or library inside the prison with exclusive access for the duration of the Cursillo. Correctional officers typically do not enter the room, leaving it one of the few spaces in the prison without commissioned correctional officers. Inside this space, volunteers shower the incarcerated with attention, love, and respect. The volunteers often return monthly to continue to develop their new relationships and to encourage participants in their Christian faith.

The administrators of Kairos hope that incarcerated people like Scott Ayd will leave the Cursillo weekend with a community unlike any they have ever had. They also intend for people to leave Kairos with a desire and with instructions to share with others their new Christian religiosity. As Nabhan-Warren described it, "This new life, the Fourth Day, entail[s] a commitment to bringing Christ into the world and sharing one's new perspectives with others in community."[21] The architects of Florida's Faith and Character-Based Completion Worksheet placed the Kairos weekend as an optional course in the Community Functioning domain for this exact reason.

The classes in the Community Functioning domain are intended to help incarcerated people become positive role models in their immediate communities. This message resonates both with neoliberalism and with larger theological impulses in the New Christian Right (NCR). Regarding the former, proponents of neoliberalism often downplay the ideas of society and the social, replacing it with what Friedrich Hayek referred to as "a person's protected personal sphere."[22] Margaret Thatcher, former British prime minister and proponent of neoliberal reforms in Britain, echoed this sentiment when she stated, "There's no such thing as society. There are individual men and women and there are families. And no government can do anything except through people, and people must look after themselves first. It is our duty to look after ourselves and then, also, to look after our neighbours."[23] The Community Functioning domain reinforces this notion as it teaches people to embrace and to engage their immediate communities for a host of concerns including social services and economic relief. This message also resonates with members of the NCR, which often calls its members to local activism in service of Christianity's political and sociocultural reforms. Their activism will either replace or greatly curtail government services with its paid professionals as volunteer religious activism becomes a hallmark of this new Christian citizenship.

In sum, the Community Functioning domain is designed to help the incarcerated reimagine their relationships with their communities, beginning in FCBIs but extending into the "real world." They learn that prosocial behaviors require them to be leaders in their communities instead of criminal leeches who take advantage of the goodwill of others. They also learn to model these behaviors in prison, where they earn credits for completing mandatory Community Service Projects inside their FCBIs. Other mandatory classes in this domain include Community Meetings, Victim Awareness Training, and Workbook. Optional courses include Civics: Restoration of Civil Rights, Civics, the Kairos Weekend Seminar, and electives applicable to this domain. Collectively, these classes teach participants in FCBIs to rely on private groups like local Christian communities for charity, social support, and social services. They also learn that they should shun government-run programs, relegating government to its "proper" place.

Marital/Family Domain

Thirteen men sat in a classroom inside the chapel at Wakulla CI, where they discussed parenthood, spousal relationships, and masculinity. Each man had to list the people who taught him how to be a father and husband, but the men were confused. That confusion, however, highlighted the lesson's point. Most of the men grew up with only one of their biological parents, and for most of the men, that parent worked multiple jobs and was rarely home. In their parents' absence, the men learned how to be a husband and father from people other than their own parents. The men tended to agree that they learned family relationships from a combination of the extended families that babysat them, media, music, pop culture, their peers who similarly grew up in split or "broken" families, and the older generation they respected and tried to model.

The men began to disagree, however, when a man named Drew asked if those influences really counted, as they did not teach the men how to be *good* husbands and fathers. Instead, it taught them to be absent, to ignore their families until they needed something from them, and to never fully commit themselves to any one partner. "That's not learning how to be in a family," he said, "it's learning how *not* be in a family, and that's not learning!"

Tyree added,

Wait, I think we did learn family relationships from our parents. I know that from my dad, I learned some things. I didn't see him very often, so I learned that you can father children and ignore them. When I did see him, I swear he was always high or drunk and angry, so I learned that you can be an addict and still be a dad. And my mom, she worked harder than any woman I ever met! Three, sometimes four jobs. I learned from her that it's a woman's job to make money for the children who are raised by other people. Those aren't good lessons, but they *are* lessons.

"Naw, man," a man named Alex responded after a brief silence, "you're missing the point. Those ain't the lessons [the inmate facilitators] wanna hear about. They wanna know who taught you how to be a *good* father and husband. They wanna hear about that."

At that point, the inmate facilitator intervened to help focus the group.

You're all right. Tyree, you are 100 percent correct that your parents taught you how not to have a healthy family. And you're right that those are lessons. Obviously, they're not good lessons, and this speaks to Drew's comment, but they are lessons. So, Alex, we do want to hear about the people who taught you how to be a *good* father and husband, but us guys in this room don't have many of those people. We got a lot of characters in our families, but ain't many of them positive role models.

Having demonstrated that the men could not look to their own families as role models, the inmate facilitator then asked, "Where, then? Where do you look to learn how to be a good husband and father? Where can you, here in prison, look to find mentors or role models who can help you learn how to be men?" For the rest of the class, the men discussed various people who could provide models of responsible family life. God was undoubtedly the most commonly mentioned source of responsible parenting, as they learn in almost all of their classes and worship services that they should take the phrase "God the Father" in the literal sense. They found admirable spousal qualities in God's kindness, in his compassion, and in the freedom he grants us to make mistakes and to learn from them. God obviously does not have a wife, but the ideal church, the men argued, provided a model of the successful wife, as the church accepts God's rules and discipline. The men also agreed that the Virgin Mary and Joseph provided ideal role models both as parents and as spouses, as evidenced by their virtue and obedience. "Adam and Eve," one man joked, "not so much." The others laughed.

Other possible sources of role models included the volunteers who visit the prison, their ministers, and the righteous correctional staff. The men also agreed that they could look to books and maybe even to television, although they acknowledged that they had to be selective with those sources, as media often contain more negative influences than positive. Finally, they all agreed that while growing up they knew at least one family who seemed to be "doing it right"—that is, both biological and heterosexual parents lived in the house where they had polite and obedient children. Several of the men found it difficult to admire or to accept those families as role models, as they previously resented those families. With God's grace, however, they intended to find both inspiration and role models.

From the facilitators' perspectives, the class was a resounding success. The men learned that their immediate families often did not provide positive role models, and instead they instilled in their children the negative values that contributed to their own broken relationships. They also learned, first, that they should find or identify new sources of responsible parents and spouses, and second, that they should actively learn from these people. In other words, they learned that they were in the early stages of a larger journey that could fundamentally alter their perceptions of family life.

Finally, the class provided the men with models of what the administrators of FCBIs consider proper and healthy family life. This model of domesticity assumes patriarchal heteronormativity as its ideal. This is particularly important as it relates to family finances, as residents in FCBIs learn, first, that as patriarchal authority figures in the house, they should manage the family's finances, and second, that Christian men have a religious obligation to be fiscally responsible.

Ike Griffin taught as much in his classes at FCBIs, as Griffin believes Jesus made finances the cornerstone of his ministry. "The most numerically prevalent subject in Jesus's teachings, are about money," he said, "how you use your money."[24] Griffin contends that Jesus taught about money because he recognized the importance of commerce and fiscal accountability. The parable of the talents provides the most common justification of this theology.

The parable of the talents appears in two of the canonical gospels. Though the accounts differ in each gospel, the basic story remains the same. A man leaves three servants in charge of his wealth while he is away. He returns to find two of the servants used the money to earn a profit, while the third servant hid the money to keep it safe. The master praises the former two and condemns the latter as being lazy and wicked. Christian theologians disagree about the meaning of this parable, but the participants in FCBIs learn that God and Jesus want them—as heads of household—to accumulate wealth and to invest it in commercial and financial activities. This theology naturalizes not only heteropatriarchal authority but capitalism as well. When coupled with the other lessons they will learn in FCBIs, the incarcerated learn to embrace alternatively regulated neoliberal capitalism as God's preferred economy.[25] The classes in the other domains reinforce this message.

The administrators and volunteers in Florida's FCBIs believe this model of marital and family life is important, not only for the sake of the incarcerated people who might someday be husbands and fathers and their families, but for society as well. Theirs is a god who calls men to be economic leaders in the era of late capitalism. The Marital/Family domain, then, includes this economic message as one of its central components.[26] The only required class in this domain is Parenting from the Inside. Optional classes include Parenting Seminar, Story Book Moms/Dads, Safe People, Financial Accountability, Premarital Study, Parenting Study, and Marriage Study. Approved electives can also count.

Healthy Choices Domain

A dozen or so incarcerated men sat in a small classroom in the chapel at Wakulla CI watching a video designed to help disrupt the decision-making process that resulted in their incarceration. One segment of the video depicted a transaction in a convenience store where a customer approached the clerk to make a purchase. During the exchange, the viewers heard a loud noise like a crash outside the store, prompting the clerk to run outside and investigate. In his haste to leave the store, he did not completely shut the cash register. Noel Illig, the inmate facilitator leading this class, paused the video on the open cash register and asked the students what they would have done in that situation.

"I would have grabbed that money and run," said one man. Another responded, "That woulda been a pay day for me, brother!" The other men laughed as they agreed that their instinct was to pocket the money and leave the store.

Ibraaheem Abu was uncharacteristically quiet during the exchange, as he stared at the television with a slight grin. He is typically one of the more outspoken men in the prison, so Noel asked what he was thinking.

I was just thinking about the times I used to run a store like that. I could smell that store, I noticed which candy bars needed restocking, I wondered which soda I would have grabbed for lunch. But to your point, yeah, I could see many of my customers taking that money. Not all of them, 'cause not everyone has the thief mentality, but when you take that money, if there's only $20 or $30 in the register, you're robbing from that guy. You're taking his house payment, his bill money, or maybe his kid's new-shoe money.

"That's right," responded Noel. "When you steal that money, you're taking his livelihood. It's easy to see how this is stealing, but can you think of other ways you can steal?"

Most of the men in this room have been incarcerated in an FCBI for over a year, so they were familiar with the question Noel asked. They knew the intended answer. Money is only one thing people steal. They can also steal memories and experiences when they commit crimes, as they deprive people of experiences associated with the items they stole. At least two convicted murderers were in the room, and one of them said, "I stole a family member from someone. With one bullet I stole someone's son, someone's boyfriend, someone's dad, and who knows how many people's friend or relative. When you commit murder, you steal someone's life, but you also steal the relationships that person had."

The men nodded solemnly, seemingly ready to move on. Noel, however, wasn't ready. "What about when you're working, can you think of ways you steal on the job? And I don't just mean taking money or things from the shelves, but how else can you steal?" Again, the men knew the answer, as Noel was revisiting a common theme. A man named William replied, "Well, if you's getting' paid but you ain't actually workin', you're stealing! That man ain't paying you to sit around and talk sports, he's payin' you to work! You gotta be working or you're straight stealin' from the man. You ain't *takin'* nothin', but you're *takin'* the labor you owe him."

"That's right," said Noel. "If you're on the clock and you're not giving the boss 100 percent of your attention, you're robbing from him. If you're on your phones, if you're playing games, if you're texting your woman, you're literally stealing!" In customary fashion, Noel then attempted to sacralize his point. "And we all agree that theft is a sin," he said as he looked directly at the only admitted agnostic in the room, "so if you're on the clock and you're not working, you're sinning! If you're on your phone, you're sinning! If you're just chattin' it up with the guys, you're sinning! It doesn't matter how bad the job is, how much you hate it, or how little you're getting paid. We have to take this seriously, gentlemen. You know why? Because God takes it seriously! How are you going to respond when God asks why you stole from your employer, you hear me?" The men nodded in agreement.

"How do we stop our sins?" he then asked the class. "How do we keep our impulses in check? I see we're out of time for the day, but we'll pick up here next week. God bless you all."

For many of the men, this class will count as an elective in the Healthy Choices domain. Collectively, the classes in the Healthy Choices domain are intended to help the incarcerated identify a set of behaviors as antisocial and undesirable, and then to take the appropriate steps to ensure that they never engage in these behaviors. Addictions of any type (including drugs, alcohol, sugar, caffeine, and of course, sex—including masturbation) are perennial objects of concern. The classes in this domain also help the students recognize and overcome their criminal instincts. As evidenced by the above exchange, these healthier choices impact every area of their lives and reflect the theological convictions of the conservative Protestants who facilitate the class and the economic concerns of neoliberal capitalism.

To assist them in this comprehensive reprogramming, participants in FCBIs have to complete three classes in this domain: Thinking for a Change, Communication and Anger, and From the Inside Out. Optional courses include Addiction Education, AA Meetings, Anger Resolution, Purpose Driven Life, Persona Exercise Discipline, Free Time Activities, Victim Awareness Training, Civics: 9/11 & the Constitution, and approved electives.

Mentoring Domain

Three years into a five-year sentence for trafficking drugs, Tyler Denver finds herself in an unusual position. Tyler is incarcerated at the FCBI at Lowell Correctional Institution (CI) for women, not only where the women in her dorm look up to her but where she allows herself to learn from others. These are relatively new dynamics for Tyler, who spent the bulk of her life avoiding relationships, as she learned at an early age that relationships often lead to harm, both emotional and physical.

Tyler's parents were never married, and her mom simultaneously worked up to five jobs, so Tyler spent most of her days being passed from one female family member to the next. On a typical day she would come home from school to her aunt's house, and her aunt would later drop her off at her grandma's, and her grandma might later leave her with another family member. Tyler described these women as "strong Baptists who didn't play," and when she acted up, corporal punishment was the norm. All of these women were active in their local church, so Tyler found herself in church more evenings than not.

When she was not with her family, she spent time with friends on the streets, where at age ten she encountered the first man who raped her. Several more men abused her over the next four years before she entered her first relationship. The assaults did not stop, however, as her new boyfriend also abused her. Fearing judgment from her Baptist community, she tried to hide the abuse, so no one was able to help her. Her boyfriend eventually broke up with her, but by now, the pattern was set. Tyler continued to date abusive men who, as she described it, pulled her hair and hit her face, routinely giving her black eyes and busted lips. One boyfriend even cut her eye while she took a shower, resulting in permanent damage. The abuse became so bad that she tried to end her life by jumping out of a moving car on the freeway.

At age nineteen, Tyler began using drugs to dull the pain—both physical and emotional—and almost ten years later she was arrested for trafficking prescription pills and cocaine. When she was incarcerated, her family effectively disowned her and will not even bring her thirteen-year-old daughter to come visit her. For all practical purposes, Tyler was alone in prison until she became active in religious programs, where she found a community of people who embraced, supported, and even loved her. Most importantly, she said, she allowed herself to feel God's love. After almost thirty years of abusive relationships, Tyler contends that God's love allowed her not only to trust again but to let others mentor her. She immersed herself in religious programs and transferred to Florida's only FCBI dorm for women, where the younger women even look up to her as a mentor. Mentors like Tyler teach outside the classes the messages, ideas, and theologies they learn inside them.

In short, Tyler now embodies the goals of the mentoring domain, which teaches incarcerated women to humble themselves enough to learn from the chaplains, the volunteers, prison administrators, and the inmate facilitators. This is no easy task, as women like Tyler have trust issues, and in FCBIs for men, many of the men struggle to let men teach them anything. Some of the incarcerated who do become mentees later become mentors for the newer inmates, where they hope to repeat the cycle that leads to the next group of mentors. Ideally, every incarcerated person develops an elaborate mentoring matrix where everyone is simultaneously a mentee and a mentor, depending on the context. These mentors will all be faith leaders who help people master religion and the economy. To achieve this goal, the incarcerated have to complete one hundred hours to fulfill the graduation requirements for the Mentoring domain, almost three times the average of thirty-four hours in the other six domains. Mandatory classes include Mentoring (four to twelve hours allowed per quarter), Work Assignment, Mentor Training, and Community Meetings. Optional courses include Character Training and Financial Accountability. This is the only domain that does not allow for approved electives.

Reentry Domain

It was the first day of the Developing Business Concepts class at Wakulla CI, and inmate facilitator Martin Syndor introduced himself and the class. Martin first established his credentials by telling the students that he is an authority on the subject, as he has a degree in business and even started an MBA program, although he never completed it. "I made one mistake and that mistake cost me my freedom, my family, and my church, but it also cost me my education," he told the students. Martin then explained the class structure—it meets twice a week for fifteen weeks, it includes fifty-five pages of homework, and before the class is over the students will develop a business concept. Successful business concepts will have a comprehensive overview of the business that includes a clear summary of the services the business will perform, a marketing plan, an analysis of the startup and maintenance costs, and a plan for raising the necessary startup capital. At the end of the term, each student will face the Gauntlet, which is a five-person panel that questions each student about the student's business and then issues a final grade based on its feasibility and the overall presentation.

Martin knew that perhaps none of these men had ever owned a business and that many were probably afraid of the prospects of self-employment. He acknowledged as much when he provided some motivational advice. "I get it," he said.

This is foreign stuff—scary stuff—to some of you. You're afraid of failure, you're afraid you might not pull it off, or who knows why you're afraid. But I'm telling you that you have to get rid of the chains that bind your mind. We see all kinds of chains in this place—chains around wrists, chains around ankles, you know what I mean. It's easy to see those chains. You can touch them, you can feel them. But you can't see the chains that bind your mind. You can't see the limits we put on ourselves to prevent us from realizing our God-given potential. God made each one of you to be a husband, a father, and a leader, and that means He wants many of you to start companies. I don't know your backgrounds, but I know your maker, and He gave each of you the potential to own your own business. If you're telling yourself otherwise, you're letting those mental chains wear you down. We can't get rid of the physical chains in this place, but we can get rid of the mental chains. And it's my job to help.

Having finished his motivational speech, Martin thought the men might want to know a little about himself. "If you haven't figured it out," he said,

I'm a spiritual man. I believe in God. I let God down when I committed a crime, but I'm a spiritual man. We even named my child after a Hebrew word. Now, you don't have to be a spiritual person to be in this class, but I am who I am, and that person is going to show up in class. I believe that God rewards the faithful with success, and this teaching, to me, is a form of ministry. So I won't preach or anything, but don't be offended if I ask God to bless you. It's one of the best ways for me to support you. Ok? Let's talk about your first assignment.

The blending of Christian theology and financial strategy is common in most of the classes in the Reentry domain. This domain is designed to identify the real and various obstacles that the incarcerated will face as they leave prison and reenter society. Employment obstacles are one of the biggest. As scholar Bruce Western noted, the formerly incarcerated routinely struggle to find work, and those who do find work typically earn less than people who were never incarcerated.[27] To help remedy this, the reentry domain routinely teaches students that self-employment is their best strategy. As one volunteer minister said, "Every job application asks if you're a convicted felon. When you show up as a business owner, though, no customer asks that question." This domain recognizes that not everyone is ready to own their own business or can even complete the necessary paperwork, so this domain also includes GED preparation and literacy courses.

Since some of the people lack technological literacy, this domain also includes courses on computer literacy.

Collectively, these classes help students create detailed plans for successful desistance. As evidenced by the previous vignette, they will learn that that the trinity of self-employment, their religious communities, and God will help them succeed outside prison, providing they are willing to put in the requisite work. Required classes in this domain include Family & Community Reintegration Plan, Portfolio: Employability Skills, Healthy Living Plan Recreation Activity, Financial Literacy and Employability, Community Service Plan, Reentry & Relapse Plan, Accomplishments List, and Managing Personal Finance. Optional courses include one-hundred-hour Life Skills Training, GED Readiness, Literacy Training, Computer Literacy Training, Computer Skills Class, Identification Project, and approved electives.

Faith Domain

The Florida Department of Corrections Faith and Character–Based Completion Worksheet lists "Faith" as a separate domain, and a relatively insignificant one at that. It contains only one required class (Core Belief Statement), and with only eighteen required hours, it contains less than half the average of forty-eight hours in each of the other six domains. Optional classes include Worship, Alpha Series, Purpose Driven Life, Personal Religious Studies, Religious Correspondence Courses, and approved electives. On paper, this suggests, first, that religious programming is one of seven discrete areas or units of study in FCBIs, and second, that it is almost an afterthought to the secular or character-based programming in the other six domains.

As the above summary of the other domains suggests, however, programming commonly associated with the NCR is a staple in every domain. Not only does each domain contain what most would consider overtly religious classes, but volunteers and inmate facilitators inject Christian theology, scriptural exegesis, prayer, and Christian rhetoric into classes that by colloquial terms would be considered secular. Collectively, this positions programming that resonates with the NCR as the default form of programming in every FCBI. To entirely avoid Christian theology and rhetoric, residents in FCBIs have to retreat to their sectarian services or study groups, to yoga classes, to meditation classes, and to independent studies. Almost all of these classes still contain religious rhetoric and theologies, but overtly Christian theology is largely absent.

As a result, Christian programming premised on neoliberal capitalism provides the dominant form of programming in FCBIs. In theory, it is possible for someone to avoid the bulk of this programming if that person enrolls in independent study courses, but a person cannot participate in the common classes if he or she wants to avoid Christian theology entirely.

Domain Summary

When Chaplain Steve Fox first organized classes into the seven domains, he did not create new classes as much as he organized existing classes into seven areas of study. This organizing reflected, first, the idea that FCBIs contain both religious and character-based programming; second, that religious programming is not sufficient for successful desistance; and third, that these seven domains provide the requisite personal, professional, and religious skills to live crime-free lives. When Florida's DOC adopted and standardized the domain approach in all of its FCBIs, it provided governmental sanction and endorsement. This raises two important issues.

First, the seven domains reflect a theory of self and subjectivity that position individual responsibility as the hallmark of civil obedience and success.[28] These seven domains—Attitude, Community Functioning, Marital/Family, Healthy Choices, Mentoring, Reentry, and Faith—emphasize personal moral responsibility and religious stewardship as the foundation of this success. In the process, the domain structure combined with the classes themselves naturalize neoliberal subjectivities with their emphasis on individual responsibility, piety, discipline, and financial accountability. They downplay structural disadvantages, shun government-run social services, and even sacralize poverty and strife. The incarcerated will hear versions of this in practically all of their classes, whether they live in FCBI dorms or prisons. Second, the question remains, which model of FCBI (dorm or prison) is most effective? This is a common debate in the community of FCBI proponents and administrators.

The Great Debate: Prisons or Dorms?

While none of my informants remember the exact date, in 2004, Governor Jeb Bush emailed his closest advisers to solicit suggestions for innovative programs during the final years of his second term as Florida governor.[29] According to Allison DeFoor—recipient of said email—Bush wanted to leave an impressive legacy based on broad reforms, and he looked to his immediate peer group to solicit ideas. Allison, a staunch proponent of faith-based corrections, offered a suggestion based on his recent visit to Florida's first faith-based prison.

Allison and the rest of the community that advocated for faith-based correctional reform in Florida were abuzz with excitement when the DOC converted Lawtey CI into the first faith-based prison in the United States, and many supporters soon visited the facility. Either by chance or according to Allison by God's providence, a few days after Bush sent his email, Henree Martin (former member of the Task Force on Self-Inflicted Crimes), Hugh MacMillan, and Allison traveled from Tallahassee to visit Lawtey CI.[30] To various degrees, the three either directly or indirectly influenced the history that led to Lawtey, and they wanted to see and experience it firsthand.

After their visit, they agreed that faith-based dorms paled in comparison with the tangible and substantive benefits that the faith-based prison offered. After years of supporting faith-based dorms, these three were diehard converts to the faith-based prison model of correctional reform. Allison was convinced that Florida's DOC should expand the faith-based prison program, and to ensure that it happened, Allison responded to Governor Bush's email where Allison suggested that the state should open additional faith-based prisons instead of more faith-based dormitories.

This anecdote highlights one of the perennial debates in Florida's FCBI program. While the proponents and administrators of Florida's FCBIs universally agree that rehabilitation is the ultimate goal, they disagree about the best means of achieving that goal. On one side of the debate are the proponents of the dorm model, who argue that the benefits of FCBI dorms dwarf any rehabilitation that occurs in the FCBI prisons. They tend to agree that the main advantage of the dorm model of faith-based correctional reform is that it allows the residents to immerse themselves almost every waking hour in FCBI programming. Recall that people in FCBI dorms have to complete their programming in eighteen months—half the time it takes people in FCBI prisons to complete their programming. People who live in FCBI dorms have to commit themselves to FCBI programming to the extent that programming takes the priority over their job assignments. Almost from the moment they wake up until the moment they fall asleep, the residents in FCBI dorms engage in extensive FCBI programming.

Proponents of the dorm model also argue that FCBI dorms potentially produce twice as many graduates in the same three-year time period. Most of the people who graduate from all FCBIs return to the general population, where they potentially have a positive impact on the larger incarcerated population. The graduates also occasionally create "alumni groups" with other FCBI graduates.[31] This continues to be an ancillary benefit to the DOC, as prison administrators argue that the alumni units help transform the mood and character of everyone in the dorm or cellblock. The proponents of the dorm model argue that since FCBI dorms produce twice as many graduates, they are more likely to make a positive impact on Florida's conventional prisons.

Proponents of the dorm model—particularly the incarcerated—will also argue that they prefer the dorm model of FCBI reform because it allows them to spend more time not only in rehabilitative space but in comfortable space. Residents in FCBI dorms spend the vast majority of their time sequestered from the larger incarcerated population either in their dorms or in the prison's chapel, where they are quite literally safer than the people who are not serving time in FCBI dorms. When they are not studying, the people in FCBI dorms are able to relax and to engage in what one man referred to as "front porch conversations" not related to incarceration or survival inside the prisons. These people prefer the dorm model of incarceration for the simple fact that they can relax.

Not only do they feel more relaxed in the FCBI dorm, but also they are more physically comfortable as they spend more time in temperature-controlled environments. With few exceptions, Florida's prisons and dormitories are not air-conditioned. Anyone who has spent time in Florida during the humid and sweltering summer months can understand the burden this places on people who spend years or even decades incarcerated in Florida's hot prisons. Residents in FCBI dorms, however, spend extended periods of time in air-conditioned rooms such as the prison's chapel or the dorm's library. The dorm's libraries typically include books, computers, and other electronic devices that need the protection of temperature-controlled space. Residents in FCBI dorms repeatedly told me that during the summer months, they spend more time than normal in the chapel or libraries, where they can escape the oppressive summer heat.

When they are not in these air-conditioned spaces, the incarcerated also spend time in their dorms. Dormitories in conventional prisons typically include windows that remain open during the summer. They also have old fans that help circulate the otherwise still, stale, and humid air. In FCBI dorms, however, these old fans are often so loud that they interfere with group work, Bible studies, and other coursework the incarcerated complete in their beds. In some of the dorms, religious communities have donated new, quieter, and more efficient fans to help facilitate Bible studies but that provide the ancillary benefit of more efficiently cooling the dorms. For all these reasons and more, some volunteers, administrators, and incarcerated people prefer the dorm model of FCBI reform to the prison model.

Equally passionate are the proponents of FCBI prisons. They readily admit that FCBI dorms allow for more rigorous immersion in FCBI programming, but they argue that the prison model of FCBI reform provides a range of unique and substantive benefits that make FCBI prisons the preferred institution. Perhaps most importantly, the FCBI prison model creates an impenetrable rehabilitative cocoon or bubble that eliminates almost all negative influences. Specifically, it isolates the dorm's residents from other incarcerated people and even from correctional staff who would potentially harm them.

To understand this point, consider that the residents in the FCBI dorms interact daily (to various degrees) with incarcerated people in conventional prisons who swear, who belittle the participants in the FCBI program, and who expose them to other behaviors and language they find offensive. Residents in FCBI dorms routinely accuse the men who are incarcerated in conventional prisons of chastising them, belittling them, and calling them chomos ("chomo" is a pejorative term in prison for a child molester). Child molesters occupy the bottom level of the informal prison hierarchy and are statistically more likely to be raped or to experience sexual abuse inside a prison.[32] FCBIs are perhaps the only correctional facilities where a person convicted of a sex crime with a minor can do his time without fear of rape, as an FCBI resident who rapes another person in an FCBI is immediately transferred from the facility and back into a conventional prison.[33] For this reason, incarcerated people in the general prison population accuse the people who live in FCBIs of being chomos who only participate in FCBIs to escape the ridicule and abuse that accompany their crimes. According to many residents in FCBI dorms, they cannot interact with anyone in the larger conventional prison without someone or even groups of people calling them chomos and telling them in detail how they want to rape them.[34] The residents in FCBI dorms not only find this language offensive but also fear the moments when the accusers will find an opportunity to fulfill their threats. People in FCBI dorms also contend that they interact with abusive correctional staff when they leave the confines of their FCBI dorm.

According to the residents in FCBI dorms, to the program administrators, and even to many of the correctional officers I interviewed while researching this book, correctional officers in conventional prisons tend to be hostile toward the incarcerated in general. The men and women incarcerated in FCBI dorms typically do not escape their wrath, as people in FCBI dorms interact with correctional staff who are either skeptical or downright hostile to the FCBI program. Consider that a large portion of the correctional officers in Florida and beyond routinely view all incarcerated people as deviants and criminals incapable of rehabilitation or redemption. An officer working at Lawtey CI suggested as much when he described how few correctional officers are capable of working in FCBIs, where they need at least a modest amount of respect for the incarcerated. Some officers, he argued, are able to embrace the concept of rehabilitative correctional facilities, but even then, he said, "it takes some time getting used to the different attitude in [FCBIs]."

The administrators of the FCBI dorms work with the senior correctional officers to identify the correctional officers who are amenable to and who support FCBI programming and rehabilitative efforts. They then assign these officers to work in FCBIs, where they help cultivate the more nurturing space that encourages rehabilitation. The incarcerated, then, feel safe and secure while inside the FCBI dorm, where the correctional staff supports their rehabilitative community. The problems occur when people in FCBI dorms interact with the correctional officers who guard the general population, a problem they potentially encounter several times a day as they move about the prisons to the chow hall, the chapel, or other places outside the FCBI dorm. People who are incarcerated in FCBI dorms routinely accuse the correctional staff of harassing them in these settings, often belittling their efforts and chastising them about their religious beliefs.

One group of incarcerated men recalled a story about a particular correctional officer who mockingly tests the men and their god by making them walk through mud puddles to see if they are "holy enough to walk on water like Jesus." Residents in multiple FCBI dorms said that correctional officers threaten to leave them alone with potential rapists either for discipline or for sport. A group of twenty inmates in the FCBI dorm at Gulf Annex Correctional Institution described how both the correctional officers and the men in the general population routinely call them soft, perverts, and chomos. "They're basically calling us women or homosexuals," one man chimed in. "They're calling us women because we display what in prison are considered 'feminine' characteristics of emotion, vulnerability, and other qualities they'd call 'soft.'"[35] Another man added, "Man, sometimes we even get served the burnt food in chow hall!" The other nineteen men in the FCBI dorm nodded in agreement to both of these statements. At no point did I hear of a correctional officer inflicting violence on any of the men in the FCBI dorms or of placing them in harm's way, but the men in FCBI dorms readily acknowledge that these threats and interactions are offensive distractions that constantly remind them of the dangers lurking outside the doors of their faith-based rehabilitative dorm. Prisons for men possess strict notions of masculinity, which do not leave much room for the displays of emotion that are common in FCBIs.[36]

The proponents of FCBI prisons, however, argue that these negative interactions with incarcerated people in the general population and with abusive or demeaning correctional staff are almost entirely absent inside the FCBI prisons. Residents in FCBI prisons live, work, worship, study, and interact with people and correctional officers already committed to the FCBI prison's rehabilitative missions. Warden Barry Reddish, warden at Lawtey CI, stated as much when he said, "The faith-based prison [as opposed to dorm] becomes a therapeutic community. You learn religious values with other inmates, you learn character with other inmates, and you eat with other inmates. All of them have the same goal."[37] And when an incarcerated person or correctional officer disrupts the prison's regime of rehabilitation, that person is transferred to a conventional prison, freeing up space for another person to transfer in. In short, an important benefit of the FCBI prison is that it provides a safe space for the incarcerated to pursue their rehabilitative efforts without the fear of violence, threat, or intimidation that the people in FCBI dorms potentially face every day.

Proponents of FCBI prisons also argue that prisons are better than dorms because participants in FCBIs have to spend twice the amount of time inside the FCBI. Recall that a person should complete the program in an FCBI dorm in eighteen months, but it literally takes someone in an FCBI prison twice as long to graduate from the program. The resident in an FCBI prison, therefore, spends twice as long inside the facility's rehabilitative bubble. Proponents of FCBI prisons typically argue that incarcerated men and women in these prisons, then, have twice as long to develop the "heart skills" or to build the "foundation of faith" that will sustain them after they leave the facility. It took years or even decades, they say, for the incarcerated to develop the patterns that brought them to prison, and it will take more than eighteen months for residents to dismantle their old selves and to acquire the new attitudes and behaviors that will help them lead crime-free lives in the future.

Not surprisingly, volunteers, the incarcerated, and staff who respectively volunteer, live, or work in FCBI prisons tend to prefer the prison model of FCBI programming, while people associated with dorms overwhelmingly prefer the dorm model, although this is not universally true. I encountered incarcerated men both in FCBI prisons and in dorms who transferred from one to the other, as they chose the facilities that they determined were best suited to their needs and preferences.

Regardless of whether someone serves time in an FCBI dorm or prison, whether a person completes more classes in a particular domain or two, or whether a person is an inmate facilitator or a resident in an FCBI, incarcerated people who serve a portion of their sentences in FCBIs will find a more or less similar experience. They will serve relatively safer and easier time, they will encounter comparably supportive fellow residents, and they will interact with administrative staff more likely to support their rehabilitative efforts. They will also devote hour upon hour to personal development, goal setting, character development, business planning, and religious programming. Collectively, these classes are designed to reduce recidivism based on models of self and subjectivity championed by members of the NCR and regulated by neoliberal capitalism.

· · · · · ·

FCBI programming—regardless of the label "faith" or "character"—consistently circulates themes about the self, its relationship with its community, and society's limited obligations to this self. These themes downplay structural and institutional analyses of oppression as they stress the importance of personal discipline, character training, and religiosity not only as the sources of successful desistance but as the foundation of the ideal society. These themes acknowledge and naturalize neoliberal capitalism as they reprogram people not only to accept but to expect the economic struggles they will experience as they reenter society.[38] Participants also learn to forgo welfare programs as they rely on the market, their communities, and their god to provide resources to survive outside prison. In the absence of these resources, they learn to either internalize scarcity as the result of personal moral failings or to sacralize it as a result of divine tribulation.

5 The Conservative Center in Faith- and Character-Based Correctional Institutions

· ·

On June 17, 2015, Dylann Roof attended a prayer service at the Emanuel African Methodist Episcopal Church in Charleston, South Carolina. Originally founded in the early 1800s, this particular church is one of oldest black churches in the United States and a staple in the surrounding black community. By his own admission, Roof, an avowed white racist, entered this church to start a race war that would "reclaim" white America.[1] To ignite that war, Roof pulled out a gun and fired indiscriminately at the attendees, killing nine people before he escaped. The Charleston shooting captured the nation's attention as Americans learned that a mass shooting occurred not only at a church but at one of the most famous and historic black churches.

Several days later, almost twenty men gathered in a classroom in the chapel at Wakulla CI for their weekly Apostolic class, a class taught by two volunteers who teach their version of biblical Christianity. The volunteers were uncharacteristically late, and the incarcerated men had heated conversations as they waited for the volunteers' arrival. The Charleston shooting was the primary topic.

The men in the Apostolic class struggled to fit the shooting into their larger view of history. They *knew* that the world would end sooner than later after a series of trials and tribulations would threaten to unravel the very foundations of society. Only then would Jesus return and usher his followers into their eternal reward. The men cited numerous examples that proved to them that biblical prophecy was unfolding before their very eyes ranging from legalized gay marriage, to the systematic murder of the unborn, to the secularizing of public schools, and according to a man named Dayton, to an oppressive federal government forcing Americans to place electronic chips in their arms. This was clearly the mark of the beast, no?

The men believed that these developments—which were bad—were necessary preconditions for Jesus's return—which is good—and the men *knew* that the Charleston shooting was one such trial or tribulation. In other words, the Charleston shooting—as appalling as it was, they agreed—

proved that the end was near; it was a necessary precondition for the ultimate triumph of good over evil. That made the church shooting a good thing, right? Or did it? In short, the men wondered how they should react to the events that precede the apocalypse, and they wanted the volunteers to help answer that question.

When the first volunteer arrived, he set his Bible on the podium and immediately addressed the shooting. "I assume you all saw what happened?" he asked. The men responded in the affirmative. The volunteer continued when he said, "Let's start today by asking God for guidance in these troubling times. Any prayer requests?"

"Let's pray for our country, and maybe for ourselves," one of the men responded. The rest of the class again nodded in agreement as the volunteer called the men to prayer.

Immediately after the prayer, Dayton raised his hand to ask a question. He apparently wanted to know more about those government chips. "I hear the government is making you get electronic chips in your forearms," he said. "That's just the beginning," the volunteer replied.

Not only that, but the government is slowly taking control of our lives. The government wants to keep all your records on these chips. When you pay for something, you scan your arm. They store all your medical records on these chips. When you want medication, you scan your arm. Our money is no longer good. At [local colleges] they're cash-free societies! You know, these chips were originally meant for pets, but now they're using them on people! It's utterly impossible for you to hide from the government. I don't even have access to my money! Do you know that my Social Security checks are just electronically deposited into my [bank] account? I have to wait for the government *and* the bank to clear it before I can even touch *my money*! The spirit of the antichrist is at large! We've lost our freedom; we've lost our freedom! We're a monarchy! You think we'd be safe in church, but you saw about that boy in that church. They're placing sensors in your car. You can't turn your car on unless you fasten your seatbelts! The other day my wife went to start her car and the ignition wouldn't turn over. She turned her key and nothing [happened]. I went to buy a battery and when I entered my phone number, it was connected to someone else's account. We're in a mess! They know all about your finances, and they control your finances! I wanted to refinance my house, so I went into the bank and they asked for everything! Business was bad and my income was down. I'd missed a few house payments and I needed a lower payment, but they wouldn't refinance it! The financial industry controls you! I can tell you how to escape this world alive, but I can't stop shootings in church or in school! I can't stop a [correctional officer] with a chip on his shoulder from beating you to death![2]

"Amen," the men collectively interrupted. Not ready to break his stride, however, the volunteer continued.

That [shooting] happened because we've opened a door for the devil. It's Obama, but it's not just Obama. It's the Senate; it's the whole government! It's the Supreme Court for thinking there's a separation of church and state. It's drugs! It's gay marriage! It's the whole lot of it! I tell you, we're in trouble! The government is in our churches! The problem is that the government is in our church! The problem is that men are not controlling the church! The problem is that men aren't controlling our families! The problem is that women are running the world! Can I get an amen?

The volunteer continued his uninterrupted speech for several more minutes as he continued to catalog the signs of the impending apocalypse. As described in the aforementioned speech, these signs include direct deposit, electronic debit, mortgage regulations, the government, gay marriage, duplicate cell phone numbers entered in corporate databases to track customer rewards, emasculated men who consent to the hegemony of female rule, and a shooting at a church that claimed nine lives (at no point did anyone in the room address that Dylann Roof was a self-proclaimed racist trying to start a race war).

With few exceptions, the volunteer's lecture contained little information I had not heard daily in faith- and character-based institutions (FCBIs). I did not know about his wife's car trouble, for example, nor was I aware of his attempted refinance. Many of these themes, however—specifically the contempt for liberals and liberal policies, hostility toward LGBTQ rights and gay marriage, the lament of the decline of male patriarchal authority, and a theology that posits sin as the source of social problems (as opposed to, say, institutionalized oppression or systemic racism)—are standard fare in FCBIs.[3] These themes combine with several others to create a dominant center or core of ideas that circulate freely and often in

Florida's FCBIs. As evidenced by the academic literature that addresses the topic, these ideas are core components of prison ministries *writ large*; that is, they are common aspects of faith-based correctional institutions and programs throughout the nation.[4]

Ideas associated with the New Christian Right (NCR) or with conservative Christians more broadly constitute a core or center that is hard to escape in FCBIs. Discussions of a dominant center or core are necessarily fraught and contentious as they conjure what are commonly deemed demons of American religious history's past. As scholar Catherine Albanese argued, white Protestant theologians in the 1800s first addressed the issue of dominant forms of religiosity in the United States where they wrote themselves and their religio-racial kin into this center.[5] These histories were overtly political as they privileged the very groups they discussed, and they silenced religious minorities, people of color, discussions of gender and sexuality, and noninstitutional religiosity.

This continued to be the dominant narrative of American religious history well into the second half of the 1900s when younger scholars influenced by the 1960s, the civil rights movement, Marxist studies, feminism, and the countercultural movement more broadly rewrote American histories to include the groups that earlier historians ignored. Though these newer histories differed from previous narratives of American religion, their histories overlapped in at least two important ways. First, they were equally political as they served to empower the groups they wrote into the center of American history. Second, they agreed that the center of American religion was politically salient as they relied on historical continuity to justify their contemporary political positions. As an extension of the second factor, scholars motivated by liberal pluralism downplayed the hegemonic status of white, male, heterosexual, conservative Protestants.

Recently, however, scholars reconsidered the historical role and influence of white Protestants in America.[6] Many agreed that white, patriarchal Protestantism occupied a position of privilege for most of America's history. Instead of celebrating this dominance, however, they criticized it as hegemonic and oppressive. In the process, these scholars provided theoretical and practical tools for addressing unequal distributions of privilege and power in American history.

Building off this insight, this chapter explores the conservative Protestants who are the numerical, ideological, and theological majority in FCBIs. Their politics and theologies constitute the dominant core that permeates the vast majority of state-sanctioned socialization in FCBIs as they routinely focus on several core issues related to theories of crime and criminality, the family, sex and sexuality, gender, individual responsibility, race, and patriarchal authority. Many of these ideas are either absent or downplayed in public schools and in government-run socialization programs.[7] They flourish, however, in FCBIs, where religion functions to create alternative regulations that allow faith-based organizations (FBOs) and religious providers to introduce content otherwise impermissible in state-run spaces. Not only does this alternatively regulated sphere of faith-based programming resonate with neoliberalism, but the content of this socialization reinforces neoliberalism itself.

The Administrative Structure in FCBIs

Christians from various denominations in the United States have long participated in prison reform, dating back to the late 1700s when evangelicals and Quakers created the first modern penitentiaries, first in Pennsylvania and later in New York. Christian administrators and volunteers subsequently proved a staple in carceral history well into the late 1970s when conservative Protestants solidified their status as the most common and influential volunteers in America's prisons. These Protestants created policies, procedures, and expectations about the role of conservative Protestantism that prison administrators routinely take for granted. Suffice it to say that for the majority of prison administrators, "religion" and "faith" are functionally synonymous with "conservative Protestants" or the NCR. These changes coincided with institutional and theological changes in conservative Protestantism—and with the Southern Baptist Convention (SBC) particularly—that proved important to Florida's Department of Corrections (DOC), where the majority of the prison chaplains are Southern Baptists.

According to the most comprehensive study of prison chaplains, the majority of America's prison chaplains are white, male, middle-aged, conservative, and Protestant.[8] The chaplains in Florida's DOC mirror the nation's prison chaplains with one important difference—the majority are not only white, male, middle-aged, conservative, and Protestant, but they are members of the SBC, and most of the chaplains who are not members of the SBC identify as evangelical, fundamentalist, or a "non-denominational Christian" and possess a functionally equivalent theology.[9] Southern Baptists constitute such a large majority of the DOC's chaplains that one scholar termed Southern Baptist ministers as "the center of gravity."[10] The Baptist hegemony was so pervasive in the 1980s that then secretary Louie Wainwright fired a senior chaplain who only hired Baptist chaplains.[11]

Baptists, like all of Florida's prison chaplains, must receive denominational endorsement as a condition of their employment. This impacted chaplains from the SBC who since 1980 had to adhere to the SBC's more conservative Statement of Faith. As many scholars and Baptist historians have documented, "moderate" Baptists controlled the SBC during most of the twentieth century.[12] In the late 1970s, a group of "conservatives" or "fundamentalists" threatened the more moderate status quo. They gained control of the SBC in 1980 when their supporters at the annual SBC meeting outnumbered the moderates' supporters, and via the democratic process, the conservatives gained control of the SBC and began to transform SBC culture to reflect their more conservative views on women, homosexuals, and of course, the importance of Jesus Christ and Christianity as the only path to salvation and the only source of universal truth. These changes are evident in the SBC's Statement of Faith, which states, among other things, that people are sinful by nature, that Satan tempts us to sin, that "all Scripture is totally true and trustworthy,"[13] that affirms the sanctity of heterosexual marriage, and that asks the wife in a marriage "to submit herself graciously to the servant leadership of her husband."[14] Ministers in the SBC must endorse this Statement of Faith and teach it in their churches and services. If they are prison chaplains, they also teach it in prisons.

These changes meant that Baptist chaplains since 1980 were more theologically conservative than their predecessors. They not only taught the SBC's Statement of Faith in Florida's prisons, but perhaps more importantly, recruited more like-minded volunteers. Recall that prison chaplains are increasingly prison administrators who do little ministering. Instead, volunteers enter prisons daily, where they lead the majority of the religious services and study groups in American prisons. As a result, these volunteers interact with most of the incarcerated more often than the incarcerated interact with the chaplains. Since most of the volunteers are similarly conservative Protestants, the combination of chaplains and volunteers creates a religio-carceral culture that overwhelmingly favors the NCR.

This culture exists in all of Florida's prisons, but it is particularly apparent in FCBIs, which rely on volunteer labor to lead many of the services, self-help groups, study sessions, and the various classes. When a facility converts to an FCBI, the chaplain invites additional volunteers to teach classes and to lead services in FCBIs. These chaplains and volunteers immediately embed the conservative core into the FCBI when they teach the first round of classes, and they perpetuate this core when they identify the incarcerated people who will assume leadership positions.

Inmate facilitators occupy the most common leadership positions in FCBIs. Inmate facilitators have no formal training or qualifications. Instead, chaplains appoint people to the position of inmate facilitator because they impress the chaplain by repeating the dominant ideas that circulate in FCBIs. Two inmate facilitators at Wakulla CI are paradigmatic examples.

Wakulla CI has several inmate facilitators, but two men named Ibraaheem Abu and Dennis Lonsdale are undoubtedly the most influential as they teach the most classes and appear to be the chaplain's most trusted assistants. The two share much in common. They are both dark-skinned African Americans, they are serving long prison sentences (Ibraaheem is serving a life sentence for murder and Dennis is serving thirty years for burglary), they are charismatic men, they are leaders in their respective congregations, and neither has a formal education beyond high school. They are also authority figures in the prison, and the other incarcerated men tend to defer to their judgment and authority.

The two make an interesting pair. Not only do they have different appearances and demeanors, they think each other is going to spend eternity in hell as one is Christian and the other Muslim. Dennis grew up in a Christian family and dropped out of high school after the tenth grade. He worked as a painter, but his real interests were drugs, alcohol, and women. "Just plain ol' livin' in sin," he told me when he described this period in his life. He started smoking marijuana and later crack cocaine. He contends that he began to commit crimes to supplement his drug habits, which led to multiple arrests and several prison sentences, including the thirty-year sentence he is currently serving, the last year of which he served at Wakulla CI. Dennis thanks God often for putting him in Wakulla, which according to him has been the "best run in [my] life; because I'm free, I'm liberated here." Dennis does not preach formal sermons—the incarcerated typically are not allowed to, although there are exceptions in certain FCBI dorms—but incarcerated Christians from various denominations approach him for spiritual guidance.

Dennis is a passionate Southern Baptist who does not speak as much as he delivers a series of rapid-fire sermons. Ask Dennis a question, and he will provide an extended response replete with Biblical citations and lessons on morality. "How are you doing on this hot Florida day?" I asked him on a particularly hot and humid afternoon. "The Bible says, 'This is the day that the Lord has made,'" he replied. "I *will* rejoice and be glad in it! Remember the Lord and his commandments today. Live a godly life and obey His commandments. And don't focus on things you can't control. This heat is nothing compared to the fires in hell."

In contrast to Dennis's boisterous personality and persona, Ibraaheem speaks softly and less often, that is, until he teaches Friday's Islamic Jumah service, where he is the resident imam at Wakulla CI. Ibraaheem grew up in a Christian household, but at age fifteen, he converted to Islam and has been a Muslim since. Before he was incarcerated, he ran a convenience store and worked part-time at a flea market and a laundromat. He contends that he was exhausted working almost twenty-four hours a day, seven days a week, when an altercation with his ex-wife led him to her house, where he shot and killed her new lover. Ibraaheem takes full responsibility for his crime, but he is adamant that it does not reflect his true character.

When Ibraaheem leads Jumah, he speaks with a stern and firm, unshakable voice. Instead of slouching, he sits upright as he surveys the men, staring each in the eye and holding each man accountable. His no-nonsense approach to Islam reminds the men that both he and Allah are watching them. "You don't see Allah," he told them, "but you do see me, and I'm watching you as well. Don't think you can halfway yourself into paradise. Be strong!" This accountability is just one of the characteristics that not only impressed his fellow Muslims, who elected him as the resident imam and liaison between the incarcerated Muslims and the chaplain, but also impressed the prison's chaplain, who trained Ibraaheem to be an inmate facilitator.

This summary of two inmate facilitators highlights how leadership and authority are constructed in FCBIs, where individual claims of religiosity trump educational training, credentialing, and institutional recognition. Consider Dennis, who when asked if he was an ordained minister, responded in the affirmative, but with a twist. "Oh, I'm ordained," he told me, "but yeah, not like you think—with degrees and whatnot. I'm ordained by God! I get my authority from the almighty who blessed me with a righteousness that don't come from any church or college!" In other words, not only does Dennis's authority come directly from God, but it surpasses any authority that results from institutional training or certification. Ibraaheem, like Dennis, has no formal credential or institutional training, but also like Dennis, his charisma and knowledge of Islam combine to position him as a leader in his religious community. Outside the FCBI, academic and institutional degrees and certificates are meant to provide evidence of competency in a particular field, be it academic, professional, or ministerial. In the faith-saturated FCBI, the claim of a personal relationship with a deity not only qualifies one for leadership but places one at the top of the religious hierarchy for like-minded believers tasked with education, socialization, and authority.

Each chaplain who administers an FCBI develops his or her own criteria for identifying people for this position. Chaplain Steve Fox described the qualifications for inmate facilitators at Wakulla CI when he said that inmate facilitators are "the most stable inmates on the compound." They must have completed 360 hours of FCBI programming, they had to excel in their classwork, they had to demonstrate superior moral character, and they had to complete each class they facilitate. Inmate facilitators at Lawtey CI— the other faith-based prison for men—have different standards, as they cannot have received a disciplinary infraction for one year, they had to be incarcerated at Lawtey for six months, they had to complete the class they will facilitate, and an existing inmate facilitator must mentor them. Other chaplains like Chaplain Faithe Liburd at the FCBI dorm for women at Lowell Annex CI simply look for incarcerated women with leadership skills and good character.

Individual chaplains, then, play a large role in creating guidelines for inmate facilitators, as the DOC lacks formal policies for people in this position. This creates a localized form of government that rests power in the hands of local religious leaders, not state bureaucrats who run the state, the DOC, or even the prison's warden. Without exception, these chaplains look for people who embrace and who perpetuate the chaplains' conservative theologies about sociocultural and political issues like gender, politics, sexuality, and LGBTQ rights. Chaplains identify these successful people and then promote them to the position of inmate facilitators, who then perpetuate the conservative core when they repeat the aforementioned ideas in their classes.

Inmate facilitators are the most common authority position for the incarcerated in FCBIs, but there are others. Some FCBI dorms, like the dorm at Tomoka CI, also contain a senior incarcerated leader called the "Grandfather." According to the Participation Manual for the people who live in the FCBI dorms at Tomoka CI, the Grandfather is a leader in the FCBI dorm who "is the person that anyone in the program should be able to go to for advice or counsel. He [is] a person possessing a high level of character."[15] The Grandfather holds a position of privilege and moral authority over the other incarcerated men, and his authority is evident in the dorm's physical layout, as while other people's beds (or bunks) are arranged in eight-person "families,"[16] the Grandfather's bed is positioned at the head of the dorm separate from the other incarcerated men. The Grandfather is the default senior inmate facilitator tasked with helping the incarcerated, volunteers, chaplains, and other program administrators whenever necessary. He is also involved in conflict resolution whenever a person violates one of the rules.

Grandfathers are leaders in several of the FCBI dorms for men, but female facilities have their own leaders. In addition to formal inmate facilitators, some of the younger and newly incarcerated women look to the informal position of prison "moms," who provide leadership and counseling. "Ma Irene" is one such mom in the FCBI dorm for women at Lowell Annex. According to Irene, the younger women look up to her, and she loves them, gives them advice, counsels them, and "give[s] hugs whenever needed."

Florida's state guidelines dictate that no incarcerated person can have authority over another incarcerated person, but inmate facilitators, Grandfathers, and to a lesser extent prison moms arguably push that regulation's boundaries as they lead classes, assign homework, and make recommendations for expulsion when someone in the FCBI does not perform to their standards. These incarcerated leaders work closely with the chaplains and with the volunteers as they help administer FCBIs. They demonstrate their abilities not by completing advanced training, by earning formal certifications, or by completing any state-approved course of study. Instead, they demonstrate their leadership capabilities by mastering the lingo, concepts, and underlying theology in the individual classes. In FCBIs, repetition demonstrates merit. The chaplains promote to leadership positions people who embrace this message, where they perpetuate the conservative core as they repeat conservative theology in their classes and to the people they mentor and advise. The remainder of this chapter explores in detail the content of this conservative core, paying particular attention to its relationship with neoliberalism.

Theories of Crime and Criminality

Scholars and others interested in crime and criminality have struggled for centuries to explain the cause of crime. In the late 1700s Cesare Beccaria and Jeremy Bentham attempted to understand crime when they created what is today called the classical school of criminology, where they argued that people are hedonistic by nature and that punishment should deter crime and punish the criminal in proportion to the crime.[17] Faced with the certainty of punishment, would-be criminals, the theory contends, will rationally choose not to commit crimes. Their theories faced their share of skeptics, but they influenced new generations of thinkers and reformers who began to think about crime.

The positivist school of criminology emerged in the early 1800s. It sought to scientifically locate crime in the biology of the criminal. Cesare Lombroso, for example, studied criminals' cadavers, looking for physical characteristics associated with crime. In the debate of nature or nurture, Lombroso and positivists stressed the former, and they prescribed medical and psychological treatment as the most effective forms of rehabilitation.

In the late 1800s, sociologist Émile Durkheim offered a novel theory of crime and criminality when he argued that crime is not an unavoidable by-product of immoral individuals, dysfunctional societies, and by implication sin. According to Durkheim, "There is no society known where a more or less developed criminality is not found under different forms. No people exists whose morality is not daily infringed upon. We must therefore call crime necessary and declare that it cannot be non-existent, that the fundamental conditions of social organization, as they are understood, logically imply it."[18] For Durkheim, crime is "normal." It is a universal and unavoidable aspect of human social life. It is also a moral issue insofar as "crime" is often synonymous with that which offends the morals of the majority or of those in power. Since regimes of power change, so too will the behaviors we deem criminal. In other words, "crime" is socially constructed. The former head of Florida's correctional department noted as much when he wrote, "In 1932, a man owning a bottle of whiskey was a criminal and a person in possession of a $20 gold piece was a respected citizen. One year later, their positions were exactly reversed!"[19]

As this summary suggests, scholars and criminologists in the early 1900s disagreed on the cause of crime, but these theories collectively highlight a growing class of scholars and reformers who applied Enlightenment-inspired principles to the study of crime. As the study of crime became professionalized, it influenced new generations of thinkers who created new theories about crime and criminality, particularly after World War II, when the rehabilitative ideal combined with environmental explanations of crime to transform many of the nation's prisons.

In the 1950s, scholars noticed that criminals tended to share socioeconomic and cultural backgrounds and patterns, suggesting that these factors influenced their criminal behavior. By this logic, prisons can rehabilitate or resocialize offenders by providing the incarcerated with the socialization skills associated with successful, crime-free living. Environmental explanations for crime peaked in different times in different locations in the United States, but by the mid-1980s, environmental explanations and the rehabilitative ideal were replaced by punitive criminal justice policies premised on the idea, first, that punitive prisons and carceral conditions will punish criminals and serve as deterrents to would-be criminals, and second, that criminals alone are responsible for crime. Bob Dole, former U.S. senator and Republican presidential candidate summarized this idea when he said, "What works in combating crime is no mystery. It begins with the understanding that the cause of crime can be explained with one simple word: Criminals. Criminals. Criminals."[20] This theory of crime and criminality justified mass incarceration, as it relied on government intervention to detain these criminals.

More recently, scholars explored an additional explanation for mass incarceration when they examined the relationship between race, racism, and incarceration. Scholars have long noted that mass incarceration disproportionately impacts black Americans, but it was Michelle Alexander's *The New Jim Crow* that catapulted race front and center to the heart of the debates concerning mass incarceration.[21] Alexander argued that black Americans have faced numerous legal, sociocultural, political, and economic obstacles throughout American history that have resulted in housing, employment, educational, and other forms of discrimination. Many Americans believe these obstacles disappeared after the 1960s, the Civil Rights movement, and the end of Jim Crow laws. Alexander, however, contends not only that racism continues to exist but that it became institutionalized in the form of mass incarceration. She wrote,

> What has changed since the collapse of Jim Crow has less to
> do with the basic structure of our society than with the language
> we use to justify it. In the era of colorblindness, it is no longer
> socially permissible to use race, explicitly, as a justification for
> discrimination, exclusion, and social contempt. So, we don't. Rather
> than rely on race, we use our criminal justice system to label people
> of color "criminals" and then engage in all the practices we supposedly
> left behind. Today it is perfectly legal to discriminate against criminals

in nearly all the ways that it was once legal to discriminate against African Americans. . . . We have not ended racial caste in America; we have merely redesigned it.[22]

Alexander persuasively argued that the war on drugs and other tough-on-crime policies targeted black Americans and that tough-on-crime rhetoric signified "black"—and more specifically "black male"—for most of white America. Perhaps the penultimate moment or example of this occurred during the 1988 presidential campaign when racial politics arguably defeated a candidate for one of the two major political parties.

In the 1988 presidential campaign, George H. W. Bush, then vice president and Republican Party presidential nominee, linked Michael Dukakis, Democratic nominee and governor of Massachusetts, to Willie Horton.[23] Horton was a convicted murderer serving a life sentence in Massachusetts, where he participated in a weekend furlough program that allowed him to temporarily leave prison. Horton did not return at the designated time, and he eventually committed multiple crimes including rape, assault, and armed robbery. Dukakis did not create the furlough program that let Horton leave the prison, although he did support it, and the Bush campaign seized on an opportunity to damage Dukakis by linking him to Horton. As Lee Atwater, adviser to Bush and future chair of the Republican National Committee, said, "By the time we're finished, they're going to wonder whether Willie Horton is Dukakis' running mate."[24] Bush defeated Dukakis and contributed to the larger processes that linked "tough on crime" with the image of the black male. This important example is but one of the numerous pieces of evidence that Alexander offered to support her larger argument.

Scholars have criticized Alexander, mainly on the grounds that she overestimated the impact of the war of drugs on mass incarceration and that she ignored the structural and political differences between Jim Crow and mass incarceration (the former was explicit, intentional, and wide reaching, while the latter operates on a covert level that is not necessarily as oppressive).[25] While these criticisms have some merit, Alexander's larger point stands: not only does race matter, but the history of mass incarceration is a history of disproportionately policing and punishing black bodies with longer and more punitive prison sentences.

Scholars today have no shortage of theories to explain crime, criminality, and mass incarceration, with most embracing a combination of the factors discussed thus far. The incarcerated, volunteers, and chaplains also explore this issue in FCBIs, but where the scholarly community fails to reach a consensus, a dominant and hegemonic theory emerges in FCBIs where crime is consistently attributed to one thing and to one thing alone: sin.

As scholars have repeatedly noted, the emphasis on sin is a common element in prison ministries run by conservative Protestants. Scholar of American religion Tanya Erzen, for example, discussed Prison Fellowship Ministries (the world's largest Christian prison reform organization), which operates several faith-based dorms in U.S. prisons under the InnerChange Freedom Initiative (IFI). As Erzen wrote, "The InnerChange program is based on the idea that sin is the root cause of imprisonment, and teaches that inmates should 'learn how God can heal them permanently, if they turn from their sinful past, are willing to see the world through God's eyes, and surrender themselves to God's will.'"[26] People serving prison sentences in FCBIs similarly not only learn that sin is the cause of crime but learn to use "sin" and "crime" interchangeably.

An incarcerated man named Avel Martin in the FCBI dorm at Gulf Annex talked about sin during a testimonial he gave on the eve of leaving prison after serving a three-year sentence. Avel described his troubled life, which began at age one when his dad committed suicide. His mom remarried, and then his stepdad abused him. Avel barely finished high school before leaving to join the Navy, but he was discharged dishonorably after testing positive for drugs. He then lived what he called a party lifestyle with women and alcohol before the night he committed the crime that landed him in prison. Avel argued with his girlfriend and fired a gun into the air, effectively discharging a firearm in public. He was arrested shortly thereafter and subsequently sentenced to prison. Given his background, Avel argued that he could blame his crime on his family, that he could blame it on his lack of education, or that he could blame it on his crazy girlfriend. "I've heard about race as an excuse [for crime and incarceration]," he also said, but he refused to accept any of these explanations. "We come into this world a broken sinner," Avel said, as he attributed all crime to sin.

At Wakulla Cl, volunteer Dan Nase similarly taught in his Spiritual Warfare class that people are "sinful in nature from our very beginning. We are predisposed to sin—to commit crime. We are sinful by nature in a condemned world. I love each and every one of you, but I have to tell that you are here because you're a sinner! Period." Several of the students in Nase's class are also inmate facilitators, and while they did not learn this idea in Spiritual Warfare, they will repeat it in the classes they teach. In Victim Awareness class, for example, Dennis Lonsdale taught, "We have to take responsibility for our crimes! It's almost in our nature to blame other people—like how Adam blamed Eve. When we sin it's our reaction to blame other people, like when we commit crimes and blame other people. We can't keep doing that. We have to fess up, to own up to our sins. They're why we're here!" His students nodded in agreement.

This idea not only explains the causes of crime and mass incarceration but prevents the incarcerated from discussing ulterior theories like institutionalized race and even racism itself. This is evident in a meeting of the Higher Standards Gavel Club. Gavel Club is a common club in U.S. prisons and beyond, where participants gather to practice public speaking. Wakulla CI hosts a Gavel Club, where during its semiannual business meeting, among other items of importance, the club's president recited various statistics about club membership including statistics about the club's racial composition. As soon as the president summarized the group's racial demographics, a black incarcerated man named Kimbrough Hall promptly raised his hand to ask a question. "Why are you even talking about race?" he asked. "We're supposed to be about higher character; higher standards. We're the *Higher Standards* Gavel Club. Why does race matter?" Race mattered, the president explained, because the prison monitors the racial composition of elective groups like the Gavel Club to ensure that they do not discriminate against racial minorities. In other words, the Gavel Club's racial composition needed to reflect the prison's racial diversity. "Well, I was just wondering," Kimbrough responded, "because we're supposed to be above all that. Amen."[27]

During this exchange, Kimbrough, himself an African American, scolded the other men for discussing race. As he said, "We're supposed to be above all that. *Amen!*" By invoking the common Christian exclamation, Kimbrough delivered more than social, political, or racial commentary as he attempted to sacralize his celebration of colorblindness. I am not sure where Kimbrough first learned to discard race as a category of social analysis and as a factor related to mass incarceration, but he had sat through numerous services and classes that reiterated and reinforced the idea that racial categories belong with other institutional analyses of social problems in the garbage dump of failed liberal social analyses.

In sum, the preceding pages summarized some of the more common aspects of FCBIs as they relate to the conservative center that all of the incarcerated encounter in FCBIs. This includes local control, freedom from the more restrictive government oversight that typically accompanies state-sanctioned socialization, teachers and leaders without academic training or professional certification, and theories not only of crime and criminality but of social justice more broadly that ignore institutionalized power structures. While none of these factors explicitly address economics, individually and collectively they resonate with neoliberal thought.

Friedrich Hayek, the Austrian economist considered one of the founders of neoliberal thought and the Chicago school of economics, helps illumine the convergence of neoliberal thought and the FCBIs' conservative center. In neoliberal classics like *The Road to Serfdom* and *Individualism and Economic Order*, Hayek argued that unregulated markets encourage individual freedom, as opposed to more restrictive socialist governments than curtail and burden individual initiative and independence. As political theorist Wendy Brown noted, while Hayek and other neoliberal thinkers did not intend for the implementation of neoliberalism as it unfolded in the 1980s in Chile, the United States, and the United Kingdom, these thinkers created a cult of the individual and a fear of government regulation that "Frankensteined" into something different that not only praises the individual and individual freedom but ignores oppressive sociocultural, economic, and political powers.[28]

Sociologist Heather Schoenfeld made a similar point about neoliberalism when she noted that the trope of individual responsibility emerged as a key component of neoliberalism's political project.[29] As neoliberal politicians dismantled welfare, attacked unions, and passed laws that benefit business, they simultaneously bolstered the rhetoric of individuality and individual responsibility.[30] They argued that the individual is solely responsible for success or failure, and by implication, for any behavior that would result in incarceration. Neoliberal theories of individuality and crime displace the theories of crime and criminality that to various degrees locate the cause of crime outside the realm of the free-willed individual.

According to scholars Michael Omi and Howard Winant, neoliberalism's cult of individuality specifically silences analyses of racism and incarceration. "Neoliberals deliberately try to avoid racial themes," they wrote, "both because they fear the divisiveness and polarization which characterized the racial reaction, and because they mistrust the 'identity politics' whose origins lie in the 1960s. They want to close the Pandora's box of race."[31]

The conservative core in FCBIs embraces the premise of neoliberal theories of crime as it agrees that the individual alone is responsible for crimes. This core differs, however, in that it contends that sin is the cause of crime and that the penitent and redeemed person stands the best chance of avoiding sin and the crimes that often accompany it. In FCBIs' epistemologies, you can identify the sinners by looking at criminals. If they are incarcerated, they have sinned. The individual is solely responsible.

The conservative core in FCBIs also overlaps with neoliberal thought as it inverts what is commonly considered expertise. Political scientist William Connolly contends that neoliberalism silences academics, academic training, and academic credentials, but this insight extends to other forms of training and expertise as well.[32] Conventional prisons typically have many leaders and authority figures, and almost all of them have extensive academic, professional, or institutional training. Doctors, psychologists, educators, chaplains, classification officers, and wardens were all vetted by multiple sources, where they displayed and highlighted their credentials, training, and expertise. In the alternatively regulated world of FCBIs, however, people are appointed to leadership positions by asserting individual claims of religiosity and by mastering the themes that constitute the conservative core.

Collectively, the volunteers and the incarcerated leaders who teach almost all the classes in FCBIs are engaging in a novel experiment that socializes incarcerated people not only to reconsider their understandings of sin, crime, and criminality but to conceive of alternate theories of expertise, leadership, the self, and society. If this socialization "sticks," the incarcerated leave FCBIs and reenter society with a different mindset, one uniquely compatible with neoliberal sociopolitical models of the self.

Gender, Sex, and Sexuality

Scholars have documented that the topics of gender and gender roles have played significant if often overlooked factors in the history of Christianity, both in the United States and beyond. The Bible itself traces these issues back to the earliest Jesus-following communities where Paul repeatedly reminded the recipients of his letters that men exercise patriarchal authority over women in matters both temporal and religious. Paul's teachings combined with other biblical prohibitions against female authority to justify patriarchal gender relations in Christian societies for some two thousand years. First-wave feminists began to challenge these ideas;[33] however, their efforts proved modestly successful, particularly as women gained the right to vote.

The issue of women's rights resurfaced in force in the 1960s when women mounted a more aggressive challenge against male dominance and oppression. They advocated for equal pay, for equal opportunities in all aspects of society, for a reassessment of the distribution of household duties, for the legal right to abortion nationwide, and for the legitimacy of female sexuality.[34] Though they never achieved their ultimate goal of complete gender equality, they did achieve modest goals. The gay rights movement similarly capitalized on the spirit of resistance as gay activists laid the foundation for the LGBTQ movement that became a dominant political force roughly fifty years later.

Not everyone supported these changes. Chief among them are the conservative Christians—both men and women—who continue to advocate for what they term traditional gender roles. As scholar R. Marie Griffith described, sex, sexuality, and gender relations became one of the more divisive issues both in the United States and in American Christianity.[35] In the contentious environment that followed the sexual revolution of the 1960s, many conservative Christians not only saw change or transformation, they identified evolving gender norms as fundamental threats that courted God's wrath, and they mobilized inside and outside their churches to restore what they called traditional gender relations. Prison ministries provide them one such opportunity, particularly in Florida's FCBIs, where conservative Christians have almost complete control over the tone and content of FCBI programming. The family becomes important in this theological milieu, where, to quote Foucault, the family is viewed as "the privileged instrument for the government of the population."[36] Discrete family units ruled by patriarchal authority figures form the basis of society.[37]

Gender and Submission in FCBIs for Men

"Marital/Family" is one of the seven domains in Florida's FCBIs. Each incarcerated person must complete thirty-two hours of classes in this domain, where, potentially, FCBI administrators, volunteers, and inmate facilitators can teach any conceivable theory about marriage and family. They can teach the incarcerated to adopt or even embrace the increasingly LGBTQ-friendly environments they will encounter when they leave prison, and they can teach the incarcerated to reevaluate patriarchal authority and gender roles. Instead, the incarcerated learn to lead the fight against evolving theories about gender and sexuality as they advocate for a return to what they believe are traditional Christian values. Numerous examples support this claim.

Consider that the Faith and Character–Based Completion Worksheet states that Marriage Study (religious or nonreligious) is an optional course in the Marital/Family domain. At Lawtey CI, that course is titled Godly Marriage Principles: God's Indestructible Plan for Marriage.[38] As its name suggests, this is an overtly Christian class that draws heavily from select verses in the Bible. To understand the Christian narratives that frame this course, consider the course description on the class's syllabus, which states, "We have a 100% chance of success in marriage, but we have to do it God's way. His perfect plan for marriage is found in the Bible (Ephesians 5:21–31), and if we will follow this plan we will have an indestructible marriage, success is assured. The reason that marriages are failing today is that we are trying to do it differently than God intended it. The primary scriptures we'll be covering in this session are: Ephesians 5:21–31; 1 Peter 3:1–7; Proverbs 31:10–31."[39] The remainder of the syllabus's first page explains "4 Reasons Why Ephesians 5:21–31 Will Be The Best Thing to Ever Happen to Your Marriage."[40]

Ephesians 5:21–31 establishes several core principles for marriage. It defends heterosexual marriage as a sacred institution ordained by God ("For this cause shall a man leave his father and mother, and shall be joined unto his wife, and they two shall be one flesh"—Ephesians 5:31), it creates a two-tiered hierarchy with Christ as the head of the church and with husbands the head of their families and wives ("Wives, submit yourselves unto your own husbands, as unto the Lord. For the husband is the head of the wife, even as Christ is the head of the church: and he is the saviour of the body. Therefore as the church is subject unto Christ, so let the wives be to their own husbands in every thing"—Ephesians 5:22–24), and it reminds men—as stewards of the godly marriage—"to love their wives as their own bodies" (Ephesians 5:28). According to these verses, the husband loves his wife but has ultimate authority over her.

The remainder of the syllabus elaborates on these themes as it addresses a number of marital issues such as communication, the importance of trust, the biblical prescription for "Indestructible Love," and an extended discussion of "Sexual Intimacy and Fulfillment." Scholars Jessica Johnson and Kelsy Burke have documented how conservative Protestants increasingly embrace sex and sexuality within the confines of heterosexual marriage.[41] Evangelicals like Tim and Beverly LaHaye wrote books that espouse the virtues of sexual pleasure, while other entrepreneurial Christians created websites that not only support this idea but that sell sex toys to Christians.[42] Sociologist Kelsy Burke described that these websites embrace and perpetuate the idea that "God created sexual pleasure to be enjoyed fully by both husband and wife."[43] The syllabus for the Godly Marriage Principles class embraces these idea as it devotes a significant amount of time to the issues of sexual intimacy and fulfillment.

The syllabus contends, "To really 'know' our wives in the Biblical sense, sex is essential."[44] The syllabus argues that God sanctifies sex between a man and woman but that He "put parameters on sex. These parameters include, [sic] no adultery, fornication, incest, pedophilia, homosexuality, bestiality, rape, and pornography."[45] Satan, the syllabus continues, will attempt to deceive us—a problem aided by the Bible's ambiguity regarding "what is or is not Godly regarding sex toys, oral sex, [and] many other contemporary sexual practices."[46] The syllabus recognizes these ambiguities and suggests that couples should discuss these issues. If the couple (in consultation with God) determines that the Bible does not clearly forbid a practice or sexual act, if husband and wife agree to do it, if it is not physically harmful, and if it does not "harm the marriage relationship," these sexual acts are permissible.[47] The couple must exercise extreme caution, however, as the devil deploys a variety of strategies to lure us into sin.

The syllabus also provides the men with knowledge about their wives' sexuality where they learn that female sexuality is linked to the couple's emotional and religious lives. The syllabus teaches that true, Bible-based spirituality and prayer are the keys to unlocking the wife's sexuality. Regarding the former, the syllabus states, "When you love your wife in a truly sacrificial [i.e., biblical] way, you will find out just how sexual she is."[48] The syllabus continues, "There is no greater level of intimacy in marriage than praying together and worshiping together. Keep in mind that one of the woman's deepest sexual needs is to have her husband pray with her."[49] In other words, a woman's sexuality hinges on her relationship both with her husband and with God, and it is the husband's responsibility to recognize these dynamics and to nurture them for the sake of his (and her) sexual fulfillment.

As this summary suggests, the elective course designed to fulfill the "Marriage Study (Religious on Non-Rel.)" elective for the religiously pluralistic FCBI prison at Lawtey CI is a thoroughly sectarian course. The Baptist chaplain Wright created the course, and it mirrors the Southern Baptist Convention's 2000 Baptist Statement of Faith, which similarly identifies Ephesians 5:21–31 (among other verses) as the biblical foundation for marriage.[50] Wright is not alone in teaching these ideas, as evidenced by many of the classes that Daryl Townsend, the most important volunteer at Lawtey CI, teaches.

The first time I visited Lawtey CI, Chaplain Wright was out of town, and I instead met with Daryl, who spends so much time at the prison that prison administrators consider him an unpaid member of the staff. In fact, in the chaplain's absence, Townsend literally had the keys to the prison's chapel. In prisons, keys are prized possessions, and I found no other instance where a non-DOC employee took possession of keys. Townsend performs a variety of duties at Lawtey CI, not limited to the classes he teaches and to the mentoring duties he performs on a weekly or even daily basis. One of his favorite classes is called Authentic Manhood, a popular course currently taught throughout the United States both inside and outside prisons, particularly in FCBIs.

Authentic Manhood is the brainchild of Dr. Robert Lewis, a successful minister and entrepreneur, who focused his ministry on the issue of masculinity.[51] Lewis argued that the 1960s and the feminist movement coincided with other factors to unleash a regime of godlessness that threatened to undermine the foundation of the Christian United States. Instead of benignly empowering women, he believed that the feminist movement produced confused and emasculated men who sacrificed their divinely ordained positions as leaders of family and community. Lewis wanted to help men reclaim their lost masculinity, but he struggled to find a place where men could come together to explore the topic. According to one spokesperson for Authentic Manhood, "If you're not on the battlefield or football field with a group of guys, then where are the opportunities for men to gather in masculine ways that seem natural for them?"[52] To help cultivate this masculine space, Lewis gathered a small group of like-minded Christian men who met every Wednesday morning at 6:00 A.M., where they aspired to identify and model "true" or "authentic" masculinity as depicted by God, biblical patriarchs, and Jesus himself.[53] By Lewis's own account, the group was successful beyond his wildest dreams, so Lewis harnessed the power of his new company, Men's Fraternity Inc., to help transform his study group into a larger movement.

Lewis's program expanded as Authentic Manhood grew "into a global movement impacting more than a million men in more than 20,000 locations worldwide."[54] This program is called The Quest for Authentic Manhood, or Authentic Manhood, for short.[55] The Authentic Manhood program currently consists of three year-long courses specifically designed to teach men to achieve authentic, Bible-based masculinity. Christian men in the United States and beyond can join the Authentic Manhood movement by purchasing the curriculum on DVDs and workbooks from Men's Fraternity. Today, volunteers like Townsend purchase the Authentic Manhood program and either teach an abbreviated version in Florida's FCBIs or train the inmate facilitators who teach it themselves. In either case, the Authentic Manhood program—much like the classes taught by Chaplain Wright—similarly teaches that God created men and women for monogamous relationships where women submit to men. In other words, this class also reinforces a conservative understanding of biblical literalism, patriarchal authority, and heteronormativity. Volunteers like Townsend teach these ideas in almost all of their classes, regardless of the topic.

Given the prevalence of conservative Protestants who administer and volunteer in FCBIs, it is not particularly surprising to find religious classes that teach biblical literalism, patriarchy, and heteronormativity. These ideas, however, are not confined to the overtly religious classes. Instead, they appear in multiple classes throughout FCBIs, including those that the DOC would classify as secular or character-based. Scholars have written at length how Christians developed and deployed the category of "secular" to their advantage.[56] Instead of creating obstacles for Protestant Christians, the category of the secular created new opportunities for Protestant socialization. In FCBIs, these (secular or character-based) courses conform to this general pattern.

Consider a course that Chaplain Wright teaches—InsideOut Dad. As scholar Richard Collier noted, fatherhood (often a synonym for masculinity) is increasingly seen as a problem that needs to be addressed,[57] and one that often results in a devaluing of mothers.[58] Scholar Melinda Cooper noted that contemporary fatherhood discourse emerged conterminously with and serves the interests of neoliberalism, as it assumes that private and patriarchal authority is responsible for socialization and for administering the families that are increasingly conceived as the foundational units of social organization.[59] Christians like Chaplain Wright embrace this model of fatherhood and teach it in classes like InsideOut Dad.

InsideOut Dad is perhaps the most common parenting course for men in American prisons. Backed by several studies that document its effectiveness,[60] InsideOut Dad boasts that it "is the nation's only evidence-based fatherhood program designed specifically for incarcerated fathers. InsideOut Dad helps reduce recidivism rates by reconnecting incarcerated fathers to their families, providing the motivation to get out and stay out."[61] According to the National Fatherhood Initiative, InsideOut Dad is taught in over four hundred correctional facilities in all fifty states, including the state of Florida, where conventional prisons and FCBIs routinely offer this course.[62]

InsideOut Dad developed both a secular and a Christian curriculum, and at Lawtey CI, Chaplain Wright teaches from the secular version, which allowed the state to purchase the course material. Wright claims that he teaches the secular option, but he "introduces a faith component" based on what he perceives to be universal religious values.[63] To avoid advocating for sectarian religion and therefore offending some of the religious people in FCBIs, Wright claims that he examined all the religions to identify their teachings about marriage. "Christians, Jews, Muslims, even Odinists," he found, "they all sanctify marriage, and they all sanctify one man–one woman marriages, with the man as head of household." This statement is verifiably false, as groups in many religions reject submission theology and support same-sex marriage and the LGBTQ movement, not limited to Wright's Christianity.[64] By appealing to these allegedly universal religious truths, however, Wright contends that he is not violating any constitutional separation of religion and state, as he avoids partisan and denominational disagreements by appealing to perennial religious values.

Chaplain Wright uses the secular program as a framework for the class, but he mines other material for additional insights that reinforce his theories about gender. He draws heavily from the bestselling book *Men Are from Mars, Women Are from Venus*, which Wright uses to help "teach [the incarcerated] how women think."[65] "I teach [the incarcerated]," he continues, "that men and women really are from different planets. God made us different so we could pair up. We have different emotions, different body parts, etc. You know, men have trouble with short-term memory, but women have better short-term memory. We complement each other."[66] In *Men Are from Mars, Women Are from Venus*—another seemingly secular book—Wright finds a theory of gender that complements what he would call the Bible-based theory of gender taught in the "Godly Marriage Principles" class. In short, the allegedly secular or character-based course similarly reinforces biblical literalism, patriarchy, and heteronormativity.

Collectively, the chaplains and the volunteers repeat these ideas in almost all of their classes, where they are ingrained in dominant FCBI culture. Not only are the incarcerated exposed to these ideas daily, but the chaplains identify the people who embrace these ideas, and they promote these people to the position of inmate facilitators. The chaplains then groom these inmate facilitators, who repeat these ideas in their classes. Numerous examples support this point.

In Celebrate Recovery, a Christian twelve-step program, an inmate facilitator taught his students that complete submission both to God and to the Bible are the keys to sobriety. "That means you have to be obedient to

God," the facilitator said. "It means you have to follow His rule, including no sex outside of marriage with your wife." A few minutes later, he revisited his theme when he said, "God made us in His image, and God isn't high or drunk! God made woman from man—from a single rib!—so they could complement and obey their husbands!" Similarly, in Anger Management, an inmate facilitator taught his students that submitting to God's love is the most effective strategy for overcoming anger, and a lesson on gender soon followed. "When you're filled with God's love," the facilitator said, "you can't be angry if you tried! You love your brothers, your sisters, your woman, even strangers. And if you're not filled with love, how can you lead your family for God?" In Commitment to Change, an inmate facilitator taught his students not only to shed their previous behaviors and mindsets but to replace them with the aforementioned Bible-based gender norms. These examples illumine a larger trend where inmate facilitators not only repeat the theories of gender they learn from chaplains and volunteers but introduce these ideas in classes that do not readily lend themselves to the topics.

Occasionally, almost an entire class would pass without an inmate facilitator or volunteer addressing gender. More often than not, however, an incarcerated student would introduce the topic, usually during a question-and-answer portion of the class, or he would simply interrupt the instructor to add his insights. During one meeting of Rev. John Spicer's Discipleship class, for example, the men watched a video that addressed what the Protestant Spicer considered papal overreach in the 1300s and 1400s. Spicer then invited the men to address the balance between effective internal church discipline and tyranny. "How," he asked, "do we enforce church discipline in the twenty-first century?" During a lively discussion that followed, one man shouted, "We can't be like the Catholics, but I hear that women are being ordained! They're wrong and their licenses should be revoked." Spicer, a member of an Anglican diocese that itself ordains women, shook his head as he seemed uncomfortable with the statement, but he did not engage or disagree verbally with the man, thereby contributing to and naturalizing the man's comments.

Gender and Submission in FCBIs for Women

Thus far, the analysis of gender has focused exclusively on FCBIs for men. For practical reasons, most of my research occurred in FCBIs for men, as I simply lived closer to those facilities. I did, however, research in every FCBI for women where I was particularly interested to learn how incarcerated women in FCBIs addressed the issue of gender submission and male authority figures.

Women are roughly half the population in the United States, but they account for only 7 percent of the incarcerated population.[67] Crime is clearly a man's game. That said, since 1985, the number of incarcerated women increased at almost twice the rate of men with black women over three times as likely as white women to be incarcerated and Hispanic women 69 percent more likely.[68] According to a report by The Sentencing Project, incarcerated women are a population in dire need of multiple forms of assistance, as "60 percent of incarcerated women were not employed full-time when they were arrested, and 37 percent had incomes under $600 in the month leading up to their arrest."[69] Additionally, 44 percent of incarcerated women have not completed high school, they were more likely than men to report drug use when they committed their offense, 57 percent of incarcerated women experienced sexual or physical abuse, and almost three-quarters (73.1 percent) of incarcerated women had mental health problems. Substance abuse tends to be a dominant issue, as drug crimes and property theft account for over 50 percent of their criminal offenses.[70] Given these statistics and dynamics, how, I wondered, do women respond to gender submission theology and patriarchal authority? The women answered my questions the first hour I met with them.

The FCBI dorm for women at Lowell Annex was the first female FCBI that I visited. After I met with the warden, he escorted me to the FCBI dorm, where I met Chaplain Faithe Liburd, the FCBI dorm's primary administrator. Chaplain Liburd arranged for me to interview several of the incarcerated women, and most of them repeated the aforementioned theories of gender and sexuality without any prompting.

An incarcerated woman named Irene Wilson was the first woman I interviewed.[71] She articulated a history of her childhood and adolescence that, combined with her experiences in prison and in the FCBI dorm, provided a familiar story that many of the women repeated, plus or minus a few details. As such, a detailed summary of her life and of her experience in the FCBI dorm is appropriate. At age fifty-seven, Irene is currently twenty-nine years into her life sentence for first-degree murder. She grew up in a Baptist family, although she did not see her biological parents very often, as both her parents worked multiple jobs to make ends meet. Instead, after school on most days her aunt took her to church, where she spent her evenings. It is not much of a stretch to say she literally grew up in church, and her Baptist faith played a central role in her upbringing. Not only did she spend most of her time in the church, but Sunday's church services also provided the only chance for Irene to spend more than a few minutes with her mom, who worked as many as five jobs simultaneously.

Irene had a half-brother who lived with her grandma since before Irene was born. They had the same mom, but when their mom remarried, her brother went to live with her grandma, as Irene's father did not think it appropriate to raise someone else's son in his house. Irene said "there was a general consensus in the community that it would be wrong for the boy to live with the new family." Irene's faith began to be tested at the age of thirteen when three of her brother's friends first sexually assaulted her. They raped her repeatedly over the next several years, but she did not tell anyone, as her community frowned upon premarital sex and she was embarrassed, ashamed, and fearful that she would be judged. The abuse stopped at age fifteen, but it came with a cost, as the abuse only ended after her brother was shot and killed. Her abusers simply stopped visiting the house. Irene described how she became angry, both because of her abuse and because of her dead brother, and God bore the brunt of her frustration. For the first time in her life, she resented her maker.

Irene finished high school several years later, and at age seventeen she married a man she had dated for two years. A year later she felt like her life was coming back together when she learned she was pregnant, but this optimism was short-lived after her baby son was born with a heart defect and died three days later. Her husband divorced her not long after, and she found herself an abused divorcee with a dead child. She dated the first man who expressed interest in her, but he, too, proved bad for Irene, as he was physically, emotionally, and sexually abusive. Irene recalled, "At first he told me what to wear, where to go, when I could leave the house, etc." His yelling gave way to pushing which turned into slapping. On multiple occasions he even punched her.

The nadir of their relationship came one night when her boyfriend came home drunk and demanded sex. She told him that she was not in the mood, and unwilling to accept "no" for an answer, he chased her through the house. At some point in his pursuit, he grabbed a knife. He caught up with Irene and grabbed her by her hair, stabbed her in the back, and then bent her over and raped her at knifepoint while she bled from the new wound. This convinced Irene to end the relationship, but over the next several months, her now ex-boyfriend stalked and abused her. One night he found her at a local bar and dragged her outside, where he pinned her against a wall and choked her. She thought he was going to kill her right then and there, but a friend saved her.

She experienced a brief reprieve when he moved to the other side of Florida for a few months. This was a particularly dark period for Irene, as she worked during the days and then spent her evenings at home alone, where she drank excessively. "I didn't trust nobody," she said. Determined to get her life back together, she overcame the residual anger she held against God and she sobered up and went back to church. Things started looking better for Irene when her ex returned to town and promised to be the man she had always wanted, so they spent the weekend together. "It was so good," she said, "I even skipped church." A month later, however, the optimism faded as her boyfriend started abusing her again. She ended the relationship for good, although the ex-boyfriend continued to stalk her. Afraid that he might try to choke her again or worse, she made the decision she still regrets today—she bought a handgun.

Several days before Christmas in 1986, Irene went shopping to purchase Christmas gifts and then she went to a ball game. On her way home, she decided to stop at a fast food restaurant for dinner. As soon as she stepped out of her car, however, she saw her ex. More importantly, he saw her and, according to Irene, he ran toward her with a deranged look in his eyes. Irene grabbed the gun from her car, which she hoped would scare him. Instead, as Irene recalled, "Me 'n him started tussin'. Next thing I know, it went off." She fled the scene and later learned that her ex-boyfriend died. The police arrested her the next day, and she has been incarcerated since.

Today, Irene is an esteemed and trusted prison "mom" in the FCBI dorm at Lowell Annex, where she is an informal leader and comforter for the other women.[72] "God loves them," Irene said; "they're daughters of the most high and they need to know that. I help them get rooted in God." She continued, "A lot of these women were mistreated by drug dealers. You know, [they were] raped, abused, [and] prostituted, so I remind them the good news that they get a new body in Christ. There's no more defilement! They're new again. I tell them how to have godly relationships with men. I always tell them about Peter and being submissive to their husbands. And that means they need to first find godly men. When you're submissive to a godly man, you find freedom in Christ." As this suggests, Irene, who has never had a positive long-term relationship with a man, now teaches other abused women to submit to men. Ironically or not, her god and the men who abused her have similar expectations—they can be distant, they claim that suffering breeds strength, and they demand her submission and obedience.

In summary, Irene not only repeated the all-too-familiar tropes about gender that I learned to expect in the men's facilities, but she also teaches them to younger women. Perhaps, I thought, she was the exception. Or maybe her positions were the norm? Subsequent interviews quickly confirmed the latter, as the women's stories predictably contained some combination of sexual abuse, drug abuse, and negative relationships with men. Almost without exception, they also grew up in Christian families (both Protestant and Catholic) and considered themselves Christians when they committed their crimes. They now believe that *true* Christians do not commit crimes, so they reconcile this contradiction by retroactively denying the religiosity of their former selves. As one woman said, "I used to blame God for the victimization that led to my crimes, but I now realize it was my fault, not God's. Had I been a better Christian, God wouldn't have allowed those bad things to happen. God casts a protective umbrella over his true children." Finally, the women also repeatedly told me that their god wants them to submit to godly men.

My experience in the FCBI dorm at Lowell Annex taught me not only that chaplains and incarcerated leaders in FCBIs teach women that God only sanctions patriarchal gender relations and heterosexual unions but that these ideas are more prevalent in the female facilities. To a certain extent, this is predictable, as the chaplains and the volunteers who teach classes at all FCBIs overwhelmingly mingle in the religious circles that teach and that circulate a core set of religious ideas—including gender submission—and they teach these ideas in various settings, including FCBIs. Incarcerated men in FCBIs learn that they will become heads of households, but women learn to become submissive, and they are also taught *how* to submit. They have to learn how to trust men, how to obey men, and how to interact with authoritative men—a recipe that has not served many of them well in the past. To break their old selves, the women learn repeatedly through intense socialization to embrace their new gendered ethics.

LGBTQ

On June 26, 2015, the U.S. Supreme Court affirmed that gay Americans have a constitutional right to marriage.[73] Writing for a slim five–four majority, Justice Anthony Kennedy opened the Court's decision when he wrote, "The Constitution promises liberty to all within its reach, a liberty that includes certain specific rights that allow persons, within a lawful realm, to define and express their identity. The petitioners in these cases seek to find that liberty by marrying someone of the same sex and having their marriages deemed lawful on the same terms and conditions as marriages between persons of the opposite sex."[74] The Constitution's expanding notion of freedom, the majority concluded, grants them that right.

I had spent the morning at Wakulla CI hoping the Court would announce its decision before I left for the afternoon, as I wanted to hear the men's reaction in real time. Without exception, the dominant culture in FCBIs virulently opposes gay marriage and homosexuality in general. From the perspectives of the incarcerated, every "advance" for LGBTQ communities further validates their idea that Satan is overtaking the United States and that Armageddon is near. Regardless of the Supreme Court's decision, the men in the FCBI would have passionate reactions. If the Court legalized gay marriage, the men would lament the triumph of evil over good. Conversely, if the Court ruled it illegal, the men would praise the decision as the triumph of good over evil. Unfortunately for me, the Court announced its decision twenty minutes after I left prison; however, I returned to the prison as soon as possible.

As expected, the men were livid, to say the least. They voiced their skepticism as soon as I entered a classroom in the prison's chapel, where one of the men shook my hand and said, "Hey, Brad, this is the greatest country in the world! Now homosexuals can marry! Can you believe it? Two percent of the population [I'd previously learned that he believes only 2 percent of people are gay, or more specifically, that they chose to 'lead a gay lifestyle'] succeeded in convincing the government to overturn God's laws." A man named Daniel responded. Daniel has a deep voice and an intense stutter, and he mumbles his words more than speaking them in articulate English. Per usual, we had trouble identifying his first several sentences until we identified the words "Sodom and Gomorrah," which caused the other men to nod their heads in agreement, presumably anticipating God's impending judgment and wrath against the United States.

A man named Bruce, however, had a different take. "I hear you, brothers," he began, "but I'm excited! God told us in the Bible that the end would come and the true believers would be saved. People have been waiting *thousands of years* for the prophecies to come true, but just look, it's happening right now! I'll tell ya, I'm excited to see it happen! I'm excited to see all the sinners get what's coming; I'm excited to see all the doubters learn how very wrong they are."

Bruce continued, and as was common in this class, the content changed to link gay marriage with a host of issues that riled the men. "What more proof do we need?" Bruce continued. "The president is a Muslim, gays can marry, and the government knows what we're doing every moment of every day! Are y'all following this about the Google cars? About how they're driving around recording everything and collecting data on everything we do? They're absorbing information from all over. They're downloading entire computers, all our personal information, because they're so observant. I tell ya, when I'm out of prison, if I see one, I'll rear-end it just to do it!"

While the men were still laughing at the joke, the first of two volunteer ministers arrived. Forgoing the usual small talk, the minister asked them to turn to Philippians 4:8, which reads, "Finally, brothers and sisters, whatever is true, whatever is noble, whatever is right, whatever is pure, whatever is lovely, whatever is admirable—if anything is excellent or praiseworthy— think about such things."

"I take it you all saw what happened—you heard about it, that is," he asked. The men nodded in the affirmative, to which he responded,

> In these trying times, we need to stay focused. We need to reclaim
> our thoughts. We need to think about anything excellent or
> praiseworthy, [because] the enemy is trying to hijack your thoughts;
> your imagination. God doesn't want this. We need to guard our
> thoughts; to reclaim our thoughts. I don't have to tell you, "Hey
> brother, the devil is trying to destroy you." You just know it! It's
> second nature! Jesus won't save your flesh, but he'll save your soul,
> if you stay focused on Him and His message. Reclaim what the devil
> seeks to destroy.

Assuming he helped the men find hope or consolation in these trying times, he addressed the more pertinent topic. "So," he began,

> they're redefining marriage in the courts! They're devaluing life! We
> don't know if men are men or if boys are boys. So much confusion!
> Let's do an honest assessment of where we stand: homosexuals can
> marry, you can legally kill babies, Christianity is illegal in the
> schools, and the schools have to let pedophiles [transgender people]
> use the bathrooms with our daughters! *How much worse does it have
> to get?* I need to remind you—this isn't too much for you to handle!
> You're here, now, for a reason! God needs you! If God knew you
> couldn't take it, you would have been born a long time ago in more
> godly times. No, my brothers, you're here in this place, in this time,
> to do His work, to be His army! You were chosen by the Almighty to

fulfill his prophecy, and if that don't give you hope and put a deep joy in your heart, then what will?

I returned to the prison almost daily the following week where volunteers, ministers, and inmate facilitators waxed and waned between extreme anger that Satan was winning in the short term and by an exuberant enthusiasm that God not only controlled but even orchestrated the long game.

Over the days and weeks that followed, the anti–LGBTQ rights sentiment slowly faded close to the pre-*Obergefell* levels. It did not disappear as much as it no longer dominated the conversations, classes, and sermons. When it did appear, however, a new level of disdain accompanied it, due largely to the Court's decision.

The anti-LGBTQ sentiment is most evident in the sectarian services and study groups where incarcerated people gather as members of their respective religions or denominations. The examples from the conservative Protestant services and study groups are simply too numerous to list, where the rhetoric of heteropatriarchal marriage was as ubiquitous as the detainment devices that separate the incarcerated from the free world. In these services, volunteer after volunteer blamed "the homosexual agenda" for everything from the broken U.S. trade policy, to declining scores on standardized tests in public schools, to the breakdown of the American family, to race problems, to mass incarceration itself (as one man said, "Is it any coincidence that the same country with prison problems is the same country that now lets gays marry?"). And when "the homosexual agenda" is not the cause of the nation's problems, it is often added to the constellation of problems that collectively harm America.[75]

Conservative Protestants, however, are not the only groups that teach these ideas in FCBIs, as some of the religious minorities share these ideas. Hebrew Israelites—as discussed later, Hebrew Israelites believe that black people are the true Hebrews—similarly believe that homosexuality and same-sex relationships offend God. This message comes straight from the group's founder, Yahweh ben Yahweh, who before he died in 2007, recorded instructional videos designed to help his organization, the Nation of Yahweh (NOY), spread its theology and recruit new members. Incarcerated Hebrew Israelites watch these videos in the prison.

In these videos, Yahweh ben Yahweh teaches the Hebrew Israelites that they are the true, biblical Hebrews, but he also teaches that homosexuality and same-sex relationships offend Yahweh. He shared these thoughts during a discussion of Yahweh University, a school owned and operated by the

NOY. Yahweh ben Yahweh boasted not only that the children are excelling in all their studies but that none of them smoke, take drugs, or drink alcohol. They do not have a problem with teen pregnancy, nor do the students have venereal diseases or AIDS. "What does that mean?" he asked. "It means we have no faggots in our school!"[76] He contrasted the students in the University of Yahweh with the larger American population, where children get abortions and even use birth control without their parents' permission. "Your children have no restraints, no inhibition," he continued. "Their parents are probably off participating in a gay parade somewhere."[77]

Messianic Jews expressed a similar sentiment when the volunteer who leads the Messianic Jewish group at Wakulla CI told the men about a bad dream he recently had, where a terrorist brought a car full of explosives to a public school. "I'm worried," he continued, "because we are under terrorist attack!" A few illegible words in my notes make it difficult to identify the person who spoke next, but either the volunteer or one of the men soon said, "Schools are particularly vulnerable because the school has aligned itself with the unholy one. The schools teach gay rights and outlaw Torah." Once again, a participant in an FCBI suggested that religious teachings conflict with LGBTQ rights, and he implied that the schools and the state embrace LGBTQ rights at their own peril.

Despite their significant differences, Messianic Jews and the NOY find common ground on this particular issue not only with each other but also with the conservative Protestant majority in FCBIs. Chaplain Fox described the importance of these seemingly ecumenical moments when he said, "We look for these moments with groups like the Hebrew Israelites. We're not going to agree on much, but if I can get them to agree on a particular point or set of ideas, then at least we're engaging each other." Fox hopes that these ecumenical moments will lead the incarcerated, in his words, to embrace Christ, but in the meantime, the various parties welcome these ecumenical moments centered primarily on issues of gender and sexuality. The people from the various religions then internalize these ideas, and inmate facilitators repeat them in their classes. The training classes for a new course titled WHYTRY provide an excellent example.

Chaplain Fox learned about a new program called WHYTRY, and after he attended an introductory class, he decided to introduce the program into Wakulla CI. WHYTRY is a class or program designed to help anyone identify goals and then find the grit—to use a popular buzzword—to persevere in pursuit of these goals. This program could potentially help anyone,

Fox reasoned, but it might particularly resonate with the incarcerated. To introduce the program into Wakulla CI, he asked two graduate students in the Social Work Department at Florida State University to teach the program to the inmate facilitators, who would later teach the class themselves. Subsequent private discussions with the two student teachers revealed that they considered the class a thoroughly secular course and that they struggled to keep a secular tone, as the inmate facilitators consistently steered the discussions toward religious issues and themes.

One day in class, the men received materials from the "WHYTRY Game Plan Journal" to help the students identify goals, to identify obstacles, and to help them achieve their goals by prioritizing behaviors most conducive to those goals. The first page of the handout included a dizzyingly elaborate maze that wove through three big words: DESIRE TIME EFFORT. The students had five minutes to complete the maze, but very few made it to the end. "The maze," one of the instructors said, "serves as a metaphor for the obstacles we face in life. A lot of you couldn't finish the maze because you kept getting stuck at the dead ends. So, what dead ends do *you* face today? What dead ends do *we* face today?" David Mollett, one of inmate facilitators at Wakulla, provided the first answer.

"Homosexuality!" he said. "It's a dead end. How many lives have been destroyed by it, how many nations have been destroyed for it? God's made his position clear, and now we're deciding it's ok? We need to return to scripture, and we'd realize real quick that it's a dead end." This conversation continued for several rounds of questions and answers where the instructors tried unsuccessfully to redirect the conversation. Realizing their failure, one of the instructors suggested they move on.

David will someday teach WHYTRY in his own classes, where he will have more control over the course's tone and contents. Until then, he teaches several classes such as Commitment to Change and Bridge Builders. In the latter, David teaches the incarcerated that part of their recovery might require them to shed their old friends and to embrace new ones. This insight resonated with a man named Isaac, who said, "We even need to practice this in prison." In prisons, he said, people group together with other people who share their problematic behavior or identity. "Bikers with other bikers," he continued, "gang members with other gang members, homosexuals with other homosexuals. Sinners group with other sinners!" To overcome their problematic behaviors, the incarcerated, he argued, need to find new friends. "And forgive me, Lord, if this is vain," he joked, "but us chapel-dwelling folk might be the best friends you'll meet in prison."

As this summary suggests, the incarcerated people who participate in popular FCBI programs are exposed to (and repeat) the idea that LGBTQ rights are anathema to American progress and are offensive to God. Not all of the incarcerated share these views, however, and they remain the silent minority in FCBIs. An incarcerated woman named Brittany is one such woman.

Brittany's story is unique because she was incarcerated at Hernando CI before it converted into an FCBI, and she witnessed the transformation that occurred as the emphasis on faith-based rehabilitation attracted more volunteers who oppose LGBTQ rights. I asked Brittany if the anti-homosexuality rhetoric increased after the conversion. "Oh yes," she replied, "[anti-LGBTQ rhetoric] increased significantly! It used to be a part of the prison, but now it *is* the prison. Today they're anti! Very anti! Extremely anti! People speak out against homosexuality in here all the time. [The old chaplain] told me I had to go to church, but I told him I don't want to go to church because they hate lesbians so much, and he told me, 'Well then, you don't go to church unless you're willing to hear it [anti-homosexuality].' So, I don't go to church."

Another woman, Jia Noel, voiced a similar response, but she added a religious justification for her position. Jia grew up in a family where the women practiced magic and other rituals she now identifies as Wiccan. Today, she also considers herself a Wiccan and practices Wicca in Hernando CI. When I asked her about homosexuality, she invoked the goddess when she replied, "I have no problem with it. The Mother wouldn't care, so why should I?"[78] Conversations with additional Wiccans revealed they, too, overwhelmingly support gay marriage and LGBTQ rights. FCBI chaplains are aware of the Wiccans' support for LGBTQ rights, and in the words of one of the chaplains, their support is just one of the many reasons Wiccans will "bust the gates of hell wide open" when they die. The same chaplain believes that every non-Christian is similarly going to hell ("I'm not really sure about the Catholics," he said. "That's entirely God's call."), but no other group provokes such sweeping condemnation. Since Wiccans embrace LGBTQ rights and have many other beliefs and rituals that offend the conservative Protestant majority, they remain isolated and shut out of the ecumenical moments that members of the other religions occasionally share with the conservative Protestant majority. As such, they remain outliers in a correctional world built to accommodate religious diversity.

Not only do some of the incarcerated people support LGBTQ rights, but some of the volunteers also support them. In the course of my research,

I talked to several volunteers and even to a volunteer minister who supports LGBTQ rights. At no point, however, did any of these people voice their support of LGBTQ rights inside the prison. And when someone in the prison made comments critical of LGBTQ rights, none of the supporters disagreed with them. For example, during a Quest meeting at Wakulla CI, the class had broken into small groups to discuss parenting responsibilities for moms and dads in an era when traditional gender roles have dissolved. Hugh MacMillan, a volunteer deeply invested in Quest, suggested that there is no correct way to distribute parental duties and responsibilities assuming the spouses agree on the distribution of labor. A man named JD responded, "Yeah, I can get with that. That's cool. I guess anything'll work as long as it ain't two dads or moms." Several men in the group nodded their heads in agreement, and the conversation continued. About an hour later, Hugh and I exited the prison together, and knowing Hugh's position on LGBTQ rights, I asked him why he did not disagree. "We're here to build bridges," he replied, "not to dig trenches." In other words, Hugh did not challenge the man because Hugh wanted the man to be open to the other ideas Hugh might teach. The broader point remains, however, that his silence reinforced the anti-LGBTQ culture in Wakulla CI.

In summary, this section highlighted the dominant anti-LGBTQ sentiment that permeates Florida's FCBIs, including both the male and female facilities. The sentiment is particularly strong in FCBI dorms, where the incarcerated participate in more classes together that incorporate this idea and where it is comparably hard for them to opt out of the many classes and programs either based on or that incorporate this sentiment. They carry these ideas across the dorm to their bunks, where they revisit them as they study into the evenings. In lieu of any dissenting voice, this sentiment is naturalized in FCBIs not only as a biblical principle but as a universal religious sentiment. The religious people who question this sentiment court passionate disagreement when they voice their opposition, so they, like the volunteers, choose to remain quiet. In the wake of their silence, some of the most persistent and vocal opposition to LGBTQ rights occurs in state-funded, -owned, and -operated FCBIs.

Disrupting Labor Relations

Hierarchies abound in prison. From carceral hierarchies that position some incarcerated people as authority figures and others as potential victims, to racial hierarchies that position some incarcerated groups as more powerful than others, to the hierarchies between the incarcerated and staff, the incarcerated are keenly aware that to successfully navigate prison, they need to know their "place" in any given situation. As discussed elsewhere in this book, FCBIs attempt to subvert and even dismantle some of these hierarchies; however, FCBIs introduce new relations of power that result in new hierarchies centered primarily, although not exclusively, on gender and sexuality. These hierarchies are common in FCBIs' alternatively regulated spaces, where the emphasis on faith is in tension with laws that relate to gender and sexuality.

One type of hierarchy involves the incarcerated in FCBIs, many of whom earn formal leadership positions. Florida's Administrative Code states, "No inmate shall be given control or authority over other inmates,"[79] although incarcerated leaders in FCBIs gain various degrees of authority over other incarcerated people in the facility. Informal leaders like prison moms and the men who are considered moral leaders influence the incarcerated, but their guidance and ability to discipline are more informal and subject to the consent of the incarcerated who look to these people for advice and guidance. Formal leaders like inmate facilitators and Grandfathers, however, teach classes, discipline students in classes, and recommend to the chaplain that people should be kicked out of a class or even the FCBI. The chaplain and prison administrators are responsible for the final decision, but chaplains appoint the inmate facilitators and typically trust their judgment. People in formal leadership positions are aware of this power dynamic and use it to their advantage.

If FCBIs create opportunities for incarcerated people to have authority over other people in the facility, it also creates conflicts where an incarcerated person can challenge other prison administrators, including correctional officers and chaplains. Regarding the former, incarcerated people in FCBIs routinely complain about the presence of gay correctional officers, primarily women, who do not perform gender or conform to conservative Christians' gendered stereotypes.[80] One incarcerated woman expressed as much when she lamented the presence of lesbian correctional officers. "It's not just wrong, it's not professional! I mean, the Bible teaches—the Jews, Christians, Muslims, they all believe that [homosexuality is] a sin! They shouldn't be here, and at least half of [the female correctional officers] are [gay]." When I asked how she knows which correctional officers are lesbians, she shook her head and responded, "How do I know they're gay? Oh, I know! Have you heard of gaydar? I'm not gay, but my gaydar is always going off in here." Men in multiple FCBI prisons and dorms expressed similar sentiments when they decried the presence of gay correctional officers. These men agree almost universally that Florida's DOC should not hire gay employees and that when it does, the DOC should only assign them to work in conventional correctional facilities as opposed to FCBIs. As one man said, "Look, I mean, they can't tell us homosexuality is a sin and then hire all these lesbians to watch us every day. They're sending us mixed messages." Not only do the incarcerated resent the presence of LGBTQ employees, but they are also more likely to be defiant or to challenge a correctional officer when the incarcerated identify a correctional officer as gay. Incarcerated people typically protest what they perceive as a gay correctional officer by shrugging, smirking, or even shaking their heads in protest when the correctional officer speaks to them or walks by.

In addition to protesting or passively resisting correctional officers, the incarcerated also occasionally challenge female chaplains when they deny these chaplains their religious authority or when they invoke the supernatural to influence chaplains. Karen Moffett is one such chaplain who worked at Lawtey CI for several years as an Other Personnel Services (OPS) chaplain[81] before she left the DOC in 2014 after budget cuts resulted in DOC downsizing. Like all FCBIs that I visited, the dominant culture at Lawtey CI teaches that women lack spiritual authority over men and that they should submit to men. This presented a potential problem for Moffett, who taught several courses and who helped Chaplain Wright administer the program at Lawtey CI. Chaplain Moffett, then, was a female religious authority figure in an environment that routinely denied her the authority guaranteed by her state employer. This presented several problems, particularly in the various classes she taught and in other interactions with the incarcerated men, where the men repeatedly told her about the theological dilemmas that resulted when virtually every volunteer, Chaplain Wright, and the Bible collectively agreed that the incarcerated men should deny Chaplain Moffett the spiritual authority she claimed. The men also told her that she lacked the authority to teach the incarcerated men about Christian theology. According to Moffett, the incarcerated specifically cited Daryl Townsend, the most trusted long-term volunteer at Lawtey CI, who repeatedly taught the men "she shouldn't be doing the things she's doing." Townsend admitted as much to me when he said, "Women don't take a leadership role in worship—I believe that and I teach it."[82] The men addressed their concerns with Moffett, who repeatedly sidestepped the issue. She told them that female submission is not a "kingdom issue," meaning one need not teach or even believe in female submission to earn a place in heaven with God. "We just don't go there," Moffett said. "I taught the inmates to eat the meat and spit out the bones," she told me, or to focus on the "kingdom issues" and disregard the superfluous.

Moffett may not think this tension is a kingdom issue, but it became a legal issue when Chaplain Wright regulated her behaviors solely on the basis of her gender. Chaplain Wright did not allow Chaplain Moffett to minister on Sundays (presumably during the "nondenominational service" OPS chaplains often teach), as he believes "there are no biblical references for women teaching over men."[83] Moffett herself did not support this decision, but as the lone voice for female ministers, she decided not to challenge the more senior administrators on this particular issue.

Chaplains also exercise authority over female volunteers, and they deny female and male volunteers equal access to the prison. Women volunteer at every FCBI I researched; however, female volunteers are typically not allowed to be formal mentors for incarcerated men. In FCBI prisons (as opposed to dorms), mentors meet in the chapel and in the chapel's classrooms to provide more counseling, guidance, and comfort. They also occasionally meet in the men's dorm and cellblocks. Chaplain Wright described how at Lawtey CI, they only allow men to be mentors "not because we're discriminating against females, but a lot of these guys were raised by women—by their moms, aunties, grandmas, and whatnot—so we want them to see and interact with successful men."[84] In other words, the FCBI prevents women from serving as mentors precisely because they are women, meaning, the facilities and the incarcerated men at Lawtey CI are not equally available to all volunteers, with gender playing the penultimate deciding role. Additionally, I interacted with several female volunteers, but at no point did I see a woman lead a service for men or preach to them. I doubt the chaplains would allow it, and the incarcerated men would probably not attend if a woman did preach.

FCBIs also disrupt the relationship between chaplains and volunteers when the chaplains are women and the volunteers are men. Female prison chaplains have a tremendous amount of authority, and they surrender some of this authority in FCBIs, primarily to male volunteers. Chaplain Faithe Liburd is a female chaplain at Lowell Annex, Florida's largest prison for women, where she is also the administrator of its FCBI dorm. Chaplain Liburd believes that men should exercise spiritual authority over women, and this creates a potential spiritual conflict inside the FCBI dorm, where many of the volunteers are men who deny Liburd's spiritual authority. Chaplain Liburd resolves or even prevents this potential conflict, as she does not attempt to exercise spiritual authority over men. Instead, she contends that she only exercises temporal authority over the male volunteers, telling them when and where they can meet, teach classes, and otherwise mentor the incarcerated. She can approve or decline their course proposals, but at no point does she exercise spiritual authority over men by correcting their theology or by disagreeing with them. As a result, at the FCBI dorm in Lowell Annex, the male volunteers—regardless of their training, credentials, or qualifications—have spiritual authority over the prison's credentialed and ordained head chaplain.

The larger issue in many of these instances relate to labor, workplace discrimination, and arguably sexual harassment. As legal scholar Marci Hamilton and others have argued, religious entities have legal exemptions that allow them to discriminate in their hiring practices and in the duties they assign to employees.[85] FCBIs, however, are not religious entities; rather, they are state owned, financed, and administered. As such, all state and federal labor laws are applicable. Prison administrators, volunteers, and even the incarcerated realize that spaces deemed faith-based provide them with opportunities to subvert some of this legislation, and they take advantage of this seemingly liminal space to run the facilities as if they were religious entities. This impacts both employee relations and opportunities for volunteers who are denied access and who have their roles limited on the basis of their gender or sexuality. FCBIs, then, and religious entities more broadly, contribute to neoliberalism's attempts to disenfranchise labor as they create local environments that either challenge or are exempt from employment discrimination laws.[86]

· · · · · ·

At first glance, the emphasis in FCBIs on heterosexual sexuality and patriarchal gender roles seems to confirm little more than that conservative Protestants exercise near hegemonic control over the content of socialization in both the overtly religious courses and in the classes intended to be secular or character-based. This analysis, however, misses the deeper implications of this content, specifically, its association with neoliberalism. These associations are extensions of what Wendy Brown termed the "architecture of reason" that united the NCR to libertarian and neoliberal thought in the second half of the twentieth century.[87] This was not a natural alliance, as the NCR and neoliberal capitalists seemingly had little in common. Historian Nancy MacLean noted one significant difference between the groups when she wrote that many influential libertarians were atheists "who looked down on those who believed in God."[88] Despite this and other differences, the two groups found common cause on a variety of issues, chief among them the importance of deregulated business and commerce. Christian leaders like Jerry Falwell and Ralph Reed were themselves entrepreneurs who had little trouble embracing neoliberalism's entrepreneurial ethos. According to MacLean, "The religious entrepreneurs were happy to sell libertarian economics to their flocks—above all, opposition to public schooling and calls for reliance on family provision or charity in place of government assistance."[89]

MacLean identifies another point of convergence when she notes that the two groups share a mutual distrust and even contempt for government programs like education and social services. Scholars repeatedly documented how many conservative Christians object to governmental programs like education, welfare, and social services. These programs—combined for some conservative Christians with the labor movement—taught Americans to seek political and institutional remedies for economic troubles instead of relying primarily on God, the family, and their extended networks of like-minded Christians. Additional factors—like feminism, abortion, and the gay rights movement—also threatened the family. Some ministers initially voiced their concerns from the pulpit and in print, but in the 1970s they increasingly sought more overtly political remedies, where they found common interest with libertarians and neoliberal capitalists.

This strategic shift overlapped with the popularization of neoliberal theories in the United States and beyond, where neoliberal thinkers sought to curtail the legislative state and welfare in service of curating free and deregulated markets.[90] Scholars like David Harvey argued that the welfare state was a common neoliberal target as neoliberal thinkers tasked other institutions with assuming responsibility for the maintenance of the social. As previously discussed, the heteropatriarchal family, many of these thinkers argued, should replace the state. Brown described neoliberal logic as it relates to the family when she wrote, "As social investments in education, housing, health, child care, and social security are decreased, the family is retasked with providing for every kind of dependent—the young, the old, the infirm, the unemployed, the indebted student, or the depressed or addicted adult."[91] In other words, the family emerges "as foundational to socioeconomic order."[92] "More than anything else," scholar Melinda Cooper wrote, "this appeal to familial responsibility sealed the working relationship between free market liberalism and social conservatism, very much defining the shape of social welfare in the contemporary era."[93] Scholars Jean and John Comaroff similarly linked neoliberalism to the NCR when they argued that "anxieties about sexuality, procreation, or family values" are themselves extensions of neoliberalism.[94]

This analysis suggests that despite their different paradigms, neoliberals and conservative Christians found common cause on several issues, including their contempt for big government and their desire to elevate the family as the foundation of socioeconomic life. Perhaps few members of the NCR overtly or explicitly champion neoliberal economics, but their policies served the interests of the neoliberal state regardless. From this perspective, the conservative core in Florida's FCBIs—with its emphasis on heteropatriarchal families—does more than simply socialize the incarcerated with conservative Christian theology. It also trains them to embrace neoliberal sociopolitical and economic thought. FCBIs, then, provide more than faith-based socialization; they create and empower state-run spaces for the perpetuation of the alliance between the NCR and neoliberalism.

6 Volunteers

. . . .

The fifteen men who stood at the gates of Wakulla Correctional Institution (CI) received a detailed script, and they intended to follow every step. They had spent the previous evening at a Baptist church in Tallahassee, Florida, where a team of coaches led by Tully Blanchard, a former professional wrestler and world tag team champion, explained the plan to a total of 126 men and women who were going to enter eight of Florida's prisons the following morning to get as many commitments to Christ as possible.

For the fifteen men visiting Wakulla CI, their plan began at 7:30 A.M., when they met outside the prison. Correctional officers greeted them at the prison's gates, where they searched every square inch of the Harley Davidson motorcycles that were also entering the facility in conjunction with the event and while a senior volunteer worked with correctional staff to arrange a PA system in the prison's yard. Within an hour or so, the volunteers would walk to the yard, where they would potentially mingle with all of the 1,397 convicted felons incarcerated at Wakulla CI.

In spite of their goal to get commitments to Christ, they were specifically instructed *not* to mention Jesus, God, religion, or anything related to Christianity—at least not at first. Instead, the men were supposed to mingle with the incarcerated and engage them in small talk, hopefully earning their trust and interest. Perhaps they could talk about sports or maybe even the weather. They could also discuss the Harley Davidson motorcycles strategically placed to capture the men's attention.

The volunteers would eat lunch with the incarcerated in prison, and then several hours later, a professional athlete would arrive and speak to them, where the athlete would list her struggles, victories, and awards. Only then, after she described in detail how she rose to the top of her field, would she attribute all her success and accomplishments to God, and only then were the volunteers allowed to invite the incarcerated to commit their souls to Christ. According to an email I received roughly a week later, 126 volunteers in eight prisons helped 710 incarcerated people either convert to Christianity or recommit their lives to Jesus.[1] In other words, the eight Bill Glass Behind the Walls events worked exactly as planned.

Bill Glass is a former professional football player who at the height of his career played defensive end for the 1964 National Football League champions.[2] Glass was long interested in the ministry, and he pursued a formal theological education between football seasons when he enrolled in Southwestern Seminary. Glass soon caught the attention of Billy Graham, who asked Glass to speak at some of Graham's rallies. Graham persuaded Glass to minister in cities, but Glass soon felt called to take his ministry into American prisons, which he officially did in 1972 when he created Bill Glass Behind the Walls. Every year since, Glass and his organization have brought hundreds or even thousands of volunteers into U.S. prisons.

Make no mistake—Glass enters a prison to help persuade the incarcerated to make "commitments to Christ." Instead of holding revivals or traditional services in the chapel (where he would most likely encounter people who already consider themselves Christians), Glass takes his sports clinics to the prison's yard, where the incarcerated exercise and socialize. In the yard, Glass's team will potentially encounter all incarcerated people in the prison, not just those who frequent the chapel. This form of stealth evangelism has proved quite successful, as it captures the attention of the incarcerated population who might never set foot in the chapel, and many of them make commitments to Christ. From Behind the Walls' perspective, commitments to Christ are the ultimate measure of success.

Prison administrators are not explicitly interested in commitments to Christ, but they have ulterior motives for inviting Behind the Walls into Florida's prisons. First and foremost, Glass and his organization do what the DOC has trouble doing on its own. Behind the Walls entertains the incarcerated at little cost to the DOC, it brings obedience into the prisons, and it organizes what is often termed the private sector's financial resources for the benefit of the incarcerated. To host a Behind the Walls event, the prison need only open its gates, inspect the volunteers and the materials they bring into the prison, and occasionally provide lunch and water for the volunteers. For the duration of the event, then, the incarcerated basically manage themselves as they interact with the volunteers. Behind the Walls organizes and pays for almost all of these benefits.

As the previous summary suggests, Behind the Walls events are expensive. Not only does the organization support a full-time staff with over a dozen employees, but the organization has to fly people around the country for each event and to pay an honorarium to the athlete speakers. These fees add up, as each event costs almost $34,000.[3] From the perspective of Florida's DOC, Behind the Walls spent over $250,000 that day when it brought eight Behind the Walls events into Florida's prisons. For a correctional department constantly struggling with budgetary issues, this is no small feat.

Behind the Walls is but one of the numerous prison ministries in the United States. These ministries range from international organizations like Prison Fellowship Ministries to national organizations like Behind the Walls. They include smaller regional ministries, ministries that exclusively work in a few prisons, single congregations that encourage their members to become active in a particular prison, and tens of thousands of volunteers who teach individual classes or who lead worship services in prisons. Collectively, these organizations and volunteers provide a stable source of socialization in American prisons, but they play an even larger role in Florida's faith- and character-based correctional institutions (FCBIs).

This chapter, first, documents the range, roles, and extent of volunteer labor in FCBIs. Specifically, it chronicles in detail the goods, services, and labor that Christian volunteers provide FCBIs as it highlights the largely successful effort to mobilize Christian labor and finances for the benefit of Florida's incarcerated Christians in FCBIs. Volunteers also support religious minorities, but for reasons discussed elsewhere, their involvement in FCBIs pales in comparison to the Christian volunteers who not only volunteer to lead worship services, Bible study groups, and other overtly Christian classes in prisons, but who also teach many of the character development classes in every FCBI. These Christians volunteer in record numbers, saturating FCBIs with volunteer labor.

Second, this chapter argues that volunteer labor fulfills neoliberalism's mandate for allegedly private and market-based solutions not only to economic issues but to providing social services as well, as volunteer labor and resources flow into Florida's FCBIs in unprecedented numbers. When the DOC applies the label "faith" to a correctional facility, that label functions as an interpolating call for Christian volunteers, the bulk of whom support the tough-on-crime policies that created mass incarceration and that removed more comprehensive programs from Florida's prisons.[4] These volunteers answer that call in spades. In the process, they not only transform the FCBI but alter their lives as well in service of the neoliberal state.

Protestant Volunteer Labor in Florida's Correctional Department

The relationship between Christian volunteers and Florida's DOC extends back to 1868, when Florida created its first state prison. Commanding

Officer (warden) Malachi Martin addressed the issue just two years later when he wrote,

> Owing to the cramped condition of our finances; the commanding officer did not consider it proper to hire a chaplain, but relied on such assistance as he could from the humane to preach gratuitously to the prisoners. In this he has been aided by the Reverend LaFayette Hargrave, of the A.M.E. Church (colored), who has held divine service in the prison on alternate Sundays. Recently, he has been transferred from this district, and we are now without assistance in this respect. Other gentlemen, amongst whom may be numbered the Honorable J. C. Gibbs, Secretary of State, and the Reverend James Page, have, when opportunity offered, preached to the prisoners. A Sunday-school has been established, which is regularly attended by about thirty of the prisoners, who take a warm interest in it, and manifest a decided change for the better.[5]

As this suggests, the administrators of Florida's correctional system welcomed Protestant socialization in its first prison. It continued to welcome volunteers and soon paid for Protestant chaplains to minister to the incarcerated men and women in the various versions of Florida's evolving criminal justice system.

While Florida's prison administrators implicitly endorsed Protestant Christianity beginning with its first prison, they explicitly endorsed it in 1923 when they printed in their biennial report, "Any reputable representative of a Protestant Church or a representative of any religious welfare society who applies . . . for the purpose of holding religious worship for the benefit of the convicts shall not be denied the privilege."[6] Florida's correctional system reproduced this call in all of its biennial reports until 1947, when it opened the prisons to "any church" as opposed to just Protestants.[7] Over the next several decades, the DOC also accommodated Catholic and Jewish volunteers, although Protestants continued to provide the vast majority of volunteer labor.

Florida's correctional department continued to grow over the next several decades. Every growth spurt created more prisons, and more prisons meant more opportunities for religious volunteers. When Louie Wainwright became director of Florida's correctional department in 1962, he embraced the idea that religious volunteers should play important roles in Florida's prisons. To administer this growing body of volunteers, Wainwright soon hired the first coordinator of religious activities.[8] This coordinator proved to be a committed and enthusiastic leader, and under his leadership, the chaplains became liaisons between the incarcerated and Florida's religious communities outside the prisons, resulting in more opportunities for Protestant volunteers.[9]

The 1970s brought the next significant change to Florida's prisons as convicted felons entered Florida's prisons in record numbers. Christian volunteers soon followed, resulting in a variety of new partnerships between Florida's prisons and its evangelical and fundamentalist communities, organizations, and volunteers. This activism coincided with larger trends in American Christianity where Christians looked beyond their congregations or even their denominations to create what sociologist Robert Wuthnow called special purpose groups.[10] These groups consisted of like-minded Christians who devoted a portion of their religious activism to Christian organizations that helped specific vulnerable populations such as orphans, the homeless, and the incarcerated. These groups drew members from various churches and denominations united by their mutual interest in helping one of these populations. Many of these groups became active in Florida's prisons.

In 1972, for example, fifty evangelical churches near Florida Correctional Institution (CI) organized a weeklong Kingdom of the Son Crusade, where 481 incarcerated men sang, wept, danced, and asked Jesus to work miracles in their lives.[11] After the crusade, Florida CI's administrators partnered with the volunteers to create a program where Christian volunteers would return to the prison to visit and otherwise minister to the incarcerated Protestants. Characteristic of each such crusade or revival, volunteers demonstrated to correctional administrators their ability to mobilize their communities, to generate funding, and to otherwise harness their resources for the benefit of the prison's Protestants. These volunteers brought the additional benefit of helping the offender reestablish ties with the community where he might find a job, a place to live, or other sources of support after his incarceration. In other words, the crusade was more than a onetime event; rather, it created a long-term partnership that linked Florida's correctional department and its incarcerated population to the Christian communities that surrounded the prisons. Florida's DOC welcomed many similar crusades.

Crusades and revivals were but one manifestation of the larger impulse to saturate Florida's correctional department with conservative Protestantism in the 1970s. This impulse also created new college-level Bible study courses, and it resulted in Christian rallies that attracted famous authors and gospel singers.[12] It also created numerous new in-prison programs which program administrators called Bible-based or Christ-based twelve-step programs, self-help programs, drug abuse programs, parenting courses, and others. It brought organizations like Campus Crusade for Christ into Florida's prisons.[13] It exposed more missionaries and ministers to a growing and captive missionary field that existed not on the other side of the planet but close to their homes. Collectively, these organizations and programs helped elevate the status of Protestantism in prisons more broadly as their combined efforts resulted in a steady flow of crusades, revivals, weekend seminars, workshops, Bible studies, and other religious services and events that collectively stressed the importance of Protestant socialization.

New Christian organizations and nonprofits also developed in the 1970s, specifically devoted to prison ministry. Some of these organizations were headquartered in Florida, but others were national or even international organizations that brought their ministries into Florida's prisons. Correctional departments welcomed these organizations as they primarily organized weekend courses, Bible study groups, or other courses and workshops designed to foster Protestantism. Three organizations specifically—the aforementioned Bill Glass Behind the Walls, Prison Fellowship Ministries, and Kairos Prison Ministry (KPM)—proved particularly important for Florida's correctional department as they brought Christianity into Florida's prisons through a variety of programs ranging from weekly meetings, to daylong sporting events, to three-day Cursillos.

The increase in religious volunteer labor coincided with rising populations of incarcerated people, the massive increase in the DOC's budget that accompanied mass incarceration, and the spread of a political ideology hostile to governmental attempts to rehabilitate the incarcerated. Prison administrators still had to provide the incarcerated with meals, housing, and clothing, and they had to pay correctional staff to monitor and discipline the incarcerated, but with fewer rehabilitative and recreational programs, incarcerated men and women became bored and potentially unruly, so prison administrators looked to Christian volunteers to help fill that void.

As a result, Christian volunteers were ubiquitous in America's prisons long before politicians like Newt Gingrich and Dick Armey called for religion to play a larger role in the delivery of social services. President George W. Bush embraced this idea and made it an important component of his presidency. Bush promised "to rally America's armies of compassion" who would help people suffering in their local communities.[14] He asked these armies to look to their neighbors and to their surrounding communities where they can identify people who need help. They should then work with their churches and other civic organizations to provide for the needy. Their actions should be results oriented and should reflect their desires to take responsibility for themselves and their communities. Bush also argued that the government should encourage this by providing government funding for faith-based organizations (FBOs) and faith-based social service providers. This funding, Bush argued, would empower the people most committed to compassionate results without corrupting them by enmeshing them with the government.

Some American Christians were disappointed with Bush's presidency, as they argued that he did not spend enough political capital to support their policies and to help them realize their version of Christian nationalism. Many FBOs also ignored Bush's call to accept government funding, as they wanted to avoid all potential entanglements with the government.[15] While large groups of Christian conservatives rejected Bush's calls to accept government funding, they were already active in their communities, where they continued to work with their churches, FBOs, and other groups who provided numerous services for America's needy. This was particularly true in Florida, where prison administrators relied on volunteer labor to provide the bulk of the rehabilitative programming in their growing FCBI program. The rest of this chapter highlights the role and extent of volunteer labor, focusing on the goods and services they provide Florida's FCBIs.

Volunteers

In the mid-1990s, Bob Rumbley learned that Florida's DOC had plans to build a major prison in Crawfordville, Florida.[16] Rumbley lived close to the proposed facility, and he objected vehemently to the idea that over 1,000 convicted felons would live so close to his home. By his own admission, Rumbley was a stereotypical tough-on-crime Christian conservative who had no problem with prisons. Quite the contrary, he wanted to lock up more criminals for longer sentences in harder prisons. He wanted criminals to suffer in prisons, just not in his backyard. What if they escaped, he thought? What would happen when they are released from prison? Will they rob the first house they see? Will they rape the first woman they encounter? And what kind of riffraff would come through the town to visit the felons at the prison?

To voice his dissent, Rumbley attended a public meeting where he objected to the facility and where he asked DOC officials to build the prison elsewhere. Florida was a big state, he reckoned, so they should have little trouble finding an alternate location. Rumbley lost the debate, and the addition of that prison—Wakulla CI—did impact his life, just not as he anticipated.

Rumbley is a deacon at his church, and almost twenty-five years ago, he and his fellow deacons prayed for new ministry opportunities. They were not ordained ministers, but they all considered themselves missionaries who could save souls. Rumbley found his opportunity when the unthinkable happened—one of his associates committed a felony and was sentenced to prison. Rumbley visited the man, where he got his first glimpse of life inside prison, and more importantly, where he first interacted with convicted felons. Over time, Rumbley increasingly saw the incarcerated as more than irredeemable and degenerate criminals. Instead, he saw broken people with horrible pasts who might not be flawed to the core. These people needed help, he reckoned, not just punishment. Most importantly, they needed the redemption and salvation that only his God can provide. Motivated by his evolving impression of the incarcerated, Rumbley began to volunteer at the prison he once opposed. In hindsight, Rumbley believes that God answered the deacons' prayers as Rumbley unknowingly fought against the answer. Instead of being a danger or a burden, Wakulla CI was a gift from God.

As Rumbley volunteered in the prison, he began to reflect on a Bible verse he had read many times. According to Matthew 25:35–36, Jesus described the behaviors that accompany the righteous when he said, "For I was hungry and you gave me something to eat, I was thirsty and you gave me something to drink, I was a stranger and you invited me in, I needed clothes and you clothed me, I was sick and you looked after me, I was in prison and you came to visit me." The righteous, Rumbley wagered, are people who help the downtrodden or the needy, including the incarcerated. Instead of avoiding prisons, Rumbley believes he has a biblical mandate to take the Gospel into prisons.

Today, Rumbley and his wife, Mary, not only teach weekly classes at Wakulla CI but run Care Tallahassee, a Christian reentry home for formerly incarcerated men. Care Tallahassee houses a disproportionate number of sex offenders. In other words, the Rumbleys subsidize and support the very group that most worried them several decades earlier.

One day I sat in the office at Care Tallahassee with the Rumbleys, where they shared their personal and professional stories, including Bob Rumbley's evolving position on crime in general, but particularly on sex crimes. In Rumbley's brand of conservative Protestantism, God has clear and strict expectations for men and women. Rumbley teaches in prisons and in Care Tallahassee that men are head of house and that sex is properly reserved for heterosexual marriages between consenting adults. People who violate these divine laws court not only eternal damnation but temporal punishments as well. Rumbley trusts that God will punish all sinners as He sees fit, but Rumbley has mixed feelings about the state's punishment, which continues to punish ex-felons after they are released from prison. "I get it," he said. "There are some bad guys who need to be in prison. But these ongoing punishments after prison—well, something has to change! You can't keep punishing people indefinitely while they're trying to get their lives back on track." "So, just to be clear," I replied, "you want the government to soften its laws on sex offenders."

"I don't know what that'd look like," he said, "but yeah. The current system is too much. It just isn't right!"

In one of my final questions, I asked Rumbley if thirty or so years ago he ever imagined that he would become an advocate for sex offenders and convicted pedophiles. The mere question prompted visceral and embodied reactions, first from Mary, who though only passively engaging in the conversation while working on a computer, simultaneously pushed her chair back, tilted her head to the ceiling, and laughed out loud—"HA!" Simultaneously, Bob grinned practically from ear to ear as he leaned forward and then backward in his chair while switching his crossed legs, vigorously shaking his head "no" while repeating himself—not once, not twice, but four times—"Not at all, not at all, not at all, not at all!" Somewhere in the process of working with the incarcerated, the incarcerated worked on him.

The example of Bob and Mary Rumbley is but one example of a larger trend common among Christians who work with the incarcerated, where tough-on-crime Christians interact with incarcerated people and subsequently soften their positions on punitive criminal justice policies, particularly as they relate to incarcerated Christians. Some of these Christian volunteers are full-time or retired ministers, and some are lay people interested in helping the incarcerated in their pursuit of Christianity. They are drawn to prison ministry for a variety of reasons, but most are introduced by friends or other associates already involved with prison ministry. For one reason or another, they agree to help or to even teach in prison. The resulting interactions expose them to a population not only that needs help but also—in the volunteers' reading of the Bible—that these volunteers have a biblical mandate to help. These Christian volunteers are typically critics of liberal welfare programs and of state-run programs more broadly, so they also see the subtle hand of God rearranging the government to accommodate their version of state-sanctioned biblical Christianity. Empowered by the combination of all of these factors, Christian volunteers like the Rumbleys provide the backbone of Florida's FCBIs. The following section documents the myriad benefits that volunteers provide every FCBI, specifically focusing on volunteer labor, material goods, discipline, and reentry services.

Volunteer Labor

Daryl Townsend is a lifelong Christian who worked for twenty years in the dairy industry before 2004, when he first set foot in one of Florida's prisons.[17] Townsend's experience in prison mirrors Rumbley's, as he encountered in Florida's prisons an incarcerated population—in his words—desperately in need of Christ. Sensing a spiritual need inside the prisons, Townsend taught weekend classes and participated in Prison Fellowship Ministries. The following year Townsend founded Off the Chains Ministries, a nonprofit 501(c)(3) organization run entirely off private donations. Today, Townsend is active in several prisons in northeast Florida, particularly Lawtey CI, where the DOC considers him an indispensable partner in the FCBI prison.

Townsend performs various services for the incarcerated both during and after their incarceration. When he is not assisting the formerly incarcerated outside the prisons, he spends numerous hours inside them, where he teaches several classes, holds worship services, leads Bible studies, serves as a mentor, provides counseling, and even baptizes the incarcerated. His typical weekly schedule at Lawtey CI begins on Sunday with worship service for up to 120 people. He returns on Tuesday night to teach his Financial Peace class. He is back in the prison the following morning, where he leads a class on the Book of Acts, and then he returns later that evening for one-on-one Bible study and counseling. Thursday morning he is back at Lawtey CI, where he teaches a class titled Minor Prophets, returning later in the evening and then again on Friday for more Bible study and counseling. If we recall that Townsend is active in several of Florida's prisons, we begin to understand why Florida's DOC considers him an essential partner. Arguably, he spends more hours in Florida's prisons than the average DOC employee. Prison administrators value Townsend because, from their perspective, he is an ideal partner, not only because he works for hours on end without DOC compensation.

Every FCBI has at least one Daryl Townsend, that is, a volunteer who is practically an unpaid DOC employee, and behind every Townsend are perhaps a dozen more volunteers who similarly volunteer many hours each week in an FCBI. There are also several hundred volunteers who might come to a particular FCBI to teach one or two classes each week, or who teach the same class in multiple prisons. Collectively, these volunteers create a steady stream of volunteer labor. Volunteer labor is not unique to FCBIs, but FCBIs have higher rates of volunteer labor than the average conventional prison. Warden Tina Roberts from Hernando CI, the only FCBI prison for women, stated as much when she said, "I've never worked with so many volunteers in my life. I never imagined I would."[18]

Consider, for example, religious volunteers at Lowell Annex, which is a conventional prison for women that also includes an FCBI dorm. Lowell Annex is capable of housing 1,500 incarcerated women, and eighty-six of those women live in the FCBI dorm, leaving 1,414 women in the conventional prison.[19] The chaplain at Lowell Annex is the senior administrator for the FCBI dorm, but she is also the chaplain for the entire prison, where she expects roughly five hundred active volunteers to visit the prison on a semiregular basis.[20] Roughly four hundred of those volunteers work with the 1,414 women in the conventional prison at Lowell Annex, but one hundred volunteers specifically volunteer and minister to the eighty-six women in the FCBI dorm. In other words, there is more than one volunteer for every woman in the FCBI dorm at Lowell Annex, compared with one volunteer for every three or four women in the rest of the prison. The administrators of several other FCBI dorms report similar volunteer-to-inmate ratios, as do the administrators of FCBI prisons who consistently report higher levels of volunteer labor, activism, and ministry after they convert the prison to an FCBI.

Prior to its conversion into an FCBI, Hillsborough Correctional Institution for women averaged 220 volunteer hours per month. After its conversion, however, that number increased 262 percent as volunteers provided an average of 796 volunteer hours per month.[21] The DOC closed Hillsborough

CI and later converted Hernando CI into an FCBI prison for women. According to the chaplain, since the conversion, Hernando averages 1,450 volunteer hours per month.[22] The chaplain has roughly five hundred registered volunteers, and around 275 will visit each month including ten "hardcore volunteers" who visit the prison multiple times each week. The FCBI prison for men at Lawtey CI has similar numbers as volunteers collectively average 719 volunteer hours per month. By comparison, Hendry Correctional Institution, a prison of similar size, averaged only 103 hours of volunteer labor per month, suggesting that FCBIs exponentially increase volunteer turnout.

Of all FCBI prisons, however, Wakulla CI boasts the highest number of volunteers, and according to the people who chose to convert this prison into the world's largest faith-based prison, this is no accident.[23] Chaplain Steve Fox at Wakulla CI maintains a list of some 1,400–1,600 volunteers who have ministered to or have worked with the incarcerated men.[24] Not all of these volunteers are active, but even a fraction of that number would flood the facility with volunteer labor. With over 11,000 hours of volunteer labor annually, it is safe to conclude that the prison is living up to its expectations.

According to the Office of Program Policy Analysis and Government Accountability, which collected data from April 1, 2008, to March 31, 2009, volunteers provided the three FCBI prisons with over 31,000 volunteer hours, or the equivalent of fifteen full-time employee hours.[25] Using the figure of $25.43 per hour, volunteers in the three FCBI prisons annually provide the state with over $788,000 of free labor.[26] Many of the volunteers would provide this labor even without the label "faith-based," but the data repeatedly suggest that volunteers are more likely to volunteer in faith-based than in conventional correctional facilities.

Coordinating all this volunteer labor is a significant undertaking, and that task usually falls on the facility's chaplain. Before a facility converts into an FCBI, it already relies on scores of volunteers who will continue to volunteer after the conversion, provided they can adjust to the religious pluralism that exists in the facilities. Not all of the volunteers are amenable to pluralism, so they are not allowed to participate in the FCBIs. Those who accept the pluralistic setting are allowed to volunteer in FCBIs, where the chaplain is tasked not only with accommodating the volunteers, their classes, and their schedules but also with recruiting additional volunteers.

Typically, the chaplains already have extensive networks of like-minded Protestant Christians—and occasionally this network includes a few members from other religions, primarily Catholics, Jews, and Muslims, in that order—and this network provides the first source of additional volunteer labor that accompanies FCBIs. The chaplains quite literally call, email, or even visit the people in their extended networks, where they solicit volunteer labor. They also ask the pool of existing volunteers to similarly recruit additional volunteers. In both scenarios, the majority of these volunteers are conservative Protestants.

Occasionally, however, volunteers from minority religions do contact FCBIs. Chaplain Fox recalled one such moment, when a member of the Reformed Egyptians called the FCBI, offering to introduce the religion into the facility. Knowing that no man in his prison identified as a Reformed Egyptian, Chaplain Fox declined his offer, saying, "It's not our job to encourage new religions; it's just our job to facilitate those already here. I did tell him, 'Hey, if we ever get one, I'll know who to call.'" Assuming, however, that a volunteer offers to support a religious minority already incarcerated at the FCBI, in theory, the FCBIs have to accommodate the volunteer, and many minority groups do have volunteers that support them. I write "in theory" because incarcerated people at all three FCBI prisons and in multiple FCBI dorms said that chaplains routinely turn away volunteers from minority religions, as the chaplains tell potential volunteers that the programming roster is already full or that there is no room to add new programs and classes.

FCBIs typically schedule FCBI programming in the chapels, classrooms, libraries, educational buildings, dormitories or cell blocks, and even the common recreational areas such as the gym and the yard. Volunteers compete for access to these limited spaces, and conservative prison chaplains routinely prioritize religious programs that reflect their denominational or theological biases. Chaplains prioritize these classes, workshops, and services, where they arguably monopolize limited prison space, leaving religious minorities without space for their sectarian services and events. Wiccans, for example, are told that they cannot hold outdoor services, but the same prison invites a prison ministry such as Bill Glass Behind the Walls into the prison, where the ministry monopolizes the same outdoor space for an entire day. Native Americans are told that the prison cannot accommodate a sweat lodge, but the prison welcomes Kairos Prison Ministry, which brings over a dozen volunteers into the prison for a three-day immersion course in Christianity. In the process, Kairos has exclusive access to some of the largest educational or indoor spaces in the prison.

In short, ethnographic research in Florida's FCBIs revealed a familiar story, where members of religious minorities claimed that chaplains routinely cite "space" concerns as legitimate reasons to deny their sectarian services, study groups, and other potential programs run by volunteers. Chapel clerks routinely admitted that the chaplains cite "space" as a reason to deny a religious minority's request for accommodation, despite the clerks' impression that the space exists. A chapel clerk serving a life sentence for murder summarized this when he said, "The chaplain knows he can pull the 'space' card anytime he wants and it makes the request go away. You just can't challenge it. If there ain't space, there ain't space! There usually is, ya know, but [the chaplain] won't admit it." In other words, this man suggested that chaplains deliberately use the prison's limited space to limit volunteer opportunities for religious minorities. Conservative Protestants, however, rarely encounter these problems.

Volunteers who are allowed into the FCBIs follow the standard volunteer-intake procedure. When they decide to volunteer, they complete the volunteer application and the DOC performs a background check.[27] This background check is potentially problematic for the many volunteers who were formerly incarcerated and who now want to help other incarcerated people find God, and the DOC has to approve these individuals on a case-by-case basis. Assuming the volunteer passes the background check, he is invited to a mandatory meeting. In Tallahassee, the DOC holds this introductory meeting at a local church.

These meetings are important, particularly for the volunteers who have never set foot inside a prison. The DOC uses the opportunity to introduce these volunteers to prisons, to educate them about standard DOC practices and expectations, and to provide them with knowledge and strategies to ensure that incarcerated people do not manipulate or endanger the volunteers.[28] These meetings are also important because the DOC has to inform the volunteers of acceptable and unacceptable behaviors. This is more important for the volunteers interested in the FCBIs (as opposed to conventional prisons), as Florida's DOC wants to avoid any potential constitutional challenges primarily related to establishment clause violations, and they fear an incarcerated person might complain if he is subjected to constant proselytization.[29] The volunteers who are most eager to proselytize are the least likely to appreciate these restrictions.

After the introductory meeting, the volunteer typically contacts a chaplain at a local prison. The local prison will deny the application if the volunteer is already on the visitation list or if the volunteer has a family member incarcerated at the facility. At FCBIs, the chaplain typically interviews the volunteer and asks if the volunteer wants to teach a course of the volunteer's choosing or if the volunteer is willing to teach a specific course the facility needs taught. Assuming the FCBI finds a class that fits with the volunteer's goals, the volunteer will enter the FCBI weekly to teach the class or to lead the service or Bible study. And since Florida's FCBIs go out of their way to ensure that volunteers teach or lead most of the faith-based programming, volunteers are a ubiquitous fixture in FCBIs.

Material Goods

It was a hot and humid day in August when I visited the FCBI dorms at To-moka CI. The FCBI dorms in Tomoka are important, not only because its faith-based dorm was the first in Florida's DOC but also because Tomoka has separate dorms, one designated "faith-based" and the other designated "character-based." This is not the norm, as most FCBI dorms are designated both faith- and character-based. By the time I made the short walk from the reception area to the dorm, I was covered in sweat. I didn't expect much of a reprieve once I entered the dorm, as few of Florida's prisons are air-conditioned, and most of them have old fans that barely do more than circu-late the hot and sticky air. Inside the FCBI dorm, however, the program coordinator ushered me into the dorm's study room, where I found a func-tional and powerful air conditioner—a rarity in Florida's correctional dor-mitories. To understand the anomalous air conditioner, consider that the study room contains several computers and that the walls in the study room are lined with videos, books, Bibles, and various self-help programs. To prevent the books from molding and to protect the electronics, the study room contains a powerful air conditioner, making it one of the few air-conditioned areas accessible to the incarcerated (but only to the people in the FCBI dorm) and one of the more desirable rooms in the prison. In other words, necessity resulted in a unique perk, as these air-conditioned rooms provide a reprieve from Florida's punishing heat. A man in the study room revealed another perk when he asked me if I wanted any coffee. Tea? Orange juice? Water?

Just a minute or so inside the FCBI dorm at Tomoka CI, I already noticed several things largely absent in conventional prisons: comfort and abun-dance. The men sat in nice chairs in the study room, they worked on com-parably modern equipment, and the air conditioner made the room feel more like a library than a prison. Other men undoubtedly sat sweating in the rest of the prison, but one would struggle to find one drop of sweat on any of the men in the study room. The comparably extensive choice of bev-erages combined with all the study materials lining the walls inside the room were similarly anomalous, as few correctional dormitories contain, well, so much *stuff*. Minus the Christian and other faith-based literature, this could have been a study room on any college campus.

Later when I toured the FCBI dorms at Tomoka CI, I continued to notice perks and benefits largely absent in conventional correctional dormitories. The living conditions themselves, for example, were more pleasant than the typical dorm. Not only did murals adorn the walls, but new and more efficient ceiling fans cooled the rooms. The old fans were so loud that they disrupted Bible studies and other study groups, so volunteers paid for new and quieter fans. As a result, the FCBI dorms were not only the quietest but also the coolest dorms in the entire prison. This undoubtedly made it easier for the people who read and studied the various books they pulled from their individual lockers which themselves were bigger than the lockers in other dorms, as the incarcerated people in FCBI dorms have more study materials and they need to store their materials in larger lockers—lockers that volunteers purchased.

As a result of all these perks or benefits, the FCBI dorms were perhaps the most comfortable places to do time in Tomoka CI. This is typically the case in all FCBI dorms, where a combination of necessity and practicality create what are commonly the most comfortable places to do time inside individual prisons. Incarcerated people in FCBI prisons similarly have access to resources not available to people incarcerated in conventional prisons, and volunteers pay for almost all of these resources, perks, and incentives.

As this summary suggests, not only do Florida's Christian volunteers donate their time, but they also mobilize the financial resources of Florida's Christian communities, which donate tens of thousands of dollars every year to incarcerated Christians interested in pursuing faith-based programming. When the DOC converted Lawtey CI into its first faith-based prison, the Beaches Chapel Church alone donated almost $30,000 in goods including "$1,163 for ceiling fans, $4,000 for musical instruments, $1,500 for a sound system, $2,500 for computers, $500 for Bibles, $840 for books, $2,500 for food, games, and candy."[30] Though the Beaches Chapel Church's donations are not typical, they highlight the range of material goods that volunteers bring into Florida's FCBIs.

Starting on the smaller side, volunteers routinely bring small and inexpensive items such as food and drinks into the FCBIs. Sometimes they will bring dessert and punch for a special event like a graduation ceremony or a special celebration at the end of a multimonth class. Some volunteers will keep a steady supply of coffee in the prison, which they prepare after class for postclass fellowship. Most Americans take something like coffee or cake for granted, but these are rare treats in U.S. prisons. To understand how important these are in prison, keep in mind that without exception, incarcerated people routinely complain about prison food. To supplement the prison food, many incarcerated people rely on parents and family members to place money into their canteen accounts, which allows them to purchase food otherwise not available. For incarcerated people with no outside support who only eat prison food, a piece of cake or even a single cookie becomes a rare delicacy.

Occasionally, a volunteer attempts to smuggle contraband into a prison by hiding it in food, and all of Florida's prisons—including FCBIs—will temporarily forbid volunteers from bringing food into Florida's prisons. During these "blackouts," some of the nonessential religious classes in FCBIs shrink in number. One man described this when he joked, "People always doubt if we're sincere, but there's a test you know? Wait 'til they outlaw outside food. If you're still showing up to the service, you're legit. The fakers drop off, but they come back when the cookies come back. I see it happen every time." In addition to food and drinks, volunteers also purchase small and comparably inexpensive items like writing materials, markers, paint, and notebooks. They also purchase tapes and videos.

Volunteers also purchase religious material by the box not only for the prison libraries but also for the individual classes they teach and for the worship services they lead. Some of the classes like The Quest for Authentic Manhood are based on specific material produced and marketed by a for-profit company, so volunteers will either purchase these materials with their own money or raise money from their religious communities. These materials are rarely cheap. The DVD and CD packs for the Quest for Authentic Manhood program alone cost $368, with an additional $9.95 for each participant's workbook.[31] This one class can easily cost over $500 with an additional $100 to $300 each subsequent course cycle, depending on the number of participants. The individual FCBIs often purchase some class-specific materials, particularly materials deemed secular like secular versions of self-help programs. Religious volunteers, however, purchase material like the Authentic Manhood program, which is marketed as a religious, or more specifically a Christian, program.

Volunteers, individual churches, and religious nonprofits have pooled their resources to purchase even more expensive items like coffee pots, VCRs, computers, computer software, recreational equipment, televisions, and other equipment such as permanent fans. They donate some of this material to the FCBI, but in other instances, they remain the owners even though they leave it in the prison where it is accessible for their class or for anyone they choose to share it with. That volunteers also purchase expensive class materials suggests that volunteers invest heavily in FCBIs.

Individual FCBIs also create unique partnerships with specific groups or organizations that provide various services to the FCBI. Two examples from Wakulla CI help illumine this larger dynamic. Steve Fox is not only the chaplain at the world's largest faith-based prison but also an aspiring author who belongs to the John 3:16 Marketing Network, which according to its website is "a Christian network that promotes Christian books through press releases, social networking, blog showcases, and charities."[32] In 2014, the network extended its efforts to Wakulla CI, where it agreed to donate between ten and fifteen Christian manuscripts or books per month to the prison. The men will then read these materials and provide written commentary and feedback to the authors. Fox justified the program when he said, "Reading takes the prisoners on a journey out of their cell into an undiscovered world. Knowing the author will personally receive each person's book review will help with prisoners' self-esteem and encourage personal growth in character. Writing book reviews will also promote job skills for the formerly incarcerated for when they are released from prison."[33] Fox contends that the program has exceeded his expectations as the men have developed personal relationships with some of the authors who engage the men as pen pals. Fox hopes that these new relationships might help the men after they leave prison, as perhaps some of the pen pals will help the men find jobs or offer other services to assist their reentry.

Chaplain Fox also partnered with Faith Radio, a Christian radio station in Florida that plays Christian music and that broadcasts Christian sermons.[34] Faith Radio's "Doctrinal Statement" of beliefs—which, among other things, affirms the Bible as the infallible word of God, virgin birth, the total depravity of man, the reality of hell, the reality of Satan, the sanctity of human life beginning with inception, and the sanctity of sexual activity between a married man and woman—positions them on the conservative end of the Protestant theological spectrum.[35] In 2006, Faith Radio donated solar-powered radios and earbuds to some of the men at Wakulla CI.[36] The prison's administrators would not allow batteries in the facility, so the radios had to be solar powered. Fox and the owners of Faith Radio wanted to ensure that the incarcerated could not use the radios to listen to untoward or even Satanic music, so the radios can only receive one radio signal—Faith Radio's. The incarcerated Christians immediately embraced the radios, as they provided the Christians with another resource to help advance their religiosity and because they also provided the incarcerated with another link to the free world.

Over time, however, additional benefits began to materialize as the incarcerated wrote letters to Faith Radio thanking them for the donations, and occasionally donating money to the company for additional radios. Ironically, the company created the radios to be, in their words, "blue mini-missionaries" (the original radios were blue) designed to evangelize to "lost inmates." The targeted population, however, is now funding additional "missionary" efforts.

Faith Radio read some of these letters live on the radio, prompting some of the listeners to write to the letters' authors. These listeners have since developed relationships with the incarcerated, where listeners send them stamps for additional communication, they mail the men religious materials, and they occasionally donate money to their canteen accounts. Chaplain Fox even contends that several men have left the prisons to join their pen pals' churches, where the congregation helps them find jobs and living arrangements. In other words, both partnerships—the John 3:16 Marketing Network and Faith Radio—not only resulted in additional resources for the incarcerated while they are in prison but also created long-term relationships that potentially help the men adjust to society and live crime-free lives.

These examples combine to tell a larger story about the relationship between Florida's Christian communities and FCBIs, which routinely subsidize incarcerated people in Florida's FCBIs. Ironically, these religious volunteers raise the bulk of this money from the same religious Floridians who support the tough-on-crime laws and policies that created and that fuel mass incarceration. While many religious Floridians relish the fact that Florida's prisons are not air conditioned, they will purchase fans and air conditioners for FCBIs. They cringe at the thought of their tax dollars supporting literacy or GED programs in prisons, but they pool their resources to purchase Bibles and Bible-based course materials by the box. They want incarcerated people to struggle through every unpleasant meal, but they donate money to the incarcerated Christians' canteen accounts so they can purchase good food at the prisons' canteens. In other words, the label "faith-based" triggers a degree of economic support, compassion, and sympathy otherwise absent in certain Christian communities. These Christians contend their God calls them to extend grace and forgiveness, but only to the penitent and to those redeemed in Christ.

Disciplining the Incarcerated

Noel Gilli has a complicated relationship with correctional officers.[37] Incarcerated for life at age seventeen, Gilli spent over a decade inside prison undermining correctional staff as he manufactured and sold prison "buck" (alcohol), taught martial arts on the side, and violated numerous other DOC rules and policies. When he became a Christian, however, he learned that he had to obey not only the prison's rules but also the correctional staff who enforced these rules. Citing Romans 13:1, Gilli believes that he has a biblical mandate to submit to every authority figure. This verse states, "Let everyone be subject to the governing authorities, for there is no authority except that which God has established. The authorities that exist have been established by God." Gilli's interpretation of this verse required him to completely rethink his impression of the correctional officers, the administrative staff, the legal system that sentenced him, and the DOC that incarcerates him. Instead of obstacles to his freedom, all these people and institutions are agents of God serving some larger and unknown role in God's master plan. Gilli described this logic when he said, "I know that God placed those officers in positions of authority, so when I disobey them, I disobey God." Gilli's Christianity, then, teaches him to obey correctional authority, and Christian volunteers repeatedly reinforce this idea.

This example highlights another benefit the volunteers provide, as they teach the incarcerated to submit to carceral authority as an extension of their submission to godly authority. Volunteer Dan Nase said as much when he told his class, "When you're under the authority of God, it makes it easier to be under the authority of man." In other words, discipline to God facilitates discipline to prison administrators.

Even when the volunteers do not explicitly teach the incarcerated to discipline themselves, discipline is an ancillary benefit that results from their various classes. Correctional staff have long noted that busy incarcerated people tend to behave better, but "tough on crime" and skyrocketing correctional budgets combined to remove many of the various programs that previously occupied the incarcerated. As they had more spare time, they had more time to violate rules. In FCBIs, however, incarcerated people spend a large portion of their days in classes. After their classes, they work on the homework and study materials. Imagine a scenario where eighty-six incarcerated people are trapped in a dorm, restless, without any evening activities. Now imagine those same people inside the dorm where every person either completes his homework or study material in silence or talks to other people about that homework or study material.

The disciplinary benefits of homework and classes are self-evident, but volunteers also provide an additional source of discipline, as incarcerated people tend to follow the prison's rules in the presence of volunteers. As stated earlier, it is hard to overstate the extent to which incarcerated people enjoy interacting with volunteers. The incarcerated live in correctional worlds where every DOC employee is tasked, first and foremost, with facilitating their confinement. Some of the employees might be interested in the religious lives of the incarcerated or in their mental health, but if push comes to shove, those employees will help detain the incarcerated, reminding them that they are prisoners. Volunteers, however—religious or otherwise—come into the prison to assist the incarcerated for no other reason than because they want to be there.

It does not really matter how or why volunteers come into the prison; their presence provides a break from the monotony of incarceration. According to Gilli, "A volunteer could just walk in this room and sit in that corner and it would make it better. Just *being here* is enough." The mere presence of a volunteer might suffice, but volunteers want to do more than simply *be there*, as they enter prisons for the purpose of helping the incarcerated. They have no financial incentive; rather, they volunteer exclusively for the benefit of the incarcerated. The volunteers' intentions are not lost on the incarcerated, many of whom cannot recall anyone ever going out of their way to help them just *because*. Doug Morgan in Wakulla CI stated as much when he said,

> Look, man, I was an accident. My parents didn't want me, and they let me know. Then my teachers were paid to teach me, but they didn't care. Then my "friends" were only around when I had money, and the police only showed interest to arrest me. The COs [correctional officers] only showed up to punish me. These volunteers, though, they're here because they care! They're here because they love me. Me! That's powerful! And I know this: they only care because they're filled with God's grace. Not to diminish them, but you know, we need to make sure that all glory goes to God.

Doug believes that volunteers provide an unprecedented level of compassion and interest, and many incarcerated people repeated this idea. The incarcerated behave better around the volunteers both out of their respect for the volunteers and because they know that prison administrators can restrict volunteer labor if the incarcerated misbehave in their presence.

Chaplain George Lajueness at Wakulla Annex seemingly doubts the sincerity of the incarcerated when they interact with volunteers, as he made clear when he said, "Inmates like to play a game or put on a show for the volunteers whenever they're around." Only the individual people know if Lajueness is correct, but either way, without exception, prison administrators argued that the volunteers' presence helps diffuse the stress that accompanies daily prison life.

Given their respect and their appreciation for the volunteers—and the break they provide from day-to-day prison life—the incarcerated have multiple incentives to behave in the presence of volunteers. For this reason, correctional staff members in FCBIs do not routinely monitor the incarcerated when they interact with volunteers. A correctional officer might stick his head into a room or peek through a window, but the majority of the time, the volunteer's presence provides a level of discipline that correctional staff would struggle to obtain. In short, for all of the reasons outlined in this section, volunteers provide more than free labor and material goods. They also provide discipline and order to a group of Americans characterized largely by their lack of discipline.

Reentry Services

Scholars and activists cannot agree on the definition of the term "reentry," but it is increasingly the focus of research, debate, and public policy.[38] Does it, as some have argued, generically reference all of the formerly incarcerated who return to society, or does it, as others have argued, refer only to the activities and programs designed to help the incarcerated readjust?[39] Either way, roughly 750,000 people leave American prisons each year to return to society, and high recidivism rates suggest the need for health care, job placement, housing, and other forms of assistance for the formerly incarcerated.

Consider that the incarcerated typically enter prison with lower educational rates than the average American. Inside prison, over half the incarcerated have mental health problems and up to 25 percent have serious mental health problems like schizophrenia.[40] The mentally ill used to be detained in mental hospitals, but since mental hospitals were defunded and closed in the 1980s, the mentally ill increasingly end up in American prisons.[41] Additionally, over 50 percent of people in prisons have substance use disorder, and incarcerated people have higher rates of sexually transmitted diseases, minor health conditions, and chronic diseases.[42] These people also have access to fewer rehabilitative programs, and those with access tend not to use them.[43]

These people also face the effects of prisonization, the process of adopting to negative conditions in prison that are not conducive to successful desistance or life outside prison.[44] Scholars routinely document the criminogenic effects of incarceration that leave the formerly incarcerated predisposed to commit crime after incarceration. Sociologist John Irwin described this when he wrote, "For long-termers, the new situation of doing time, enduring years of suspension, being deprived of material conditions, living in crowded conditions without privacy, with reduced options, arbitrary control, disrespect, and economic exploitation is excruciatingly frustrating and aggravating. Anger, frustration, and a burning sense of injustice, coupled with the crippling processing inherent in imprisonment, significantly reduce the likelihood [that prisoners can] pursue a viable, relatively conventional, non-criminal life after release."[45]

When people do finally leave prison, they encounter what scholars often call "invisible punishments" that make successful reentry more difficult than in the past.[46] Cut off from many welfare programs, almost 80 percent of the formerly incarcerated are without health insurance, and many are homeless.[47] They also underperform in the labor market, as almost half remain without a job up to a year after they leave prison.[48] Criminologist Joan Petersilia described the bleak situation the formerly incarcerated encounter when she wrote, "The average inmate coming home will have served a longer prison sentence than in the past, be more disconnected from family and friends, have a higher prevalence of substance abuse and mental illness, and be less educated and less employable than those in prior prison release cohorts."[49] Because of these obstacles, the formerly incarcerated are more likely to commit suicide when they leave prison, they are almost thirteen times more likely to die in the first two weeks following release, and they are 129 times more likely to die of an overdose.[50]

Collectively, these statistics describe a cycle where the average person enters prison with the characteristics associated with high rates of crime. Inside prison, prison culture provides incentives for incarcerated people (primarily men) to adopt prison codes associated with future criminality.

Once the person leaves prison, the person faces obstacles that prevent complete reintegration into society. For these reasons, "reentry" is one of the most popular topics in criminology and in the broader worlds of criminal justice and corrections, as prison administrators look to partner with people and with organizations who will help the formerly incarcerated stay out of prison in the future. Perhaps every prison in the country has various partnerships with religious groups, churches, and FBOs, but these partnerships are particularly important to FCBIs, who rely on Christian reentry homes and services. The example of Bob and Mary Rumbely's Care Tallahassee helps demonstrate the potential benefits the Rumbleys offer the formerly incarcerated.

To create Care Tallahassee, the Rumbleys purchased an old motel and converted it into a reentry home. The Rumbleys originally liked the building because it provided an affordable facility capable of housing thirty-two men, but Rumbley soon came to believe that God led him to this particular building, as its specific location allows him to house sex offenders and even convicted pedophiles, the classes of the formerly incarcerated that typically face the harshest reentry obstacles. Sometimes sex offenders literally have no place to live when they leave prison. Their families and friends have either rejected them or died, so without places like Care Tallahassee, life on the streets is seemingly their only option. The Rumbleys sometimes invite specific formerly incarcerated people to live in the facility, but prison administrators will occasionally call the Rumbleys to ask if they will admit someone with nowhere to live but the street. In other words, agents of the state actively solicit the Rumbleys' help.

Assuming both parties agreed, residents would live by the house's strict rules. They live rent free until they find a job, at which point they pay $100 weekly. All residents have to attend the almost nightly services and study groups, they have to obey the strict curfew, they are escorted to and from work the first month, and they have to wait thirty days before they are allowed to have a phone. Bob explained his justification for the latter when he said that "the men get phones and they're more likely to get involved with women. When they get relationships with women, they lose focus."[51] Focus and dedication are particularly important, as Care Tallahassee has a strict zero-tolerance policy. The irony is not lost on the Rumbleys, who readily admit that they regulate and impose restrictions in Care Tallahassee that are almost as strict as the restrictions their residents encountered in prison. Care Tallahassee also provides its residents with three meals a day, but unlike in prison, the residents look forward to these meals.[52]

Regardless of the person's crime, Care Tallahassee admits any formerly incarcerated person the Rumbleys deem a good fit for the facility. Due to Care Tallahassee's unique zoning and the Rumbleys' familiarity with Wakulla CI, however, Care Tallahassee disproportionately houses men from Wakulla CI. This gives Christians at Wakulla CI special access to the Rumbleys and to the facility they operate. The relationship between Care Tallahassee and Wakulla CI is not the only special relationship between a particular FCBI and a Christian reentry home.

Daryl Townsend and Lawtey CI have a similar relationship, as Townsend owns several transition homes capable of housing ten men. Newly released people live rent free until they have jobs, and once they have jobs they pay a modest rent. Every facility also has hospitality night once a week where the tenants' families join them for dinner. Townsend also meets with all of his tenants once a week to address their budgets and to ensure that they spend their money responsibly. He helps the tenants get their driver's licenses, shuttles them to jobs, helps them find jobs, buys them work clothes or other items they will need for their jobs, and does anything else he can to help the ex-convicts reintegrate into society.

Townsend also helps some of his tenants become homeowners. The process begins when Townsend purchases a small home that he rents to individual ex-convicts. He deposits their rent checks into escrow accounts, and after several years, the ex-convicts accumulate enough money for a down payment, allowing them to purchase the homes from Townsend. Once the house sells, Townsend purchases another home and repeats the process.

Similar to Care Tallahassee, Townsend's homes also have strict rules, as residents have to avoid masturbation, sexual activity outside marriage, drugs, alcohol, and homosexuality. They also have to complete several nightly classes such as Bible study and a Christian twelve-step program. Residents who ignore or violate these guidelines are asked to leave. It is the rare occasion when someone is actually expelled from the homes, however, as Townsend handpicks the people who will live in these houses, giving particular attention to people "solid in their faiths" and committed to successful reentry based on what Townsend considers a Christian lifestyle. Many of these men served a portion of their prison sentences in FCBIs, where they participated in peer-based accountability programs, and they bring this mindset into Townsend's transition homes, where they support each other in Christian-based desistance and where they establish new roots outside the prison based on their Christian identities and networks.

The Rumbleys and Townsend are just two examples of the numerous Christian reentry homes and programs in America. The Rumbleys and Townsend are unique because they also volunteer in FCBIs, where people in these facilities have a greater chance of living in one of these homes after they leave prison. Increased access to Christian reentry homes is just one of the benefits that volunteers bring to FCBIs, and it is part of the larger process where volunteers assist in reentry.

Volunteers also connect formerly incarcerated people to churches, to jobs, and occasionally to a room or even a house for rent. Individual volunteers or even their churches might help the formerly incarcerated purchase groceries, buy clothes, or even pay a few bills while the person adjusts to society and becomes self-sufficient. All of these services help formerly incarcerated people stay out of prison, potentially reducing recidivism and the extensive costs associated with recidivism. Volunteers who help with reentry continue to benefit Florida's DOC long after someone leaves an FCBI.

· · · · · ·

Bob Rumbley and Daryl Townsend are not ordained ministers, yet they have devoted their lives to Christian ministry. Prisons provide their missionary fields, and in the era of mass incarceration, those fields are particularly fertile. This motivates volunteers like Townsend, who earns his living as a prison minister, and Rumbley, for whom prison ministry is essentially a retirement project, to work countless hours in Florida's prisons for the benefit of Florida's incarcerated Christians. It also motivates their friends and colleagues to subsidize their ministries as they provide money, labor, and material goods to Christians who proselytize to incarcerated people in Florida.

Florida's politicians and prison administrators learned that when they apply the label "faith" to a correctional facility, that label issues an interpolating call to prison administrators, sympathetic politicians, and activists to support rehabilitative prisons. The label "faith" also calls conservative Christians to action as they volunteer in record numbers, and it impacts their larger communities who support their efforts. In the process, the label "faith" motivates entire communities who change their lives to benefit Christians in the faith-based context. The incarcerated themselves are not immune from this "calling." Consider that most of the people who reside in FCBIs come from dysfunctional families and have troubled pasts. They associate the government with their arrest, their incarceration, and their subsequent discipline. Many of these people experience compassion and love for the first time in the faith-based context, and they leave FCBIs associating the government with punishment and privatized faith with redemption. Many of them even go into the ministry themselves. In short, the label "faith" might not call "armies" to action, but it does successfully mobilize many people to behave differently in service of their religion. Their extra-government action fulfills one of neoliberalism's central mandates to organize what it labels the private, and in this regard, it is quite successful as volunteers provide labor, goods, and resources at no or minimal cost to the state.

Conclusion

Spiritual Entrepreneurs in Florida and Beyond

On a cold and windy January 5, 1999, Jeb Bush, newly elected governor of Florida, sacralized his election when he began his inaugural address by saying, "I thank God for the opportunity to be here today and for the blessings that have been bestowed upon us all."[1] This would be the first of many references to Bush's God. "At the core of our understanding," Bush continued, "must be a fundamental humility born of the recognition that we owe all to our Creator." Bush suggested that people, communities, and even the government have a sacred obligation both to recognize the Creator as the source of everything good and to foster private relationships with the "Divine Giver," the "wellspring from which goodness flows."

The remainder of the speech outlined not only a legislative agenda but a comprehensive theory of self, society, citizenship, and government. Bush acknowledged that his election occurred on the eve of the new millennium, and he wanted his office to spearhead the changes that would re-create government and society in the coming new age, an era where the state would reposition and realign itself to empower Bush's God and His preferred sociocultural, political, and even economic policies.

Bush then summarized Florida's conflicted history, a history, he wagered, that included both incredible growth and unrealized opportunities. In the previous century, Bush continued, the state of Florida transformed from a largely untamed frontier into a political, economic, technological, and educational juggernaut whose size and accomplishments dwarfed most countries. Despite these many accomplishments, however, Florida had not realized its full potential. Weak communities and an educational system that failed to provide young people "with the lessons that will make them better adults" were just a few of the problems. These problems, Bush suggested, were attributable primarily to big government and "the crushing weight of taxes, regulations, and mandates on Florida's families and entrepreneurs."

Suggesting that his government would address these problems, Bush asked a rather straightforward question: "What's best?" That is, what are the best and most enduring ideas and institutions to help Florida thrive as it strengthens both its communities and its economy? The answer, he argued, lied in a smaller government that deferred to, protected, and nurtured the enduring and seemingly private trinity of "faith . . . family . . . friends. These are what's best. These will endure. We should trust in these more than we trust in government. State government, now and forever, must respect and nurture and rely on these enduring institutions so that we can unleash their amazing potential."

To empower these "enduring institutions," Bush articulated a theory of society and sociality premised on religious and community-engaged citizenship, where a seemingly smaller government curates, relies on, and even defers to this faith-based private sphere. "Let us not be afraid," he argued, "to engage our churches and synagogues and spiritual entrepreneurs to enhance care for the needy and to fill the hollow hearts. State government can draw much from these reservoirs of faith." In short, Bush envisioned a future where the government simultaneously empowered and deferred to "spiritual entrepreneurs" who, motivated by private religious convictions and market savvy, would replace the government at the local level and throughout the state.

For the rest of his administration, Bush attempted to implement this vision as he worked to reduce state government's size, payroll, and influence; to lower taxes; to reduce regulations; and to champion faith-based reforms.[2] Regarding the latter, not only did Bush support the growing faith-based correctional facilities program, but his administration trained hundreds of state employees in faith-based social service reforms as he diverted tax dollars to support a host of faith-based programs including religious educational programs for children, a voucher program, religious marriage counseling, and religious foster care and adoption services, to name but a few of Bush's many faith-based reforms. While these reforms were allegedly open to all religions, conservative Christians who shared Bush's sociopolitical epistemology were the primary benefactors of the overwhelming majority of these partnerships.

While Jeb Bush remade Florida's state government, his brother, President George W. Bush, embraced and implemented a similar agenda at the federal level. As discussed earlier, President Bush tackled faith-based reforms just days into his tenure as U.S. president when he signed executive orders that established the White House Office of Faith-Based and Community Initiatives (WHOFBCI), which supported at the federal level what supporters later termed "the quiet revolution" that is state-funded faith-based social services.

Every U.S. president in the twenty-first century supported a version of "the quiet revolution," although each modified the program to reflect his values and priorities. President Bush wanted to create the legal and administrative infrastructures to support faith-based reforms while protecting the autonomy of faith-based organizations (FBOs). President Obama renamed the WHOFBCI when he created the White House Office of Faith-Based and Neighborhood Partnerships. Obama did not challenge FBOs' autonomy; rather, he wanted to protect the beneficiaries receiving faith-based social services by requiring faith-based social service providers to make "reasonable efforts" to provide lists of alternative providers to consumers who did not share the FBOs' religiosity. President Trump subsequently created the White House Faith and Opportunity Initiative, where he doubled down on Bush's efforts by eliminating both the alternative-provider requirements and the documentation that informed beneficiaries of their rights to religious freedom.[3] In the balancing act between the rights of FBOs and potential beneficiaries, the Trump administration protected the former.

In short, "the quiet revolution" continues to progress as a core component of state and federal legislation. Its critics bemoan its successes, while its staunchest supporters lament that it has not progressed more rapidly. In a comparably short period of time, however, faith-based reforms were naturalized as legitimate and legal forms of state-sanctioned socialization. This naturalization is evident not only in Florida's faith- and character-based correctional institutions (FCBIs) but in the faith-based correctional facilities that are active in most of the nation's criminal justice systems and in numerous other partnerships between religion and state. These partnerships document how "the quiet revolution" continues to grow, even as the majority of the nation ignores its existence. Its supporters envision a not-too-distant future where FBOs and private organizations provide the majority, if not all, of social services, including, but not limited to, state-funded schools and educational programs, the various services offered to people experiencing homelessness, pregnancy prevention programs, policy research, sex education programs, addiction treatment and recovery centers, adoption agencies, and community management groups. The laws and policies that apply to Florida's FCBIs will similarly guide and influence these programs, although organizations deemed FBOs will have even more autonomy than state-run FCBIs or private organizations deemed secular. FBOs (whether they receive state funding or not) will have comparably unlimited freedom to provide social services on their terms, in their facilities, using employees of their choice, to recipients who conform to their morals and standards, and with content entirely of their choosing. If "the quiet revolution's" supporters succeed, this will result in a fundamental reorganization of social services, society, and the state itself. This reorganization, however, is precisely the goal.

The growth of state-sanctioned faith-based reforms reflects a significant moment in the relationship between the category of religion and state, but faith-based reforms have not occurred in a vacuum. As Governor Bush's inaugural address demonstrates, proponents of faith-based reforms tether these reforms to the larger sociocultural, political, and economic trends and transformations that scholars often term neoliberalism. As discussed earlier, neoliberal reforms began as economic theories designed to stimulate the market. Neoliberal economists lamented government regulation, high taxes, and other policies that stifle economic freedom and the potential for growth. As neoliberalism grew and developed, it became associated with larger hostilities to the government in general as proponents of neoliberalism questioned the government's role not only in the market but in society writ large. The new neoliberal government, proponents suggested, would downsize almost across the board, creating a vacuum of sorts that would open new and more effective markets. Neoliberal economics required neoliberal societies, and members of the New Christian Right (NCR) helped create them.

Proponents of neoliberalism found in the NCR a theological agenda that resonated with neoliberalism's embrace of the free market and its hostility to government-run socialization efforts. Generally speaking, the members of the NCR shared the social imaginary that divided the world into a private and public sphere, and they positioned religion or faith in the former category, even as they claimed that the former informed the latter. The resonance machine between neoliberals and the NCR worked to create a space for seemingly private faith-based reforms as but one piece of larger neoliberal transformations.

The example of Florida's FCBIs suggests that the state-funded social services that constitute "the quiet revolution" are compatible with neoliberalism where they exist within the alternatively regulated world of state-sanctioned social service providers. These regulations allow local FBOs greater freedom to police and regulate participation in state-sanctioned social services. They also create an alternatively regulated sphere of state-sanctioned socialization where the state subsidizes messages and content that are otherwise frowned upon or illegal in state-funded programs that do not prioritize faith-based providers and content. As employers, FBOs also have greater freedom to discriminate in their hiring practices and to fire employees who violate the organization's ethics. In short, if neoliberalism seeks to empower what it deems the private, state-funded FBOs embody this empowerment.

In addition to thriving in the culture of neoliberalism, FCBIs and potentially other FBOs perpetuate this culture when they take the incarcerated—the majority of whom struggled prior to their incarceration to participate in white, Protestant, capitalist society—and mold them into neoliberal subjects through intense socialization laden with neoliberal tropes and culture. This socialization includes a model of localized patriarchal authority figures who shun government services in favor of religious activism, community-based providers, and private notions of citizenship and civic participation. To this end, these patriarchal figures claim that they surrender the market to their deity, who uses the market to incentivize obedience, to punish the disobedient, and to reward the just. In short, faith-based socialization in facilities like FCBIs creates neoliberal subjects and citizens as it conditions the incarcerated to embrace neoliberalism and the culture that sustains it. If Florida's FCBIs resemble other state-funded FBOs, "the quiet revolution," then, is more than a revolution in religion-state relations; it also entails a significant reorientation of the state's priorities and of the state's relationship to its polity. Critics of this transformation will undoubtedly see "the quiet revolution" as a step backward, but proponents see Florida's FCBIs and the faith-based initiative as a success—a work in progress but encouraging in the short term.

Finally, dominant theories of faith and religion as private and removed from the state and from the public help enable the transformation that is the subject of this book. For many members of the NCR, "faith" as a category justifies their hostility to the government, it triggers compassion for otherwise tough-on-crime Christian conservatives, it calls many Christians to help fellow Christians in faith-based facilities, it encourages members of the NCR to donate their financial and personal resources to Florida's FCBIs with the goal of replacing the state, and it allows them to teach messages of their choice in state-owned spaces. Instead of regulating or even being hostile to these "spiritual entrepreneurs," in FCBIs, the state welcomes and encourages their faith-based reforms. One of the most significant aspects of "the quiet revolution" is not that it successfully remakes the government, but that it reshapes the polity as it forms and fashions notions of subjectivity that prioritize the private, of which faith is conceived as a necessary and constituent element.

It remains to be seen if the dynamics described in this book apply to faith-based reforms in other states. Florida is in many ways a large and outlier swing state with competing cultures, with a citizenry with diverse interests, and with state politicians who abhor the other side's accomplishments. It is difficult to compare the diverse people and regions within Florida, much less with other states, their citizens, and their states' policies.

That said, the literature on faith-based correctional reforms in other states suggests that the carceral trends outlined in this book are more the norm than the anomaly.[4] Prisons throughout the country are bursting with incarcerated Americans, and prison administrators increasingly look to so-called private solutions to replace the dearth of programming in American prisons. Faith-based correctional programs are the most common solution, and with faith-based correctional reforms come the conservative Christians who were one of the primary objects of study in this book. If faith-based reforms across the nation empower the neoliberal economy and culture that accompanied—and arguably fueled—mass incarceration, scholars would be well served to survey "the quiet revolution" to look for points of convergence and for discrepancies between "the quiet revolution" and the "spiritual entrepreneurs" who feed and are fed by neoliberal thought.

Notes

Introduction

1. In this book, I document and cite formal interviews, but I omit citations for casual conversations and for information and quotations obtained from individual classes, workshops, revivals, worship services, and other events in Florida's prisons. Additionally, all of the incarcerated have pseudonyms, as do some of the volunteers who provided verbal but not written consent to participate in this project. Finally, the incarcerated people whom I interviewed provided detailed histories of their pasts, including their crimes. In a few instances, an astute researcher might be able to identify two of the interviewees based solely on my description of their histories. To protect their privacy, I altered small details that preserve their stories but that hopefully make it impossible to determine their identity.

2. For additional information on Wakulla Correctional Institution, see Wakulla Correctional Institution, Florida Department of Corrections, accessed September 16, 2020, http://www.dc.state.fl.us/ci/118.html.

3. This figure reflects the number of FCBIs at the time of publication. Florida's Department of Corrections operates over fifty correctional facilities, and many senior administrators would like to create an FCBI in every prison, so it is quite likely that the number of FCBIs has increased since the publication of this book.

4. White House, *The Quiet Revolution: The President's Faith-Based and Community Report: A Seven-Year Progress Report,* Office of Faith-Based and Community Initiatives (2008), iii, https://georgewbush-whitehouse.archives.gov/government/fbci/The-Quiet-Revolution.pdf.

5. Center for Public Justice, *A Guide to Charitable Choice* (Washington, DC: Center for Public Justice, 1997), 18.

6. The issue of religious employers' rights appears to be in flux in light of two factors. First, the Supreme Court's decision in *Hosanna-Tabor Evangelical Lutheran Church v. EEOC* arguably broadened the category of "minister," particularly in Justice Clarence Thomas's and Justice Samuel Alito's concurring opinions, where the justices, respectively, urged the Court to "defer to a religious organization's good-faith understanding of who qualifies as a minister" and to apply the term "minister" to similar positions in non-Christian religions (Hosanna-Tabor Evangelical Lutheran Church v. EEOC, 312 S. Ct. 694, 710 [2012]). Second, the addition of Justices Neil Gorsuch and Brett Kavanaugh in all likelihood created a court more sympathetic to exemptions for religious employers, although the current Court has yet to rule on any cases related to this issue.

7. See George W. Bush, *Rallying the Armies of Compassion* (Washington, DC: Executive Office of the President, 2001). See also Rebecca Sager, *Faith, Politics, and Power: The Politics of Faith-Based Initiatives* (Oxford: Oxford University Press, 2010).

8. Broadly speaking, my thoughts on socialization are influenced by Émile Durkheim, who wrote that "it is patently obvious that all education consists of a continual effort to impose upon the child ways of seeing, thinking, and acting which he himself would not have arrived at spontaneously" (Émile Durkheim, *Rules of Sociological Method and Selected Texts on Sociology and Its Method*, ed. Steven Lukes, trans. W. D. Halls [New York: Free Press, 1982], 53–54). Building off this insight, all socialization efforts, including those directed at adults, contribute to this process.

9. For a good summary of existing and relevant legislation, see Ira C. Lupu and Robert W. Tuttle, *The State of the Law 2008: A Cumulative Report on Legal Developments Affecting Government Partnerships with Faith-Based Organizations* (Albany: Nelson A. Rockefeller Institute of Government, State University of New York, 2008). Alexander Volokh argued that faith-based prisons are of dubious legality; however, he argues that a prison voucher system would position more firmly with the constitutional framework. See Alexander Volokh, "Prison Vouchers," *University of Pennsylvania Law Review* 160, no. 3 (February 2012): 779–863. For additional discussions of the legality of faith-based correctional facilities, see Lynn S. Branham, "'The Devil Is in the Details': A Continued Dissection of the Constitutionality of Faith-Based Prison Units," *Ave Maria Law Review* 8, no. 35 (September 2008): 409–41; Lynn S. Branham, "'Go and Sin No More': The Constitutionality of Governmentally Funded Faith-Based Prison Units," *University of Michigan Journal of Law Review* 37 (2004): 291–352; and Richard P. Nathan and David J. Wright, "Is 'Charitable Choice' Compatible with the First Amendment? Is It a Good Idea? Does It Work?," Rockefeller Institute of Government, Roundtable on Religion and Social Welfare Policy (September 2003).

10. Ira C. Lupu and Robert W. Tuttle, "The Faith-Based Initiative and the Constitution," *DePaul Law Review* 55, no. 1 (Fall 2005): 203.

11. See Susanna Dokupil, "A Sunny Dome with Caves of Ice: The Illusion of Charitable Choice," *Texas Review of Law and Politics* 2 (2000): 150–208. For information on foreign partnerships between religion and state, see J. Bruce Nichols, *The Uneasy Alliance: Religion, Refugee Work, and U.S. Foreign Policy* (Oxford: Oxford University Press, 1988).

12. Elbert Lin, Jon D. Michaels, Rajesh Nayak, Katherine Tang Newberge, Nikhil Shanbhag, and Jake Sullivan, "Faith in the Courts? The Legal and Political Future of Federally-Funded Faith-Based Initiatives," *Yale Law & Policy Review* 20, no. 1 (2002): 183–225.

13. Several scholars have studied faith-based correctional programs in American prisons. Winnifred Sullivan studied the constitutionality of a faith-based dorm in Iowa (see Winnifred Sullivan, *Prison Religion: Faith-Based Reform and the Constitution* [Princeton, NJ: Princeton University Press, 2011]); Joshua Dubler discussed the chapel in a particular prison (see Joshua Dubler, *Down in the Chapel: Religious*

Life in an American Prison [New York: Farrar, Straus and Giroux, 2013]); Tanya Erzen provided a survey of faith-based correctional programs (see Tanya Erzen, *God in Captivity: The Rise of Faith-Based Prison Ministries in the Age of Mass Incarceration* [Boston: Beacon, 2017]); and several scholars studied the in-prison seminary in Angola Prison in Louisiana (see Michael Hallett, Joshua Hays, Byron Johnson, Sung Joon Jang, and Grant Duwe, *The Angola Prison Seminary: Effects of Faith-Based Ministry on Identity, Transformation, Desistance, and Rehabilitation* [New York: Routledge, 2017]). None of these works, however, specifically and extensively explore the compatibility of faith-based correctional reforms and neoliberalism.

14. Some might take issue with my use of the term "ethnography," which traditionally refers to a degree of immersion that I, as a nonincarcerated person, was not able to achieve. I did, however, spend numerous hours inside the prisons, where I ate with the incarcerated, attended worship services and rehabilitative programs with the incarcerated, visited and even spent time with them in their dorms and in the prisons' yards, and spent time with the incarcerated during down time. I remained the consummate outsider in the sense that I could never be "one of them," but I did everything with the incarcerated I could, short of sleeping in the prison and being punished with them during lockdowns.

15. The term "New Christian Right" (NCR) is a term scholars commonly use to describe politically active, conservative Christians that emerged in the second half of the twentieth century. For an example of early usage of the term, see Robert C. Liebman and Robert Wuthnow, eds., *The New Christian Right* (New York: Aldine, 1983). Collectively, members of the NCR span the politically, socially, and theologically conservative end of the spectrum of Christians. They identify as evangelical, fundamentalist, nondenominational, or simply Christian. They also reject some of these terms but embrace the theologies commonly associated with evangelicalism and fundamentalism. To avoid the debate regarding definitions of evangelicals and fundamentalists, I simply use the term "NCR."

Scholars have acknowledged the relationship between religion and the economy since the likes of Karl Marx and Max Weber. More recently, various scholars cited throughout this book have explored the relationship between religion and the economy; however, it was anthropologist Erica Bornstein who especially called scholars to explore the relationship between the economy and faith-based development. See Erica Bornstein, *The Spirit of Development: Protestant NGOs, Orality, and Economics in Zimbabwe* (Stanford, CA: Stanford University Press, 2005).

16. Allison DeFoor (volunteer and supporter of Florida's FCBIs), personal correspondence with the author, June 2014.

17. In addition to the literature listed elsewhere in this book, my thinking on neoliberalism is influenced by the following scholars: Monica Prasad, *The Politics of Free Markets: The Rise of Neoliberal Economic Policies in Britain, France, Germany, and the United States* (Chicago: University of Chicago Press, 2006); David Harvey, *A Brief History of Neoliberalism* (New York: Oxford University Press, 2007); Philip Mirowski and Dieter Plehew, eds., *The Road from Mont Pèlerin: The Making of the Neoliberal Thought Collective* (Cambridge, MA: Harvard University Press, 2009); Jamie Peck, *Constructions of Neoliberal Reason* (New York: Oxford University

Press, 2010); Manfred B. Steger and Ravi K. Roy, *Neoliberalism: A Very Short Introduction* (New York: Oxford University Press, 2010); Pierre Dardot and Christian Laval, *The New Way of The World: On Neoliberal Society*, trans. Gregory Elliott (New York: Verso, 2013); Robert van Horn, Philip Mirowski, and Thomas A. Stapleford, eds., *Building Chicago Economics: New Perspectives on the History of America's Most Powerful Economics Program* (Cambridge: Cambridge University Press, 2013); Daniel Stedman Jones, *Masters of the Universe: Hayek, Friedman, and the Birth of Neoliberal Politics* (Princeton, NJ: Princeton University Press, 2014); and Adam Kotsko, *Neoliberalism's Demons: On the Political Theology of Late Capital* (Stanford, CA: Stanford University Press, 2018).

18. The literature on this topic is quite voluminous and well documented. For histories of the modern category of "religion," see Talal Asad, *Formations of the Secular: Christianity, Islam, Modernity* (Stanford, CA: Stanford University Press, 2003); Peter Harrison, *"Religion" and the Religions in the English Enlightenment* (Cambridge: Cambridge University Press, 2002); and Brent Nongbri, *Before Religion: A History of a Modern Concept* (New Haven, CT: Yale University Press, 2013).

19. This project approaches the study of religion as described, critically, by Nancy Levene, who wrote, "The shift is from the question of what religion is to the question of who is speaking and what are the social and political stakes of identification" (Nancy Levene, "Marx's Eleventh Thesis and the Politics of the Study of Religion: Lessons from *The Sacred Is the Profane*," *Journal of Religion* 98, no. 2 [2018]: 225). Levene was criticizing the work of William Arnal and Russell McCutcheon, who wrote, "It is important to bear in mind when studying those who divide up their social world in [any way] the principle that, after describing the participant's own use of such designators, scholarship requires us to redescribe all such first-order or folk classification systems, seeing them as instances of other, far wider, cross-cultural or historical processes—processes that do not necessarily share a common identity but which, instead, serve as analogies exemplary of something the scholar finds curious" (William E. Arnal and Russell T. McCutcheon, *The Sacred Is the Profane: The Political Nature of "Religion"* [New York: Oxford University Press, 2013], ix). Religious Studies scholar Tisa Wenger described part of the rationale for this approach when she wrote, "Ultimately no discourse is singular in meaning or limited in the kinds of cultural work it can perform, and no ideal can be contained by its history or the apparent logic of its significations" (Tisa Wenger, *Religious Freedom: The Contested History of an American Idea* [Chapel Hill: University of North Carolina Press, 2017], 239). Building off this insight, this book explores the neoliberal implications of the discourse on "faith" in the era of the faith-based initiative.

20. As Steven Lukes noted, notions of individuality are "social and indeed historically specific" (see Steven Lukes, *Individualism* [Oxford: Basil Blackwell, 1973]).

21. Peter Metcalf, *They Lie, We Lie: Getting on with Anthropology* (New York: Routledge, 2002).

22. My thinking on critical ethnography is influenced by Nikolas Rose's theory of critical history. See Nikolas Rose, *Inventing Our Selves: Psychology, Power, and Personhood* (New York: Cambridge University Press, 1998).

23. H. L. Goodall Jr., *Writing the New Ethnography* (Lanham, MD: AltaMira, 2000).

24. Jim Thomas and Aogan O'Maolchatha, "Reassessing the Critical Metaphor: An Optimistic Revisionist View," *Justice Quarterly* 6, no. 2 (June 1989): 143–72.

25. Jim Thomas, *Doing Critical Ethnography* (Newbury Park, CA: SAGE, 1993), 2–3.

26. George W. Noblit, Susana Y. Flores, and Enrique G. Murillo Jr., eds., *Postcritical Ethnography: Reinscribing* Critique (Cresskill, NJ: Hampton, 2004), 3. For additional information on this topic, see James Clifford and George E. Marcus, eds., *Writing Culture: The Poetics and Politics of Ethnography* (Berkeley: University of California Press, 2010).

27. D. Soyini Madison, *Critical Ethnography: Method, Ethics, and Performance* (Thousand Oaks, CA: SAGE, 2005).

28. I disclosed my intentions to all informants, and despite this disclosure, only one person decided not to participate in the project.

29. Bruce Lincoln, "Theses on Method," *Method and Theory in the Study of Religion: Twenty-Five Years On* (Boston: Brill, 2013), 165–67.

30. As I will argue throughout this book, conservative Christians are the majority in Florida's FCBIs. In addition to Christians, however, Florida's FCBIs do include members of other religions, and all of those religions—with one exception—allowed me to observe their sectarian services. Odinists were the sole exception. Generally speaking, Odinists are polytheists who celebrate their Nordic ancestry and who advocate for racial segregation. For this reason, groups like the Southern Poverty Law Center often label them extremists, a hate group, and a white-power prison gang masquerading as a religion (see "Neo-Volkisch," Southern Poverty Law Center, accessed September 16, 2020, https://www.splcenter.org/fighting-hate/extremist -files/ideology/neo-volkisch). Odinists talked to me repeatedly, but they would not let me observe their sectarian services on the grounds that I, as a nonbeliever, would introduce impurities into their service.

31. To a large extent, this relationship is the subject of Aaron Griffith's book. See *God's Law and Order: The Politics of Punishment in Evangelical America* (Cambridge, MA: Harvard University Press, 2020).

32. Pew Forum on Religion and Public Life, *U.S. Religious Landscape Survey: Religious Affiliation; Diverse and Dynamic* (Washington, DC: Pew Research Center, 2008), 1.

33. Scholars of American religious history debate the idea that Americans have always displayed high levels of religiosity (these debates typically ignore the idea that "religion" is a socially constructed category with no inherent meaning or stable referent), but the debate over American religiosity is evident in the first grand narratives of American religious history. For example, see Sydney E. Ahlstrom, *A Religious History of the American People* (New Haven, CT: Yale University Press, 1972); Robert Baird, *Religion in America* (New York: Harper & Row, 1970); Sidney E. Mead, *The Lively Experiment: The Shaping of Christianity in America* (New York: Harper & Row, 1963); and Philip Schaff, *America: A Sketch of Its Political, Social, and Religious Character* (Cambridge, MA: Harvard University Press, 1961).

Regarding Supreme Court justices, in 1952 Justice William Douglas famously (or infamously) wrote, "We are a religious people whose institutions presuppose a Supreme Being" (Zorach et al. v. Clauson et al., Constituting the Board of Education of the City of New York, et al., 343 U.S. 306, 313 [1952)]). Supreme Court justices repeated this statement in subsequent court cases such as *Engel et al. v. Vitale et al.*, 370 U.S. 421, 442 (1962); *School District of Abington Township, Pennsylvania, et al. v. Schempp et al.*, 374 U.S. 203, 231 (1963); *Lynch, Mayor of Pawtucket, et al. v. Donnelly et al.*, 465 U.S. 668, 675 (1984); and *Marsh, Nebraska State Treasurer, et al. v. Chambers et al.*, 463 U.S. 783, footnote 29 (1983), among others. Recent court cases affirm the idea that we are a religious people, even when they do not explicitly cite Justice Douglas (see Town of Greece, New York, Petitioner v. Susan Galloway et al., 134 S. Ct. 1811 [2014]).

34. See Michael W. Flamm, *Law and Order: Street Crime, Civil Unrest, and the Crisis of Liberalism in the 1960s* (New York: Columbia University Press, 2005). Some people question if crime rates actually increased or if the government more effectively tracked crime (Heather Schoenfeld, *Building the Prison State: Race & the Politics of Mass Incarceration* [Chicago: University of Chicago Press, 2018]).

35. Political scientist Naomi Murakawa persuasively argues that the concern with law and order predates the 1960s. See Naomi Murakawa, *The First Civil Right: How Liberals Built Prison America* (New York: Oxford University Press, 2014).

36. Jeremy Travis, Bruce Western, and Steve Redburn, *The Growth of Incarceration in the United States: Exploring Causes and Consequences* (Washington, DC: National Academies Press, 2014), 34. See also Bert Useem and Anne Morrison Piehl, *Prison State: The Challenge of Mass Incarceration* (New York: Cambridge University Press, 2008).

37. Travis, Western, and Redburn, *Growth of Incarceration*, 34.

38. Travis, Western, and Redburn, 33. U.S. incarceration rates have since decreased to 655 incarcerated people per 100,000 Americans. See Roy Walmsley, *World Prison Population List*, 12th ed., Institute for Criminal Policy Research (London: Birkbeck, University of London, 2013), 6. As Elliott Currie wrote, "What we have witnessed in the past quarter century is nothing less than a revolution in our justice system—a transformation unprecedented in our own history, or in that of any other industrial democracy" (Elliott Currie, *Crime and Punishment in America* [New York: Picador, 2013], 9).

39. Walmsley, *World Prison Population List*.

40. Walmsley, 11.

41. Travis, Western, and Redburn, *Growth of Incarceration*, 37.

42. This is an often-cited statistic. Among others, see Adam Liptak, "U.S. Prison Population Dwarfs that of Other Nations," *New York Times*, April 23, 2008; Carolyn W. Deady, *Incarceration and Recidivism: Lessons from Abroad* (Newport, RI: Pell Center for International Relations and Public Policy, 2014), 1; and *The Punishing Decade: Prison and Jail Estimates at the Millennium* (Washington, DC: Justice Policy Institute, 2000), 1.

43. Ron Walmsley, *World Female Imprisonment List*, 2nd ed., International Centre for Prison Studies (London: University of Essex, 2012), 1.

44. A number of scholars use this term, but it figures predominantly in the work of Marie Gottschalk, *The Prison and Gallows: The Politics of Mass Incarceration in America* (New York: Cambridge University Press, 2006); Marie Gottschalk, "The

Carceral State and the Politics of Punishment," *The SAGE Handbook of Punishment and Society*, ed. Jonathan Simon and Richard Sparks (Los Angeles: SAGE, 2013), 205–41; Joe Sim, *Punishment and Prisons: Power and the Carceral State* (London: SAGE, 2009); and Loïc Wacquant, *Punishing the Poor: The Neoliberal Government of Social Insecurity* (Durham, NC: Duke University Press, 2009).

45. When discussing the compatibility of Christianity and neoliberalism, Wendy Brown argued that moralism and Christian conservatism "conjoin familiar elements of neoliberalism (licensing capital, leashing labor, demonizing the social state and the political, attacking equality, promulgating freedom) with their seeming opposites (nationalism, enforcement of traditional morality, populist antielitism, and demands for state solutions to economic and social problems)" (Wendy Brown, *In the Ruins of Neoliberalism: The Rise of Antidemocratic Politics in the West* [New York: Columbia University Press, 2019], 2). See also Joshua Dubler and Vincent Lloyd, *Break Every Yoke: Religion, Justice, and the Abolition of Prisons* (New York: Oxford University Press, 2020).

46. Wendy Brown, *Undoing the Demos: Neoliberalism's Stealth Revolution* (New York: Zone Books, 2015). See also James Dennis LoRusso, *Spirituality, Corporate Culture, and American Business: The Neoliberal Ethic and the Spirit of Global Capital* (New York: Bloomsbury, 2017). Some even question neoliberalism's existence.

47. Harvey, *Brief History of Neoliberalism*, 2.

48. Dennis LoRusso, "Towards Radical Subjects: Workplace Spirituality as Neoliberal Governance in American Business," in *Spirituality, Organization and Neoliberalism: Understanding Lived Experiences*, ed. Emma Bell, Anca Simionca, and Scott Taylor (Northampton, MA: Edward Elgar Publishing, 2020), 3.

49. Doreen Massey similarly argued that "vocabularies of the economy" become governing principles that ripple beyond the economy. See Doreen Massey, "Vocabularies of the Economy," *Soundings: A Journal of Politics and Culture* no. 54 (Summer 2013): 9–22.

50. Lisa Duggan, *The Twilight of Equality: Neoliberalism, Cultural Politics, and the Attack on Democracy* (Boston: Beacon, 2003).

51. Brown, *In the Ruins of Neoliberalism*, 19.

52. See Julilly Kohler-Hausmann, *Getting Tough: Welfare and Imprisonment in 1970s America* (Princeton, NJ: Princeton University Press, 2017); Brown, *Undoing the Demos*; and Jason Read, "A Genealogy of Homo-Economicus: Neoliberalism and the Production of Subjectivity," *Foucault Studies* no. 6 (2009): 25–36; and Barbara Cruikshank, "Revolutions Within: Self-Government and Self-Esteem," in *Foucault and Political Reason: Liberalism, Neo-Liberalism, and Rationalities of Government*, ed. Andrew Barry, Thomas Osborne, and Nikolas S. Rose (Chicago: University of Chicago Press, 1996), 231–52.

53. As Wendy Brown wrote, "The contemporary attack on society and social justice in the name of market freedom and moral traditionalism is thus a direct emanation of neoliberal rationality, hardly limited to so-called 'conservatives'" (*In the Ruins of Neoliberalism*, 13).

54. Wacquant, *Punishing the Poor*. For a criticism of Wacquant's theory of the causes of mass incarceration, see Bert Useem and Anne Morrison Piehl, *Prison*

State: The Challenge of Mass Incarceration (New York: Cambridge University Press, 2008).

55. Harvey, *Brief History of Neoliberalism*, 3.

56. Quinn Slobodian, *Globalists: The End of Empire and the Birth of Neoliberalism* (Cambridge, MA: Harvard University Press, 2018).

Chapter One

1. M. K. Sawyer, "A Message from the Superintendent," *S.C.I. Sound* 1 (July 2, 1982): 1.

2. M. K. Sawyer, "Superintendent's Message to SCI Staff," *S.C.I. Sound* 1 (July 9, 1982) 1.

3. M. K. Sawyer, "Superintendent's Message to Inmate," *S.C.I. Sound* 1 (July 9, 1982): 1.

4. Inmate Richard Gilliland, "Unity Gavel Club," *S.C.I. Sound* 2 (August 12, 1983): 1. Scholars today typically try to avoid referring to the incarcerated as inmates. While I am sympathetic to this, I included the word "inmate" in front of incarcerated authors, as their names appear in the documents themselves.

5. Inmate Michael Allen, "Toastmasters and Jaycees—At It Again!," *S.C.I. Sound* 1 (July 9, 1982): 4; Inmate Steven Aleo, "Jaycees Chess Tournament," *S.C.I. Sound* 1 (September 8, 1982): 1.

6. Inmate Michael Allen, "Defending Softball Champs C-Dorm Rip Food Service," *S.C.I. Sound* 1 (July 9, 1982): 4.

7. Inmate Michael Allen, "SCI Boxing Tournament," *S.C.I. Sound* 1 (July 9, 1982): 4; Inmate Michael Allen, "S.C.I. Weight Lifters Defeat Brooksville Road Prison," *S.C.I. Sound* 1 (July 9, 1982), 5.

8. Inmate Kenneth Ford, "The Changing Face of S.C.I.," *S.C.I. Sound* 1 (July 2, 1982): 1.

9. Ms. B. Jacobs, "Computer Bug Bites SCI," *S.C.I. Sound* 1 (July 9, 1982): 1.

10. Inmate Kenneth Ford, "The Changing Face of Sumter," *S.C.I. Sound* 1 (August 25, 1982): 1.

11. Inmate Andre Griesinger, "Welding Shop Outfits Firetruck," *S.C.I. Sound* 1 (October 8, 1982): 1.

12. Inmate Steven Aleo, "Sign Up Now for G.E.D. Testing," *S.C.I. Sound* 1 (September 8, 1982): 1.

13. Inmate Anthony Relano, "Masterpiece in Wood," *S.C.I. Sound* 1 (December 8, 1982): 1.

14. Inmate James Kirkland, "SCI Graphic Arts (Print Shop)," *S.C.I. Sound* 2 (December 9, 1983): 1.

15. Inmate James Kirland, "New Vocational Masonry Instructor at SCI," *S.C.I. Sound* 2 (February 3, 1983): 1.

16. "SCI Students Complete Computer Course," *S.C.I. Sound* 1 (September 8, 1982): 1.

17. For example, see J. C. Panzetta, "Gospel Echoes Team," *S.C.I. Sound* 1 (July 16, 1982): 6.

18. "Religion," *S.C.I. Sound* 1 (July 2, 1982): 5. The administration in Florida's DOC in the 1980s typically conceived of religious diversity as it related to four religious groups: Protestants, Catholics, Muslims, and Jews. The religious services at SCI reflected this understanding of religious diversity.

19. Inmate Elijah Mack, "Introduction to Islam," *S.C.I. Sound* 1 (September 8, 1982): 7.

20. Inmate Elijah Mack, "The Light of Truth in Islam," *S.C.I. Sound* 1 (September 8, 1982): 7.

21. John C. Panzetta, "The Centrality of Christ in Your Life," *S.C.I. Sound* 1 (September 8, 1982): 7.

22. Inmates Dexter Bryant and John Boddle, "'What Is There in Hell That You Want,'" *S.C.I. Sound* 1 (August 18, 1982): 7.

23. Incarcerated people who violated the rules received disciplinary punishments, but these were usually short term, and the incarcerated returned to the general population after a team of administrators (including the facility's psychologists and physicians) deemed it appropriate. For example, at S.C.I. residents who violated the prison's policies were transferred to the Behavior Modification Wing, where they ate and showered separately from other people. They were allowed "one set of state issued clothing, toilet articles, pictures, a bible, and assorted religious material provided by the Chaplains during their visits" (Inmate Steven Aleo, "Behavior Modification Wing," *S.C.I. Sound* 1 [October 28, 1982]: 1).

24. See Angus Burgin, *The Great Persuasion: Reinventing Free Markets since the Depression* (Cambridge, MA: Harvard University Press, 2012).

25. Nikolas Rose, "Governing 'Advanced' Liberal Democracies," in *Foucault and Political Reason: Liberalism, Neo-Liberalism, and Rationalities of Government*, ed. Andrew Barry, Thomas Osborne, and Nikolas Rose (Chicago: University of Chicago Press, 1996), 45.

26. Louie Wainwright (retired Florida Department of Corrections secretary), in discussion with the author, April 2014.

27. U.S. Department of Justice, Office of Justice Programs, *Survey of State Prison Inmates, 1991*, NCJ 136949 (Washington, DC: Government Printing Office, 1993), 27.

28. "Faith-Based Programming," *Corrections Compendium* 28, no. 8 (2003): 8–20.

29. The following scholars discussed the religious roots of the modern penitentiary: Jennifer Graber, *The Furnace of Affliction: Prisons & Religion in Antebellum America* (Chapel Hill: University of North Carolina Press, 2011); Adam J. Hirsch, *The Rise of the Penitentiary: Prisons and Punishment in Early America* (New Haven, CT: Yale University Press, 1992); Orlando F. Lewis, *The Development of American Prisons and Prison Customs, 1776–1845: With Special Reference to Early Institutions in the State of New York* (Albany: Prison Association of New York, 1922); and David J. Rothman, *The Discovery of the Asylum: Social Order and Disorder in the New Republic* (Boston: Little, Brown, 1971).

30. Samuel L. Knapp, *The Life of Thomas Eddy; Comprising an Extensive Correspondence with Many of the Most Distinguished Philosophers and Philanthropists of This and Other Countries* (New York: Conner & Cooke, 1834), 56.

31. For a general history of the modern penitentiary, see Norval Morris and David J. Rothman, eds., *The Oxford History of the Prison: The Practice of Punishment in Western Society* (New York: Oxford University Press, 1998).

32. Douglas A. Blackmon, *Slavery by Another Name: The Re-Enslavement of Black Americans from the Civil War to World War II* (New York: Anchor Books, 2008).

33. U.S. Const. amend. XIII, § 1 (italics added).

34. Ruffin v. Commonwealth, 62 Va. 790, 796 (1871). "The bill of rights is a declaration of general principles to govern a society of free men, and not of convicted felons" (Ruffin v. Commonwealth, 62 Va. 790, at 796).

35. Florida was the last state to close its convict lease system.

36. The prison abolition movement continues to exist. Joshua Dubler and Vincent Lloyd recently argued that the prison abolitionist movement needs to be rooted in American religiosity. See Joshua Dubler and Vincent Lloyd, *Break Every Yoke: Religion, Justice, and the Abolition of Prisons* (New York: Oxford University Press, 2019).

37. Michel Foucault, *Discipline and Punish: The Birth of the Prison* (New York: Vintage Books, 1995).

38. National Advisory Commission on Criminal Justice Standards and Goals, *Task Force Report on Corrections* (Washington, DC: Government Printing Office, 1973), 597.

39. National Advisory Commission on Criminal Justice Standards and Goals, 358.

40. David Rothman, *The Discovery of the Asylum: Social Order and Disorder in the New Republic* (Boston: Little, Brown, 1971), 295.

41. Norval Morris, *The Future of Imprisonment* (Chicago: University of Chicago Press, 1974), 268.

42. Marie Gottschalk, *Caught: The Prison State and the Lockdown of American Politics* (Princeton, NJ: Princeton University Press, 2015), 14. See also David Garland, ed., *Mass Imprisonment: Social Causes and Consequences* (London: SAGE, 2001); and Bert Useem and Anne Morrison Piehl, *Prison State: The Challenge of Mass Incarceration* (New York: Cambridge University Press, 2008).

43. Jerome Miller, "Does Nothing Work?," in *Offenders or Citizens? Readings in Rehabilitation*, ed. Philip Priestley and Maurice Vanstone (New York: Willan, 2010), 185.

44. Charles E. Silberman, *Criminal Violence, Criminal Justice* (New York: Vintage Books, 1978), 3–4.

45. Silberman, 4–5.

46. See Katherine Beckett, *Making Crime Pay: Law and Order in Contemporary American Politics* (New York: Oxford University Press, 1999), chaps. 2 and 3.

47. Christian Parenti, *Lockdown America: Police and Prisons in the Age of Crisis* (New York: Verso, 1999), 7.

48. Dan Baum, *Smoke and Mirrors: The War on Drugs and the Politics of Failure* (Boston: Back Bay Books, 1996), 11–12.

49. James Q. Wilson, *Thinking About Crime* (New York: Basic Books, 1975), 170.

50. Douglas S. Lipton, Robert Martinson, and Judith Wilks, *Effectiveness of Correctional Treatment: A Survey of Treatment Evaluation Studies* (New York: Praeger, 1975).

51. The Christian Right's embrace of "tough on crime" was not unanimous, as evidenced by figures like Charles "Chuck" Colson, an otherwise partisan Christian and former special counsel to President Richard Nixon who served seven months in prison as a punishment for his role in the Watergate scandal. Colson emerged from prison as a staunch advocate for prison reform. Colson's work would later influence the Right on Crime movement. Right on Crime is an organization consisting primarily of conservative Christian Republicans who previously supported "tough on crime" policies but who now support criminal justice reforms. See www.rightoncrime .com. See also Aaron Griffith, *God's Law and Order: The Politics of Punishment in Evangelical America* (Cambridge, MA: Harvard University Press, 2020).

52. These terms are increasingly problematic, not only because scholars cannot agree on a set definition for either term but also because some people reject the labels even when the objects of those labels embrace the principles and behaviors associated with the term "evangelical" or "fundamentalist." Instead of parsing definitions and labels, the term "NCR" refers to politically active conservative Christians who began to mobilize and support conservative politics in the final decades of the twentieth century.

53. For additional information on Christian nationalism, see Esther Kaplan, *With God on Their Side: How Christian Fundamentalists Trampled Science, Policy, and Democracy in George W. Bush's White House* (New York: New Press, 2004); Kevin Phillips, *American Theocracy: The Peril and Politics of Radical Religion, Oil, and Borrowed Money in the 21st Century* (New York: Viking, 2006); Michelle Goldberg, *Kingdom Coming: The Rise of Christian Nationalism* (New York: W. W. Norton, 2007); and Andrew L. Whitehead and Samuel L. Perry, *Taking Back America: Christian Nationalism in the United States* (New York: Oxford University Press, 2020). Also, Bruce Schulman argues that from its beginning, the groups that constituted the NCR embraced the free-market economy. See Bruce J. Schulman, *The Seventies: The Great Shift in American Culture, Society, and Politics* (New York: Free Press, 2001).

54. Michael Tonry, *Punishing Race: A Continuing American Dilemma* (New York: Oxford University Press, 2011), 9.

55. James Q. Whitman, *Harsh Justice: Criminal Punishment and the Widening Divide between America and Europe* (New York: Oxford University Press, 2003), 6.

56. Aaron Griffith, "'Jesus Christ Is the Only Control': Crime, Delinquency, and Evangelical Conversion in the Postwar Era," *Fides et Historia* 50, no.1 (2018): 35–59.

57. Cf. Griffith, "'Jesus Christ Is the Only Control,'" 44.

58. Khalil Gibran Muhammad, *The Condemnation of Blackness: Race, Crime, and the Making of Modern Urban America* (Cambridge, MA: Harvard University Press, 2010). Heather Schoenfeld adds insights to this topic in *Building the Prison State: Race & the Politics of Mass Incarceration* (Chicago: University of Chicago Press, 2018).

59. Griffith, "'Jesus Christ Is the Only Control,'" 56.

60. Cf. Griffith, 55.

61. Cf. Griffith, 56.

62. All quotes from the candidacy speech are from "Ronald Reagan's Announcement for Presidential Candidacy," Ronald Reagan Presidential Library and Museum,

"Ronald Reagan's Major Speeches, 1964–89," accessed June 2015, https://www.reaganlibrary.gov/11-13-79.

63. "Ronald Reagan's Major Speeches, 1964–89." Reagan, here, referred to the "essential services" that he wanted to keep in place, which include "the system of benefits which flow to the poor, the elderly, the sick, and the handicapped."

64. "National Affairs Campaign Address on Religious Liberty," American Rhetoric, accessed June 2015, https://www.americanrhetoric.com/speeches/ronaldreaganreligiousliberty.htm.

65. Steven P. Miller, *The Age of Evangelicalism: America's Born-Again Years* (New York: Oxford University Press, 2014), 62.

66. Kevin Kruse, *One Nation under God: How Corporate America Invented Christian America* (New York: Basic Books, 2015); and Darren Dochuk, *From Bible Belt to Sunbelt: Plain-Folk Religion, Grassroots Politics, and the Rise of Evangelical Conservatism* (New York: W. W. Norton, 2010).

67. David Harvey, *A Brief History of Neoliberalism* (New York: Oxford University Press, 2007), 50.

68. For information on the prosperity gospel, see Kate Bowler, *Blessed: A History of the American Prosperity Gospel* (New York: Oxford University Press, 2013).

69. William E. Connolly, *Capitalism and Christianity, American Style* (Durham, NC: Duke University Press, 2008), 40.

70. Bethany Moreton, *To Serve God and Wal-Mart: The Making of Christian Free Enterprise* (Cambridge, MA: Harvard University Press, 2009), 4.

71. Linda Kintz, *Between Jesus and the Market: The Emotions that Matter in Right-Wing America* (Durham, NC: Duke University Press, 1997), 30.

72. See Michelle Alexander, *The New Jim Crow: Mass Incarceration in the Age of Colorblindness* (New York: New Press, 2012); Katherine Beckett, *Making Crime Pay: Law and Order in Contemporary American Politics* (New York: Oxford University Press, 1997); Angela Y. Davis, *Are Prisons Obsolete?* (New York: Seven Stories, 2011); Stephanie Gaskill, "Moral Rehabilitation: Religion, Race, and Reform in America's Incarceration Capital" (PhD diss., University of North Carolina at Chapel Hill, 2017); Mark Mauer, *Race to Incarcerate* (New York: New Press, 1999); Robert Perkinson, *Texas Tough: The Rise of America's Prison Empire* (New York: Macmillan, 2001); and Heather Schoenfeld, *Building the Prison State: Race & the Politics of Mass Incarceration* (Chicago: University of Chicago Press, 2018).

73. The Anti-Drug Abuse Act of 1986 and the Anti-Drug Abuse Act of 1988 further extended these policies at the exact moment that the federal government decreased funding for drug prevention programs such as the National institute on Drug Abuse (whose budget dropped from $274 million to $57 million from 1981 to 1984) and from antidrug funding in the Department of Education (cut from $14 million to $3 million). See Alexander, *New Jim Crow*, 49–50.

74. Alexander, *New Jim Crow*, 49.

75. Nancy Reagan, "Address to the Nation on the Campaign against Drug Abuse," Ronald Reagan Presidential Library and Museum, accessed May 2018, https://www.reaganlibrary.gov/research/speeches/091486a.

76. Parenti, *Lockdown America*, 50.

77. John Pfaff, *Locked In: The True Causes of Mass Incarceration—and How to Achieve Real Reform* (New York: Basic Books, 2017), 77.

78. U.S. Department of Justice, Bureau of Justice Statistics, *Bureau of Justice Statistics Bulletin: Prisoners in 1980* (May 1981), 1.

79. U.S. Department of Justice, Bureau of Justice Statistics, *Bureau of Justice Statistics Bulletin: Prisoners in 1990* (May 1991), 1, 2.

80. See Harold G. Grasmick, Elizabeth Davenport, Mitchell B. Chamlin, and Robert J. Bursik Jr., "Protestant Fundamentalism and the Retributive Doctrine of Punishment," *Criminology* 30, no. 1 (1992): 21–45; Michael A. Hallett, *Private Prisons in America: A Critical Race Perspective* (Champaign: University of Illinois, 2006); Tonry, *Punishing Race*; Mark Warr, "What Is the Perceived Seriousness of Crimes?," *Criminology* 27, no. 4 (1989): 795–822; Whitman, *Harsh Justice*; and Harry Coverston, "Religious Ideation and Capital Practice: A Study of the Florida legislature" (unpublished PhD diss., Florida State University, 2000).

81. It is generally accepted that American prisons became more punitive in the 1980s and 1990s. A minority, however, questions this. See Roger Matthews, "The Myth of Punitiveness," *Theoretical Criminology* 9, no. 2 (2005): 175–201, who argues that American prisons are too diverse to justify the idea that prisons are more punitive.

82. Michael W. Flamm, *Law and Order: Street Crime, Civil Unrest, and the Crisis of Liberalism in the 1960s* (New York: Columbia University Press, 2005), 124.

83. Michael Tonry, *Penal Reform in Overcrowded Times* (New York: Oxford University Press, 2001), 59.

84. Governor Bill Clinton, "The New Covenant: Responsibility and Rebuilding the American Community," remarks to students at Georgetown University, October 23, 1991, http://www.dlc.org/ndol_ci4c81.html?kaid=127&subid=173&contentid=2783.

85. Melinda Cooper, *Family Values: Between Neoliberalism and the New Social Conservatism* (New York: Zone Books, 2017).

86. President Bill Clinton, "State of the Union Address," 1996, https://clinton whitehouse4.archives.gov/WH/New/other/sotu.html.

87. See Melinda Cooper, "All in the Family Debt: How Neoliberals and Conservatives Came Together to Undo the Welfare State," *Boston Review*, May 31, 2017, 2; and Paul Apostolidis, *Stations of the Cross: Adorno and Christian Right Radio* (Durham, NC: Duke University Press, 2000).

88. The following scholars highlight the role of liberal Democrats in laying the political and cultural groundwork for mass incarceration and for supporting many of the policies that fueled it: Naomi Murakawa, *The First Civil Right: How Liberals Built Prison America* (New York: Oxford University Press, 2014); Elizabeth Hinton, *From the War on Poverty to the War on Crime: The Making of Mass Incarceration in America* (Cambridge, MA: Harvard University Press, 2016); Heather Schoenfeld, *Building the Prison State: Race & the Politics of Mass Incarceration* (Chicago: University of Chicago Press, 2018). Similarly, Michael Fortner argues that African Americans, many of whom were liberal or Democrats, similarly supported the policies that created mass incarceration. See Michael Fortner, *The Rockefeller Drug Laws and the Politics of Punishment* (Cambridge, MA: Harvard University Press, 2015).

89. Henry A. Giroux, "Zero Tolerance, Domestic Militarization, and the War against Youth," *Social Justice* 30, no. 2 (2003): 59–65.

90. For a transcript of Clinton's speech, see Deborah Kalb, Gerhard Peters, and John T. Woolley, *State of the Union: Presidential Rhetoric from Woodrow Wilson to George W. Bush* (Washington, DC: CQ, 2007), 977–90.

In 1993, Washington became the first state to pass a "three strikes and you're out" law, followed soon by several other states. Three years later, twenty-four states and Congress had all adopted some version of a three-strikes law. As John Clark et al. discussed, each state law contained distinct standards defining what crimes constituted a "strike." See U.S. Department of Justice, National Institute of Justice, *Three Strikes and You're Out: A Review of State Legislation*, by John Clark, James Austin, and D. Alan Henry, NCJ 165369 (Washington, DC: Government Printing Office, 1997).

Political theorist Wendy Brown argues that three-strikes laws themselves embody neoliberal logics. See Wendy Brown, "American Nightmare: Neoliberalism, Neoconservatism, and De-Democratization," *Political Theory* 34, no. 6 (December 2006): 690–714.

91. This theory of crime and criminality conflicted with academic theories and with other religious approaches to crime. "Religion," in this context, typically referred to conservative Christianity, as not all religious groups embraced the "tough on crime" approach. For example, the proponents of religious progressivism historically associated with social gospel Christianity often did support crime prevention and rehabilitation programs. For historical works that address social gospel/social Christianity, see Sydney E. Ahlstrom, *A Religious History of the American People* (New Haven, CT: Yale University Press, 1972); M. Bowman, "Sin, Spirituality, and Primitivism: The Theologies of the American Social Gospel, 1885–1917," *Religion and American Culture* 17, no. 1 (2007): 95–126; Charles H. Hopkins, *The Rise of the Social Gospel in American Protestantism, 1865–1915* (New Haven, CT: Yale University Press, 1940); George Marsden, "The Gospel of Wealth, the Social Gospel, and the Salvation of Souls in Nineteenth-Century America," *Fides et Historia: Official Publication of the Conference on Faith and History* 5, no. 1 (1973): 10–21; Paul T. Phillips, *A Kingdom on Earth: Anglo-American Social Christianity, 1880–1940* (University Park: Pennsylvania State University Press, 1996); Martin E. Marty, *Modern American Religion* (Chicago: University of Chicago Press, 1986); and William R. Hutchison, "The Americanness of the Social Gospel; An Inquiry in Comparative History," *Church History* 44, no. 3 (September 1975): 367–81.

92. Honorable William P. Barr, "Crime, Poverty, and the Family," The Heritage Foundation, Heritage Lecture no. 401 (1992), 6.

93. Honorable George Allen, "The Real War on Crime: States on the Front Lines," Heritage Lecture no. 497 (August 10, 1994); Barr, *Crime, Poverty, and the Family*; Mary Kate Cary, "How States Can Fight Violent Crime: Two Dozen Steps to a Safer America," *State Backgrounder* no. 944/S (June 7, 1993); Patrick F. Fagan, "The Real Root Causes of Violent Crime: The Breakdown of Marriage, Family, and Community," Heritage Foundation *Backgrounder* no. 1026 (March 17, 1995); Robert Rector, "A Comprehensive Urban Policy: How to Fix Welfare and Revitalize America's

Inner Cities," Heritage Foundation Memo to President-Elect Clinton no. 12 (January 18, 1993); James Wootten and Robert O. Heck, "How State and Local Officials Can Combat Violent Juvenile Crime," *State Backgrounder* no. 1977/S (October 28, 1996); and Fagan, "Real Root Causes of Violent Crime."

Authors of various Heritage Foundation reports repeatedly argued that churches and faith-based organizations should play larger roles in America's fight against crime. This is the central argument of the following Heritage Foundation report: Patrick F. Fagan, Claudia Horn, Calvin W. Edwards, Karen M. Woods, and Collette Caprara, *Outcome-Based Evaluation: Faith-Based Social Service Organizations and Stewardship*, Heritage Foundation Special Report no. SR-13 (March 29, 2007).

94. Justin Watson, *The Christian Coalition: Dreams of Restoration, Demands for Recognition* (New York: St. Martin's, 1997); and Mark J. Rozell and Clyde Wilcox, *God at the Grass Roots, 1996: The Christian Right in the American Elections* (Lanham, MD: Rowman & Littlefield, 1997). Rozell and Wilcox argue that the Christian Coalition achieved only limited success; however, I include them in my narrative as part of a larger movement linking the NCR with larger political changes in the mid-1990s.

95. Ralph Reed Jr., *Contract with the American Family* (Nashville, TN: Moorings, 1995), ix.

96. Reed, 141.

97. Reed, 142.

98. Reed, x.

99. James Q. Wilson, *Two Nations*, December 4, 1997, (Washington, DC: AEI Press), 10.

100. Wilson, 17.

101. Wilson, 14.

102. According to one scholar, conservatives favor these partnerships more than liberals, but liberals tend to use them more often. See Mark Chaves, "Religious Congregations and Welfare Reform: Who Will Take Advantage of 'Charitable Choice'?," *American Sociological Review* 64, no. 6 (December 1999): 836–46.

103. Center for Public Justice, *A Guide to Charitable Choice* (Washington, DC: Center for Public Justice,1997), 18.

104. "Taking Back Our Streets Act," Wayback Machine, accessed September 16, 2020, http://web.archive.org/web/19991023011622/http://www.house.gov/house /Contract/safetyd.txt.

105. Michael Ross, "GOP Begins Revision of '94 Crime Bill Congress: House Passes First of Seven Measures Designed to Rewrite Legislation Approved Last Session. Debate Gets Off to a Non-Controversial Start," *Los Angeles Times*, February 9, 1995, http://articles.latimes.com/1995-02-08/news/mn-295299_1_crime-bill.

106. *Taking Back Our Streets Act of 1995: Hearings before the Subcommittee on Crime of the Committee on the Judiciary, House of Representatives, One Hundred Fourth Congress, First Session, on H.r. 3 . . . January 19 and 20, 1995* (Washington, DC: Government Printing Office, 1996). By 2002, seventeen states adopted determinate sentence policies, which resulted in mandatory minimum sentences for more crimes. Kevin R. Reitz, "The Disassembly and Reassembly of U.S. Sentencing

Practices," in *Sentencing and Sanctions in Western Countries*, ed. Michael Tonry and Richard S. Frase (New York: Oxford University Press), 222–58. As the Bureau of Justice Statistics noted, determinate sentencing stemmed at least partially from a desire to reduce sentence disparity, but it most often resulted in longer mandatory prison sentences.

107. "A Decade of Dramatic Change," *Annual Report 1980–1990* (Tallahassee, Florida), 31.

108. "Louie Wainwright's Nine Lives," *Saint Petersburg Times*, May 6, 1980, A10.

109. "Prisons Chief Has Survived Two Decades of Criticism," *Miami Herald*, September 12, 1982, http://infoweb.newsbank.com.proxy.lib.fsu.edu/resources/doc/nb/news/0EB359B4DB0A60EE?p=AWNB.

110. Louie L. Wainwright (retired Florida Department of Corrections secretary), in discussion with the author, April 2014.

111. Interviews with Louie L. Wainwright (retired Florida Department of Corrections secretary), in discussion with the author, April 2014; James Crosby (former Florida Department of Corrections secretary), in discussion with the author, June 2014; and Frank Metcalf and Carolyn Metcalf (retired Florida Department of Corrections head chaplain and his wife), in discussion with the author, April 2014).

112. "Dugger Outlines Future Goals for Corrections," *Correctional Compass* 14, no. 4 (April 1987): 2, 7.

113. Richard L. Dugger, "Secretary's Message: Awarding Gain Time Is Short-Term Solution," *Correctional Compass* 14, no. 6 (June 1987): 4.

114. Steven C. Tauber and William E. Hulbary, "Florida: Too Close to Call," in *The 2000 Presidential Election in the South: Partisanship and Southern Party Systems in the 21st Century*, ed. Robert P. Steed and Laurence W. Moreland (Westport, CT: Praeger, 2002), 150.

115. Michael Barone and Grant Ujifusa, *Almanac of American Politics 2000* (Washington, DC: National Journal, 1999), 386.

116. Katherine Pennington, "1995 Legislative Update," *Correctional Compass* 22, no. 7 (July 1995): 4.

117. Florida Department of Corrections, *1994–95 Annual Report: The Guidebook to Corrections in Florida* (Tallahassee, Florida), 23.

118. Pennington, "1995 Legislative Update," 4–5, 7.

119. For a general summary of three-strikes laws, see James Austin, John Clark, Patricia Hardyman, and Alan Henry, *Three Strikes and You're Out: The Implementation and Impact of Strike Laws*, March 6, 2000, https://www.ncjrs.gov/pdffiles1/nij/grants/181297.pdf.

120. For the DOC's summary of this bill, see Pennington, "1995 Legislative Update," 4–5, 7.

121. L. L., "Other Legislative Items of Interest," *Correctional Compass* 23, no. 7 (July 1996): 6.

122. Florida Department of Corrections, *Annual Report 1986–1987* (Tallahassee, Florida), 7, 8, 78.

123. Florida Department of Corrections, *Annual Report 1996–1997: The Guidebook to Corrections in Florida* (Tallahassee, Florida), 33.

Chapter Two

1. Hugh MacMillan (former executive director of the Foundation for Partnerships in Correction Excellence), in discussion with the author, July 2014.

2. Pierre Bourdieu, *Outline of a Theory of Practice* (New York: Cambridge University Press, 1977), 169. Bourdieu discusses *doxa* as it relates to social and economic classes; however, his insights extend beyond class analyses.

3. The culture that disdains credentialing is a stark reverse of the history that Walter Trattner described when he documented how charity workers in the early 1900s sought credentials to legitimize their work. See Walter I. Trattner, *From Poor Law to Welfare State: A History of Social Welfare in America* (New York: Free Press, 1974).

4. For an analysis and criticism of the cliché that "religion is a private matter," see Robyn Faith Walsh, "Religion Is a Private Matter," in *Stereotyping Religion: Critiquing Clichés*, ed. Brad Stoddard and Craig Martin (New York: Bloomsbury, 2017), 69–82.

5. Ronald Reagan, "August 12, 1986 Quotes and Speeches," Reagan Foundation, accessed September 16, 2020, https://www.reaganfoundation.org/ronald-reagan/reagan-quotes-speeches/news-conference-1/.

6. More specifically, scholars have highlighted the association of religion, the private, and neoliberal thought. See Jessica Johnson, *Biblical Porn: Affect, Labor, and Pastor Mark Driscoll's Evangelical Empire* (Durham, NC: Duke University Press, 2017); William Connolly, *Capitalism and Christianity, American Style* (Durham, NC: Duke University Press, 2008); and Sean McCloud, *American Possessions: Fighting Demons in the Contemporary United States* (New York: Oxford University Press, 2015).

7. See Russell T. McCutcheon, *The Discipline of Religion: Structure, Meaning, Rhetoric* (New York: Routledge, 2003); and Craig Martin, *Masking Hegemony: A Genealogy of Liberalism, Religion, and the Private Sphere* (New York: Routledge, 2010).

8. Scholars and the courts agree that the First Amendment prevents a religious establishment. They disagree, however, on the meaning and contours of religious establishment.

9. Winnifred Sullivan, "Religion, Law, and the Construction of Identities," *Numen* 43, no. 2 (1996): 135.

10. Joan Wallach Scott, *Sex and Secularism* (Princeton, NJ: Princeton University Press, 2017), 4. Scott references the discourse of secularism; however, her larger point applies to the discourse of religion as well.

11. Michel Foucault, "Governmentality," in *The Foucault Effect: Studies in Governmentality: With Two Lectures by and an Interview with Michel Foucault*, ed. Graham Burchell, Colin Gordon, and Peter Miller (Chicago: University of Chicago Press, 1991), 87–104. Foucault is often rightfully criticized for tracking historical change without identifying the relevant actors and their agency in creating these changes. This book uses Foucauldian insights but tries to avoid the aforementioned criticism by identifying the individual people who implement the changes discussed in this book and the prisons, study groups, and classes in which they do it.

12. "Governor Appoints Singletary Department of Corrections Secretary," *Correctional Compass* 18, no. 5 (May 1991): 1.

13. "Governor Appoints Singletary," 1.

14. "Governor Appoints Singletary," 4.

15. "How Budget Reductions Are Affecting the Department of Corrections," *Correctional Compass* 19, no. 1 (March 1992): 1.

16. Florida Department of Corrections, *1991/92 Annual Report* (Tallahassee, Florida), 91.

17. The inmate population increased by 1.7 percent in the 1991–92 fiscal year. See Florida Department of Corrections, "Population History Summary Table," accessed June 11, 2015, http://www.dc.state.fl.us/oth/timeline/pop.html.

18. Florida Department of Corrections, *1992/93 Annual Report* (Tallahassee, Florida), 1.

19. Wendy Brown, *In the Ruins of Neoliberalism: The Rise of Antidemocratic Politics in the West* (New York: Columbia University Press, 2019), 32.

20. Florida Department of Corrections, *1991/92 Annual Report*, 3.

21. Harry K. Singletary Jr., "Letter to the Governor and Members of the Florida Legislature," *1992/93 Annual Report*, Florida Department of Corrections, Bureau of Research, Planning, and Statistics, 1992: unnumbered page.

22. Tyrone Boyd (former Florida Department of Corrections head of chaplaincy services), in discussion with the author, April 2014. Boyd helped the DOC find cheaper toothpaste after a Muslim inmate complained that the toothpaste had pork in it.

23. Florida Department of Corrections, *1991/92 Annual Report*, 24.

24. Florida Department of Corrections, *1992/93 Annual Report*, 27.

25. Florida Department of Corrections, 27.

26. Frank Metcalf and Carolyn Metcalf (retired Florida Department of Corrections head chaplain and his wife), in discussion with the author, April 2014; and Tyrone Boyd (former Florida Department of Corrections head of chaplaincy services), in discussion with the author, April 2014.

27. Harry K. Singletary Jr., "Secretary's Message," *1996/97 Annual Report*, Florida Department of Corrections, 5.

28. Harry K. Singletary Jr., "Secretary's Message," *1994/95 Annual Report: The Guide to Corrections in Florida*, Florida Department of Corrections, 2.

29. As Katherine Beckett argued, "Representations of crime and punishment are not influenced by criminological knowledge, but rather are constructed for political gain, usually to support a wider political ideology" (Katherine Beckett, *Making Crime Pay: Law and Order in Contemporary American Politics* [New York: Oxford University Press, 1997], 42). Theodore Caplow and Jonathan Simon similarly argued that U.S. politicians have relied on a "governing through crime" strategy to win elections (Theodore Caplow and Jonathan Simon, "Understanding Prison Policy and Population Trends," in *Prisons*, vol. 26, ed. Michael Tonry and Joan Petersilia [Chicago: University of Chicago Press, 1999], 63–120). As Michael Tonry described the situation, "In order to win elections and thereby to govern,

politicians have addressed crime issues in polemical and stereotyped ways" (Michael Tonry, *Penal Reform in Overcrowded Times* [New York: Oxford University Press, 2001], 9).

30. Kristy Nabhan-Warren provided the most comprehensive history of the Cursillo movement in America. See Kristy Nabhan-Warren, *The Cursillo Movement in America: Catholics, Protestants, and Fourth-Day Spirituality* (Chapel Hill: University of North Carolina Press, 2013). Chapter 6, "Feeding Bodies and Souls," explicitly discusses Kairos Prison Ministry. For additional information about KPM, see Jonathan Burnside, *My Brother's Keeper: Faith-Based Units in Prison* (New York: Routledge, 2011).

31. "Timeline Horizon," personal correspondence from Ike Griffin. For additional information on KPM's Cursillos in Florida's prisons, see "Religious Events Well Received," *Correctional Compass* 2, no. 3 (October–November 1976): 5.

32. Ike Griffin (former executive director of Horizon Communities), in discussion with the author, February 2014.

33. For an extensive discussion of the "controls" and their impact on studies that address faith-based programming, see Alexander Volokh, "Do Faith-Based Prisons Work?," *Alabama Law Review* 63 (2011): 1–43.

34. Florida Statute 944.803, Committee Substitute for S.B. no. 310, 16–17. Full text available at State Archives and Archives of Florida, accessed August 26, 2020, http://laws.flrules.org/1997/78.

35. Florida Statute 944.803, 16.

36. Florida Statute 944.803, 17.

37. Florida Statute 944.803, 17.

38. Florida Statute 944.803, 17.

39. Florida Department of Corrections, Harry K. Singletary Jr., Secretary, *A Report of Faith-Based Programs in Correctional Facilities* (December 1997).

40. Specifically, the report stated, "Four attributes of religion make it especially attractive to the prison population. First, religion is explanatory, explaining both the society and the place of the prison in society, making a statement about the cultural roles of society and moral foundation supporting them. Second, religion is prescriptive, a discipline within a disciplined world, often incompatible with the discipline taught by the inmate code found in most prisons. Third, religion is experiential. Inmates are surrounded by constant reminders of their lack of freedom. The spiritual experiences of religion can be a dynamic symbol of freedom from worry about worldly matters. Fourth, religion is social. It is one of the positive social forces that helps inmates adjust to the prison environment" (Florida Department of Corrections, Harry K. Singletary Jr., Secretary, *Report of Faith-Based Programs in Correctional Facilities*, 1). Todd Clear and Marina Myhre identified these four attributes. See Todd R. Clear and Marina Myhre, "A Study of Religion in Prison," *International Association of Residential and Community Alternatives Journal on Community Corrections* 6, no. 6 (1995): 20–25. Scholars of religion might recognize that this understanding of religion resembles the seven dimensions of religion as articulated by Ninian Smart. For Smart, religion consists of doctrinal,

mythological, ethical, ritual, experiential, institutional, and material dimensions. See Ninian Smart, *Dimensions of the Sacred: An Anatomy of the World's Beliefs* (Berkeley: University of California Press, 1998).

41. Florida Department of Corrections, Harry K. Singletary Jr., Secretary, *Report of Faith-Based Programs in Correctional Facilities*, 6, 8.

42. Florida Department of Corrections, Harry K. Singletary Jr., Secretary, *Report of Faith-Based Programs in Correctional Facilities*, 14.

43. Allen Trovillion (former Florida state representative, former chair of the House Committee on Corrections), in discussion with the author, March 2014.

44. Florida House of Representatives Committee on Corrections, *Faith Based Programs in Florida Prisons* (1998), 26.

45. Florida House of Representatives Committee on Corrections, 26.

46. Florida House of Representatives Committee on Corrections, 27.

47. Multiple people who worked with Governor Jeb Bush suggested that Bush was an enthusiastic supporter of Florida's faith-based correctional program. Allison DeFoor documented one instance when Governor Bush personally intervened to address and assuage potential constitutional concerns (Allison DeFoor, "Creating a Church behind the Gates of Hell: A Prison Ministry Project in the Episcopal Diocese of Florida" [PhD diss., Florida Center for Theological Studies, 2005], app. G, 102–5).

48. For Secretary Michael Moore's thoughts on 10–20-Life, see "Secretary's Message: 'Public Safety Is Our Number One Mission,'" *Correctional Compass* (July–August 1999). Repr. in Florida Department of Corrections, *Annual Report for Fiscal Year 1998–99* (Tallahassee, Florida), 4.

49. "Michael Moore Named New Secretary," *Correctional Compass* 26, no. 2 (February 1999), 1.

50. "Michael Moore Named New Secretary," 1.

51. Michael Moore Named New Secretary," 1. Moore said, "I do not see the offender as a victim. . . . The worst thing we can do is to make excuses for criminal behavior. If we make excuses, we reinforce the negative behavior."

52. "Secretary's Message: 'Public Safety Is Our Number One Mission,'" *Correctional Compass* (July–August 1999). Reprinted in Florida Department of Corrections, *Annual Report for Fiscal Year 1998–99*.

53. See Florida Department of Corrections, *2006–2007 Annual Report* (Tallahassee, Florida), 38, 72.

54. "Kairos Prison Ministry at Tomoka CI," *Correctional Compass* (December 1999).

55. "Kairos Prison Ministry at Tomoka CI."

56. A full draft of the bill is available at http://archive.flsenate.gov/cgi-bin /View_Page.pl?File=sb1266er.html&Directory=session/2000/Senate/bills/billtext /html/&Tab=session&Submenu=1&p=2. The "Senate Staff Analysis and Economic Impact Statement" is available at Florida State Senate Archive, accessed August 26, 2020, http://archive.flsenate.gov/data/session/2000/Senate/bills/analysis/pdf /SB1266.cj.pdf.

57. *Task Force on Self-Inflicted Crimes: Final Report Submitted to the Governor, the Senate President, and the Speaker of the House*, State of Florida (January 1, 2001), 5.

58. *Task Force on Self-Inflicted Crimes*, 5.

59. *Task Force on Self-Inflicted Crimes*, 20.

60. The authors of the bill requested that I refer to them as "The Staff at the Senate Criminal Justice Committee." The Staff at the Senate Criminal Justice Committee (Florida State Senate Criminal Justice Committee), in conversation with the author, May 2014.

61. Quoted in Advisory Task Force on Faith-Based Community Service Groups, *Faith in Action . . . A New Vision for Church-State Cooperation in Texas* (December 1996), v.

62. George W. Bush, Executive Order GWB 96–5, *Relating to Faith-Based and Community Groups* (May 2, 1996), https://lrl.texas.gov/scanned/govdocs/George%20W%20Bush/1996/GWB96-5.pdf.

63. The exact verbiage called for the task force to "(i) examine the role of faith-based programs in Texas and determine how Texas can best create an environment in which these organizations can flourish and most effectively help those in need; (ii) determine which state laws, regulations, or procedures impede the effectiveness of such organizations; and (iii) provide specific recommendations as to how Texas law could best accommodate the programs and activities of the affected community organizations" (Bush, Executive Order GWB 96–5, *Relating to Faith-Based and Community Groups*, 1).

64. Bush, Executive Order GWB 96–5, *Relating to Faith-Based and Community Groups*, 2.

65. Advisory Task Force on Faith-Based Community Service Groups, *Faith in Action . . . A New Vision for Church-State Cooperation in Texas* (December 1996), ii.

66. The task force's membership roster reads like a "who's who" of influential and politically connected advocates for FBOs in Texas. With the exception of one Jewish participant, all the members are Catholics and Protestants. Without exception, every task force minister either was an ordained minister or was affiliated with a faith-based social service provider, and many were both. For example, Rev. Msgr. Dermot Noel Brosnan was a Catholic priest who founded Patrician Movement, a faith-based drug treatment center. (For a comprehensive list of the task force members and their backgrounds, see *The Texas Faith-Based Initiative at Five Years: Warning Signs as President Bush Expands Texas-Style Program at National Level*, Texas Freedom Network, 2002, app. B, http://www.tfn.org/site/DocServer/TFN_CC_REPORT-FINAL.pdf?docID=201.) Another member, "Brother Cecil Hawkins," was an ordained minister and director of African American Men of Peace, a faith-based social service provider for at-risk youth ("Governor Bush Announces New Task Force on Faith-Based Programs," Press Release, Office of Governor George W. Bush, May 2, 1996). These men are representative of the other members of the task force, as they were active proponents of FBOs. Collectively, this task force fulfilled the obligations outlined in Governor Bush's executive order.

67. "This virtue," they wrote, "which rests at the heart of the Second Commandment's call to love your neighbor, is inseparable from the call to love God. It is direct, personal, immediate; not something that can be farmed out. Like the Good Samaritan, we are called to 'suffer with' our broken brothers and sisters, not to sub-contract

with paid professional substitutes" (Advisory Task Force on Faith-Based Community Service Groups, *Faith in Action*, vii).

68. Advisory Task Force on Faith-Based Community Service Groups, *Faith in Action*, vii. The bifurcation of government programs as bureaucratic and faith-based programs as personal and a more authentic form of compassion is a common idea among proponents of faith-based reforms. For example, John DiIulio, the first director of President George W. Bush's White House Office of Faith-Based and Community Initiatives, similarly argued this point. See John DiIulio, "With Unconditional Love," *Sojourners* (September–October 1997), vii.

69. Burnside, *My Brother's Keeper*, 242. See also Michael Eisenberg and Brittani Trusty, *Overview of the InnerChange Freedom Initiative: The Faith-Based Prison Program within the Texas Department of Criminal Justice* (Austin: Criminal Justice Policy Council, 2002).

70. S.B. 912, Sess. of 2001 (Flo. 2001): 3–4. Full text of S.B. 912 is available at http://archive.flsenate.gov/data/session/2001/Senate/bills/billtext/pdf/s0912c2.pdf.

71. S.B. 912, Sess. of 2001, 3.

72. S.B. 912, Sess. of 2001, 6.

73. S.B. 912, Sess. of 2001, 37.

74. Florida's state Senate voted in favor of the CRA on March 22, 2001, by a vote of thirty-six yeas to no nays, with four abstentions. On May 4, the House approved the bill by a vote of 111 yeas, three nays, and six abstentions. For a full summary of the bill's history, see http://archive.flsenate.gov/Session/index.cfm?Mode=Bills&Sub Menu=1&Tab=session&BI_Mode=ViewBillInfo&BillNum=0912&Chamber=Senate &Year=2001&Title=-%3EBill%2520Info%3AS%25200912-%3ESession%25202001.

75. "Historical Summary of Faith Based Dorm Programs in Florida," document provided by Chaplain Alex Taylor.

76. "Faith and Character Based Residential Programs," Florida's Department of Corrections, http://www.dc.state.fl.us/oth/faith/.

77. Thomas B. Pfankuch, "Corrections Chief Moore Resigns," *Florida Times-Union*, December 5, 2002, http://jacksonville.com/tu-online/stories/120502/met_11144687 .shtml.

78. Unless otherwise noted, all biographical information regarding James Crosby obtained from the following sources: James Crosby (former Florida Department of Corrections secretary), in discussion with the author, June 2014; and "Jimmy Crosby— Personal Testimony," video formerly posted on YouTube. Several of my sources referred to Crosby as a "good ol' boy," in the sense that he comes from a small town and talks with a country twang.

79. James Crosby (former Florida Department of Corrections secretary), in discussion with the author, June 2014.

80. Statistics compiled from Florida Department of Corrections, *Florida Department of Corrections 2002–2003 Annual Report* (Tallahassee, Florida).

81. According to the DOC, "Television coverage included major national outlets such as CNN and Fox News, and MSNBC as well as television stations across the state of Florida. Newspaper coverage included major dailies such as *New York Times*, *Washington Post*, all Florida papers and daily papers from Aberdeen South Dakota

to Santa Fe, New Mexico." "What Other People Are Saying," *Correctional Compass* (January–February 2004).

82. William Wright (chaplain at Lawtey Correctional Institution), in discussion with the author, June 2014.

83. Paul Pinkham, "Bush Dedicates Nation's First Faith-Based Prison," *Florida Times-Union,* December 25, 2003, http://jacksonville.com/tu-online/stories/122503 /met_14389635.shtml.

84. Pinkham, "Bush Dedicates Nation's First Faith-Based Prison."

85. "Faith-Based Florida Prison Is Dedicated," *Los Angeles Times,* December 26, 2003, http://articles.latimes.com/2003/dec/26/nation/na-prison26.

86. "US Gets First Faith-Based Prison," *Al Jazeera,* December 25, 2003, http:// www.aljazeera.com/archive/2003/12/2008410143621745338.html.

87. "US Gets First Faith-Based Prison."

88. See Abbie Boudreau and Scott Zamost, "Ex-Florida Prison Boss: Drunken Orgies Tainted System," CNN, February 22, 2008, http://www.cnn.com/2008/CRIME /02/11/prison.boss/index.html?eref=yahoo; and "Bush: FBI Asked Me to Wait Before Firing Prisons Head," *St. Augustine Record,* July 11, 2006, http://staugustine.com /stories/071106/state_3950862.shtml.

89. John-Thor Dahlburg, "Web of Scandal Ensnares Florida Prison System," *Los Angeles Times,* April 2, 2006, http://articles.latimes.com/2006/apr/02/nation/na -prisons2.

90. Dahlburg.

91. James Crosby (former Florida Department of Corrections secretary), in discussion with the author, June 2014.

92. James Crosby (former Florida Department of Corrections secretary), in discussion with the author.

93. "DOC Opens Female Faith-Based Prison," *Correctional Compass* (May–June 2004).

94. Steve Bousquet, "Sadness, Resentment at Closing of Hillsborough Prison," *Tampa Bay Times,* March 19, 2012, https://www.tampabay.com/news/publicsafety /crime/sadness-resentment-at-closing-of-hillsborough-prison/1220816/.

95. Danny Valentine, "Faith, Character Program Introduced at Women's Prison in Hernando," *Tampa Bay Times,* October 9, 2013, https://www.tampabay.com/news /publicsafety/faith-character-program-introduced-at-womens-prison-in-hernando /2146363/?template=amp%3FoutputType%3Damp%3FoutputType%3Damp ?outputType=amp.

96. David Crary, "Faith-Based Prisons Multiply," *USA Today,* October 13, 2007, http://www.usatoday.com/news/religion/2007-10-13-prisons_N.htm.

97. James Holguin, "Rehabilitation through Religion," *CBS Evening News,* June 20, 2005, http://www.cbsnews.com/news/rehabilitation-through-religion/.

98. See "Faith-Based Prison Programs," Americans United for the Separation of Church and State, accessed June 11, 2015, http://www.au.org/issues/faith-based -prison-programs.

99. See Winnifred Sullivan, *Prison Religion: Faith-Based Reform and the Constitution* (Princeton, NJ: Princeton University Press, 2009). Rev. Barry Lynn (executive

director of Americans United for the Separation of Church and State), in discussion with the author, August 2014.

100. At least one law professor disagrees with this decision. See James A. Davids, "Putting Faith in Prison Programs, and Its Constitutionality under Thomas Jefferson's Faith-Based Initiative," *Ave Maria Law Review* 6, no. 2 (2008): 341–87.

101. Press release, "Governor Bush Dedicates Florida's Third Character and Faith–Based Prison," Florida Department of Corrections, November 23, 2005, http://www.dc.state.fl.us/secretary/press/2005/FaithBasedWakullaPR.html.

Chapter Three

1. Information regarding the transition of Lawtey Correctional Institution (CI) to the nation's first faith-based prison obtained from James Crosby (former Florida Department of Corrections secretary), in discussion with the author, June 2014; William Wright (chaplain at Lawtey Correctional Institution), in discussion with the author, June 2014; and Alex Taylor (head chaplain, Florida Department of Corrections), in discussion with the author, February 2014.

2. Many of the incarcerated men at Lawtey CI contend that the prison has so much class space because it used to be a school for African Americans during the era of segregation. I was not able to confirm this rumor, but it is a common rumor in the prison. Some of the incarcerated men even claimed that they were incarcerated at Lawtey CI with an inmate who used to be a student at the school when he was younger and who later served time in the prison.

3. Journalists noted that faith-based correctional facilities in Texas exclude sex offenders and incarcerated people with bad disciplinary records. See "Faith-Based Prisons Multiply across U.S.," Associated Press, October 13, 2007, https://www .foxnews.com/story/faith-based-prisons-multiply-across-u-s.

4. Nancy G. LaVigne, Diana Brazzell, and Kevonne Small, *Evaluation of Florida's Faith- and Character-Based Institutions* (Washington, DC: Urban Institute Justice Policy Center, 2007), 41.

5. Émile Durkheim suggested that systems of regulation and the means of punishing transgressors are necessary preconditions for stable societies (see Émile Durkheim, *The Rules of Sociological Method* [New York: Free Press, 1964]; and Émile Durkheim, *Suicide, A Study in Sociology* [Glencoe, IL: Free Press, 1951]). These systems of regulation marginalize and punish people who threaten or potentially undermine dominant values and goals. More recently, Stanley Fish reached similar conclusions when he specifically addressed the issue of religious toleration. Fish argued that proponents of religious toleration "are always performing the exclusionary acts for which they stigmatize others" (Stanley Fish, "Mission Impossible: Settling the Just Bounds between Church and State," *Columbia Law Review* 97, no. 8 [December 1997]: 2256–57). But unlike Durkheim, Fish expected people to know what they were doing. He continued, "I do not fault them for so performing, but for thinking and claiming to be doing something else" (Fish, "Mission Impossible," 2257).

Wendy Brown provided additional insight when she argued not only that pluralism and toleration are discriminatory but that regimes of pluralism tend to privilege the Protestants who often control the discourses about religion, as they create a regime of toleration that privileges Protestants' understandings of religion. (Admittedly, Wendy Brown is describing religious toleration; however, her insights apply to religious pluralism as well. See Wendy Brown, *Regulating Aversion: Tolerance in the Age of Identity and Empire* [Princeton, NJ: Princeton University Press, 2006]). According to Brown, religious toleration is inherently exclusionary, as it "designates certain beliefs and practices as civilized and others as barbaric, both at home and abroad; it operates from a conceit of neutrality that is actually thick with bourgeois Protestant norms" (Brown, 7). Collectively, these scholars provide theoretical insights that we can apply to the regime of religious pluralism mandated by the Supreme Court and implemented in Florida's pluralistic correctional facilities. For additional critiques of religious pluralism, see Timothy Fitzgerald, *The Ideology of Religious Studies* (New York: Oxford University Press, 2000); and Russell T. McCutcheon, *Manufacturing Religion: The Discourse on Sui Generis Religion and the Politics of Nostalgia* (New York: Oxford University Press, 1997).

6. See Mark Blyth, *Great Transformations: Economic Ideas and Institutional Change in the Twentieth Century* (Cambridge: Cambridge University Press, 2002).

7. In this regard, neoliberalism conflicts with ordoliberalism, which explicitly calls for government intervention to create and sustain the economy.

8. Eddy is paraphrasing John Howard. See Jennifer Graber, *The Furnace of Affliction: Prisons & Religion in Antebellum America* (Chapel Hill: University of North Carolina Press, 2011), 35.

9. J. C. Powell, *The American Siberia: Or, Fourteen Years' Experience in a Southern Convict Camp* (Chicago: Homewood, 1891), 8.

10. Powell, 10.

11. Powell, 8.

12. For a description of these boxes, see Norman R. Yetman, ed., *When I Was a Slave: Memoirs from the Slave Narrative Collection* (New York: Dover, 2002).

13. Powell, *American Siberia*, 9.

14. Greg Allen, "Record Number of Inmate Deaths Has Florida Prisons on the Defensive," National Public Radio, March 18, 2015, http://www.npr.org/2015/03/18/393862617/record-number-of-inmate-deaths-has-florida-prisons-on-the-defensive.

15. Julie K. Brown and Mary Ellen Klas, "Inmate Reports Threats by Guard, Turns up Dead," *Miami Herald*, October 7, 2014, http://www.miamiherald.com/news/state/florida/article2564576.html.

16. Julie K. Brown, "Behind Bars, a Brutal and Unexplained Death," *Miami Herald*, May 17, 2014, http://www.miamiherald.com/news/local/community/miami-dade/article1964620.html.

17. Julie K. Brown, "Prisoner: I Cleaned Up Skin of Inmate Scalded in Shower; Human-Rights Groups Call for Federal Intervention," *Miami Herald*, June 25, 2014, http://www.miamiherald.com/news/local/community/miami-dade/article1972693.html.

18. Ed Payne, "KKK-Linked Florida Prison Guards," CNN, April 3, 2015, http://www.cnn.com/2015/04/03/us/florida-kkk-corrections-murder-plot/.

19. Several scholars noted that prison administrators routinely acknowledge that correctional staff needs to treat the incarcerated with respect if faith-based rehabilitation is going to work. See Michael Hallett, Joshua Hays, Byron Johnson, S. J. Jang, and Grant Duwe, "'First Stop Dying': Angola's Christian Seminary as Positive Criminology," *International Journal of Offender Therapy and Comparative Criminology* 61, no. 4 (2015): 1–19.

20. LaVigne, Brazzell, and Small, *Evaluation of Florida's Faith- and Character-Based Institutions*, vii.

21. Call-outs are mass movements of inmates.

22. Steve Fox (chaplain at Wakulla CI), in discussion with the author, May 2014. The emphasis on faith is misleading, as if the correctional officers resemble the rest of Florida's residents in that they are overwhelmingly religious (by common definitions of religion, that is). According to the Pew Research Forum, 76 percent of Floridians identify with a specific religion (Pew Research Forum, "Adults in Florida," accessed September 16, 2020, https://www.pewforum.org/religious-landscape -study/state/florida/). Only 7 percent identify as agnostic or atheist, leaving the remaining 17 percent who would most likely identify as either spiritual or religious but not affiliated with any particular religious group or denomination. That potentially means that 93 percent of Floridians self-identify as religious or spiritual. So, either the bulk of Florida's correctional officers come from the 7 percent who identify as atheist or agnostic or correctional officers reflect the religious and spiritual identities consistent with the larger population and are therefore overwhelmingly religious. Assuming the latter is correct, when Chaplain Fox said that he used to choose "men and women of faith," he most likely chose religious correctional officers who embraced the FCBIs' regime of rehabilitation, while he excluded the religious correctional officers who rejected it and who continued to harass, undermine, and even abuse the incarcerated.

23. Susan Davis (assistant warden at Lawtey CI), in discussion with the author, May 2014.

24. Major Brown (correctional officer at Gulf Coast CI), in discussion with the author, June 2014.

25. River (Wiccan volunteer), in discussion with the author, August 2014.

26. For an analysis of prison chaplains in the United States, see Winnifred Sullivan, *A Ministry of Presence: Chaplaincy, Spiritual Care, and the Law* (Chicago: University of Chicago Press, 2014); and Pew Research Center, *Religion in Prisons: A 50-State Survey of Prison Chaplains* (Washington, DC: Pew Forum on Religion and Public Life, 2012).

27. Pew Research Center, *Religion in Prisons*.

28. For a summary of prison chaplains' responsibilities, see Jody L. Sundt, Harry R. Dammer, and Francis T. Cullen, "The Role of the Prison Chaplain in Rehabilitation," *Journal of Offender Rehabilitation* 35, no. 3, 4 (2002): 59–86.

29. William Wright (chaplain at Lawtey CI), in discussion with the author, June 2014.

30. David Smith (chaplain at Gulf Coast CI), in discussion with the author, June 2014.

31. David Smith (chaplain at Gulf Coast CI), in discussion with the author, June 2014.

32. Interview with Alex Taylor, "Forgiveness and Restoration," *Pentecostal Evangel.*

33. For a brief discussion of evangelical hostility toward religious pluralism, see Sean McCloud, *American Possessions: Fighting Demons in the Contemporary United States* (New York: Oxford University Press, 2015), chap. 1.

34. Joshua Dubler described prison chapels as perhaps the most religiously diverse space on the planet. See Joshua Dubler, *Down in the Chapel: Religious Life in an American Prison* (New York: Farrar, Straus, and Giroux, 2013).

35. One chaplain, who wished to remain anonymous, spoke of having to be converted to pluralism. His change of heart, so to speak, continues to be a problem in his church, where many of his friends believe he is sinning.

36. LaVigne, Brazzell, and Small, *Evaluation of Florida's Faith- and Character-Based Institutions,* 10.

37. Florida Department of Corrections, "Religious Diversity in Florida's Faith and Character-Based Institutions." Accessed online April 11, 2012, http://www.dc.state.fl.us/oth/faith/stats.html.

38. Florida Department of Corrections, "Faith and Character–Based Residential Programs Procedure 506.033" (March 23, 2004), 6.

39. Florida Department of Corrections, *Faith and Character Based Program Phase One: Workbook.*

40. Alex Taylor (head chaplain, Florida Department of Corrections), in discussion with the author, February 2014.

41. See "Faith Formation," *Faith and Character Based Program Phase One: Workbook,* 39–55.

42. "Faith Formation," 48–50. Italics appear in original.

43. Alex Taylor (head chaplain, Florida Department of Corrections), in discussion with the author, February 2014.

44. According to Head Chaplain Alex Taylor, the DOC had excess beds only when it converted conventional correctional facilities into FCBIs. There are occasionally fewer incarcerated people on the waitlist than there are beds.

45. LaVigne, Brazzell, and Small, *Evaluation of Florida's Faith- and Character-Based Institutions,* 10.

46. LaVigne, Brazzell, and Small, 10.

47. LaVigne, Brazzell, and Small, 10n10.

48. Karen Moffett (former other personnel services chaplain at Lawtey CI), in discussion with the author, May 2014.

49. Daniel Crawford (classification officer at Lawtey CI), in discussion with the author, May 2014.

50. Karen Moffett (former other personnel services chaplain at Lawtey CI), in discussion with the author, May 2014. OPS chaplains are hourly employees with no benefits.

51. Horizon Communities in Prison, *Participant's Manual: Emphasizing Growth through Transition and Education in the Rehabilitation Process,* 24.

52. Horizon Communities in Prison, 24–26.

53. For a summary of the Matthew 18 process, see Horizon Communities in Prison, *Participant's Manual*, 3, 32.

54. Daniel Crawford (classification officer at Lawtey CI), in discussion with the author, May 2014.

55. Horizon Communities in Prison, *Participant's Manual*, 24 (capitalization appears in the original). The "Horizon Faith and Character-Based Programs Orientation Awareness Form," a document that informs new inmates of Horizon's expectations, states, "I ALSO UNDERSTAND THAT AS OF JULY 2, 2020 THE HORIZON FAITH AND CHARACTER BASED PROGRAMS WILL BE TOBACCO FREE. I WILL BE ALLOWED TO PURCHASE THESE PRODUCTS BUT IF I AM CAUGHT USING THEM INSIDE THE BUILDING I WILL BE REMOVED FROM THE PROGRAM IMMEDIATELY" (capitalization appears in the original).

56. Alice Goffman described "clean people" who are not incarcerated. Many of her insights and descriptions about these people apply to the incarcerated as well. See chap. 7 in Alice Goffman, *On the Run: Fugitive Life in an American City* (Chicago: University of Chicago Press, 2014).

57. "Responding to Sexual Abuse of Inmates in Custody: Addressing the Needs of Men, Women, and Gender Nonconforming Populations," National PREA Resource Center, April 2014, https://www.prearesourcecenter.org/sites/default/files/content/mod_10.pdf.

58. Brenda V. Smith, "Analyzing Prison Sex: Reconciling Self-Expression with Safety," *Human Rights Brief* 13, no. 3 (2006): 17–22.

59. David Merritt Johns, "Free Willy: Should Prison Inmates Have the Right to Masturbate?," *Slate*, January 12, 2012, https://slate.com/technology/2012/01/should-prison-inmates-have-the-right-to-masturbate.html.

60. Faithe Liburd (chaplain at Lowell Annex), in discussion with the author, June 2014.

61. See Human Rights Watch, "Ill-Equipped: U.S. Prisons and Offenders with Mental Illness" (New York: Human Rights Watch, 2003). For additional information on mental illness and the incarcerated, see also Paula M. Ditton, *Mental Health and Treatment of Inmates and Probationers* (Washington, DC: U.S. Department of Justice, Bureau of Justice Statistics, 1999). Joan Petersilia argued that mental illness is itself criminalized as a result of these changes. See Joan Petersilia, *When Prisoners Come Home: Parole and Prisoner Reentry* (New York: Oxford University Press, 2003), 36–40.

62. Stories like this convinced several researchers to conclude that Florida's FCBIs do not address mental health issues. See LaVigne, Brazzell, and Small, *Evaluation of Florida's Faith- and Character-Based Institutions*, 27.

63. This statistic is confirmed by multiple classification officers. For example, Gloria White (classification officer at Hernando CI), in discussion with the author, June 2014; and Daniel Crawford (classification officer at Lawtey CI), in discussion with the author, May 2014.

64. Inmates might voluntarily transfer out of a FCBI for several reasons. For example, they might want to be closer to a sick relative or to other family members,

or they might want to focus on vocational rehabilitation instead of faith-based rehabilitation.

65. Michael Crews (former secretary of Florida's Department of Corrections), in discussion with the author, February 2014.

66. Steve Fox (chaplain at Wakulla CI), in discussion with the author, May 2014.

67. Ike Griffin (former executive director, Kairos Prison Ministry), email to the author, February 14, 2014.

68. Ike Griffin, in discussion with the author, February 2014.

69. The decision in *Americans United for Separation of Church and State, et al., Appellees, v. Prison Fellowship Ministry, Inc., et al., Appellants* 509 F.3d 406 (2007), provides a court's most comprehensive analysis of the legality of faith-based correctional facilities.

70. Barry Reddish (warden, Lawtey CI), in discussion with the author, May 2014.

Chapter Four

1. Michel Foucault, "4 April 1979," in *The Birth of Biopolitics: Lectures at the Collège de France, 1978–1979* (New York: Picador, 2010), 267–90.

2. Antonio Negri, *The Politics of Subversion: A Manifesto for the Twenty-First Century*, trans. James Newell (Oxford: Polity, 1989).

3. Donald Clemmer, *The Prison Community* (New York: Rinehart, 1958). See also Geoffrey Hunt, Stephanie Riegel, Tomas Morales, and Dan Waldorf, "Changes in Prison Culture: Prison Gangs and the Case of the 'Pepsi Generation,'" *Social Problems* 40, no. 3 (August 1993): 398–409. Gresham Sykes noted that the incarcerated share a particular code, which itself seeks to undermine correctional officers' authority (see Gresham Sykes, *The Society of Captives: A Study of a Maximum Security Prison* [Princeton, NJ: Princeton University Press, 2007]). This code itself is part of what Clemmer called prisonization.

4. David Skarbek, "Governance and Prison Gangs," *American Political Science Review* 105, no. 4 (November 2011): 702–16; and David Skarbek, *The Social Order of the Underworld: How Prison Gangs Govern the American Penal System* (New York: Oxford University Press, 2014).

5. For a discussion of "unwritten" rules and codes of conduct in American prisons, see Earlonne Woods, Antwan Williams, and Nigel Poor, "Unwritten," *Ear Hustle*, podcast audio, September 13, 2017. Additionally, David Skarbek discussed the role that race and ethnicity play in these unwritten rules. See Skarbek, *Social Order of the Underworld*.

6. Interview with Alex Taylor, "Forgiveness and Restoration," *Pentecostal Evangel*. Additional information obtained from Alex Taylor (head chaplain, Florida Department of Corrections), in discussion with the author, February 2014.

7. Jody L. Sundt, Harry R. Dammer, and Francis T. Cullen, "The Role of the Prison Chaplain in Rehabilitation," *Journal of Offender Rehabilitation* 35, no. 3/4 (2002): 72.

8. See also Nancy G. LaVigne, Diana Brazzell, and Kevonne Small, *Evaluation of Florida's Faith- and Character-Based Institutions* (Washington, DC: Urban Institute

Justice Policy Center, 2007), 26. Robert Maginnis surveyed prison wardens and found that they overwhelmingly prefer literacy programs, educational programs, drug treatment programs, and vocational training. See Robert L. Maginnis, "Faith-Based Prison Programs Cut Costs and Recidivism," *Insight* (Washington, DC: Family Research Council, 2005).

9. Ike Griffin (former executive director, Kairos Prison Ministry), in discussion with the author, February 2014.

10. Dale White (founder, The Living Harvest), in discussion with the author, January 2018.

11. Byron Johnson, *More God, Less Crime: Why Faith Matters and How It Could Matter More* (West Conshohocken, PA: Templeton, 2011), 166.

12. Allison DeFoor (proponent of Florida's faith-based correctional program), in conversation with the author, June 2014.

13. For an abbreviated list of scholars who acknowledge this, see A. Y. Branch, *Faith and Action: Implementation of the National Faith-Based Initiative for High-Risk Youth* (Philadelphia: Public/Private Ventures, 2002); Johnson, *More God, Less Crime*; and LaVigne, Brazzell, and Small, *Evaluation of Florida's Faith- and Character-Based Institutions.*

A recent study of Florida's FCBIs even concluded that the secular or "character-based" classes are more popular than religious programming, and it similarly documents that the incarcerated want more of these programs (LaVigne, Brazzell, and Small, *Evaluation of Florida's Faith- and Character-Based Institutions,* 26).

Scholars and proponents of faith-based reform do not even agree on whether a program is faith based or secular. See Daniel P. Mears, Caterina G. Roman, Ashley Wolff, and Janeen Buck, "Faith-Based Efforts to Improve Prisoner Reentry: Assessing the Logic and Evidence," *Journal of Criminal Justice* 34 (2006): 351–67; and David R. Hodge and Jason Pittman, "Faith-Based Drug and Alcohol Treatment Providers: An Exploratory Study of Texan Providers," *Journal of Social Service Research* 30 (2003): 19–40. For this reason, some scholars advocate for the term "faith-related" instead of "faith-based" (Steven Rathgeb Smith and Michael R. Sosin, "The Varieties of Faith-Related Agencies," *Public Administration Review* 61 [2001]: 651–70). Some organizations classified by the White House Office of Faith-Based and Community Initiatives even reject the label "faith-based" (see Gary Stern, "Faith-Based Confusion," *[New York] Journal News,* January 8, 2006).

14. LaVigne, Brazzell, and Small, *Evaluation of Florida's Faith- and Character-Based Institutions.*

15. The possible exception to this might be a version of the in-prison seminary programs that are growing in American prisons. These seminaries ordain the incarcerated, and some even offer degree programs. I am not aware of any FCBI having an explicit partnership with an organization that offers these programs, although it is possible that one or more do.

16. Scholars have argued culture, laws, and policies influence and empower neoliberalism. For example, Libby Adler and Janey Halley argued that child support laws empower neoliberalism. See Libby Adler and Janey Halley, "'You Play, You Pay': Feminists and Child Support Enforcement in the United States," in *Gover-*

nance Feminism: Notes from the Field, ed. Janet Halley, Prabha Kotiswaran, Rachel Rebouché, and Hila Shamir (Minneapolis: University of Minnesota Press, 2019), 287–316.

17. Florida Department of Corrections, "Faith and Character-Based Completion Worksheet," form number DC5-323.

18. Kristy Nabhan-Warren, *The Cursillo Movement in America: Catholics, Protestants, and Fourth-Day Spirituality* (Chapel Hill: University of North Carolina Press, 2013), 2.

19. Kairos of Indiana, "Kairos Cookie Recipe," accessed September 16, 2020, http://www.kairosofindiana.org/docs/cookies.pdf.

20. Ike Griffin (former executive director, Kairos Prison Ministry), in discussion with the author, February 2014.

21. Nabhan-Warren, *Cursillo Movement in America*, 86.

22. Friedrich A. Hayek, *The Constitution of Liberty* (Chicago: University of Chicago Press, 1960), 206.

23. Margaret Thatcher, interviewed by *Women's Own*, 1987.

24. Ike Griffin (former executive director, Kairos Prison Ministry), in discussion with the author, February 2014.

25. Embracing capitalism is more common and the focus of academic research in American religion. See William E. Connolly, *Capitalism and Christianity, American Style* (Durham, NC: Duke University Press, 2008); Darren Dochuk, *Anointed with Oil: How Christianity and Crude Made Modern America* (New York: Basic Books, 2019); Darren Dochuk, *From Bible Belt to Sunbelt: Plain-Folk Religion, Grassroots Politics, and the Rise of Evangelical Conservatism* (New York: W. W. Norton, 2010); Nicole C. Kirk, *Wanamaker's Temple: The Business of Religion in an Iconic Department Store* (New York: New York University Press, 2018); Linda Kitz, *Between Jesus and the Market: The Emotions that Matter in Right-Wing America* (Durham, NC: Duke University Press, 1997); Kevin M. Kruse, *One Nation under God: How Corporate America Invented Christian America* (New York: Basic Books, 2016); Craig Martin, *Capitalizing Religion: Ideology and the Opiate of the Bourgeoisie* (New York: Bloomsbury, 2014); Bethany Moreton, *To Serve God and Wal-Mart: The Making of Christian Free Enterprise* (Cambridge, MA: Harvard University Press, 2009); and Amanda Porterfield, Darren E. Grem, and John Corrigan, eds., *The Business Turn in American Religious History* (New York: Oxford University Press, 2017).

26. Wendy Brown described neoliberalism's emphasis on the family when she wrote, "As social investments in education, housing, health, child care, and social security are decreased, the family is retasked with providing for every kind of dependent—the young, the old, the infirm, the unemployed, the indebted student, or the depressed or addicted adult" (Wendy Brown, *In the Ruins of Neoliberalism: The Rise of Antidemocratic Politics in the West* [New York: Columbia University Press, 2019], 39).

27. Bruce Western, "The Impact of Incarceration on Wage Mobility and Inequality," *American Sociological Review* 67, no. 4 (August 2002): 526–46.

28. The domains also naturalize the "self" as a project constantly in need of development. According to Carla Freeman, this notion of the self is itself an extension of

neoliberalism. See Carla Freeman, *Entrepreneurial Selves: Neoliberal Respectability and the Making of the Caribbean Middle Class* (Durham, NC: Duke University Press, 2014). See also Nikolas Rose, *Governing the Soul: The Shaping of the Private Self* (London: Routledge, 1990).

29. Allison DeFoor (proponent of Florida's faith-based correctional program), in conversation with the author, June 2014. Personal correspondence, June 30, 2017.

30. Hugh MacMillan and Allison DeFoor confirmed this story.

31. Kyle McQuillen (transition coordinator, Horizon Communities), in discussion with the author, August 2014.

32. For additional information on hierarchies in corrections, see John Irwin, *Prisons in Turmoil* (Boston: Little, Brown, 1980). Lee H. Bowker argued that one's crime determines one's place in the hierarchy (*Prisoner Subcultures* [Lexington, MA: Lexington Books, 1977]), and Donald Clemmer argued that there is limited room for mobility in this hierarchy (Donald Clemmer, "Informal Inmate Groups," in *The Sociology of Punishment and Correction*, ed. Norman Johnston, Leonard Savitz, and Marvin E. Wolfgang [Toronto: John Wiley & Sons, 1970], 423–28).

33. Residents in FCBIs are aware of this stigma, and they acknowledge that some child molesters are incarcerated in FCBIs, but they contend that child molesters are proportionately incarcerated in conventional and faith-based facilities.

34. Initially, I was skeptical of the claim that residents in FCBI dorms were constantly harassed and called chomos; however, over time, I came to believe them. Not only did multiple people in FCBI dorms repeat that, but a colleague at Florida State University had a family member incarcerated in a Florida prison, and my colleague often talked to the family member about my research. According to my colleague, when her family member first learned about my research, the family member commented, "Oh, he's researching the chomos!" My colleague subsequently revisited that idea with her family member after I heard it directly from the incarcerated, and the family member, too, acknowledged that it is a common idea.

35. See Jessica J. B. Wyse, "Rehabilitating Criminal Selves: Gendered Strategies in Community," *Gender and Society* 27, no. 2 (April 2013): 231–55.

36. See Don Sabo, Terry A. Kupers, and Willie London, eds., *Prison Masculinities* (Philadelphia: Temple University Press, 2001).

37. Barry Reddish (warden, Lawtey CI), in discussion with the author, May 2014.

38. As Judith Butler argued, people in economically precarious situations are particularly vulnerable to neoliberal economics. See Gareth Davies, "Judith Butler Speaks about Vulnerability and Resistance," *Warscapes* (blog), February 16, 2015, http://www.warscapes.com/blog/judith-butler-speaks-about-vulnerability-and-resistance.

Chapter Five

1. See Ray Sanchez, "Charleston Church Shooting: Who Is Dylann Roof?," CNN, December 16, 2016, https://www.cnn.com/2015/06/19/us/charleston-church-shooting-suspect/index.html.

2. This quote resonates with the work of Robert Fuller, who persuasively argued that conservative Protestants have evoked the Antichrist against liberalism to further their religious, political, economic, and sociocultural reforms. See Robert Fuller, *Naming the Antichrist: The History of an American Obsession* (New York: Oxford University Press, 1995). Jason Bivins contends that shifts in capitalism itself fuel the fear that animates the New Christian Right. See Jason C. Bivins, *Religion of Fear: The Politics of Horror in Conservative Evangelicalism* (New York: Oxford University Press, 2008).

3. See Stephanie Gaskill, "Moral Rehabilitation: Religion, Race, and Reform in America's incarceration Capital" (PhD diss., University of North Carolina at Chapel Hill, 2017).

4. See Winnifred Sullivan, *Prison Religion: Faith-Based Reform and the Constitution* (Princeton, NJ: Princeton University Press, 2009); and Tanya Erzen, *God in Captivity: The Rise of Faith-Based Prison Ministries in the Age of Mass Incarceration* (Boston: Beacon, 2017).

5. Catherine Albanese, *American Religious History: A Bibliographic Essay* (Washington, DC: U.S. Department of State, Bureau of Educational and Cultural Affairs, 2002).

6. See, for example, Tracy Fessenden, *Culture and Redemption: Religion, the Secular, and American Literature* (Princeton, NJ: Princeton University Press, 2013); and David Sehat, *The Myth of American Religious Freedom* (New York: Oxford University Press, 2011).

7. This analysis does not imply that this programming is more restrictive than what is colloquially called secular programming. As Joan Wallach Scott persuasively argued, discourses of secularity can contain their own restrictions on issues like gender, sexuality, and religion. Instead of arguing that faith-based spaces are more restrictive, this chapter documents the convergence of faith-based programming and deregulation, specifically as it empowers members of the New Christian Right. See Joan Wallach Scott, *Sex and Secularism* (Princeton, NJ: Princeton University Press, 2017).

8. The statistics on the categories are 85 percent male, average of fifty-seven years old, 70 percent white, and 85 percent Christian (44 percent are evangelical Protestants). Fifty-three percent describe themselves as conservative on social issues and 55 percent on political issues. Pew Research Center, *Religion in Prisons: A 50-State Survey of Prison Chaplains* (Washington, DC: Pew Forum on Religion and Public Life, 2012), 12.

9. See Sullivan, *Prison Religion*.

10. Edward L. Queen, *In the South the Baptists Are the Center of Gravity: Southern Baptists and Social Change, 1930–1980* (Brooklyn, NY: Carlson, 1991).

11. Louie Wainwright (retired Florida Department of Corrections secretary) in discussion with the author, April 2014.

12. There is an extensive literature that discusses the evolving SBC, most of which is authored by the more liberal Baptists. See Arthur E. Farnsley, *Southern Baptist Politics: Authority and Power in the Restructuring of an American Denomination*

(University Park: Pennsylvania State University Press, 1994); Glenn Feldman, ed., *Politics and Religion in the White South* (Lexington: University Press of Kentucky, 2005); Barry Hankins, *Uneasy in Babylon: Southern Baptist Conservatives and American Culture* (Tuscaloosa: University of Alabama Press, 2002); Bill Leonard, *Baptists in America* (New York: Columbia University Press, 2005); Queen, *In the South*; Walter B. Shurden, *The Struggle for the Soul of the SBC: Moderate Responses to the Fundamentalist Movement* (Macon, GA: Mercer University Press, 1993); and Walter B. Shurden and Randy Shepley, *Going for the Jugular: A Documentary History of the SBC Holy War* (Macon, GA: Mercer, 1996).

For an analysis of the impact on Baptist theology and its evolving mission statement, see Douglas K. Blount and Joseph D. Wooddell, *The Baptist Faith and Message 2000: Critical Issues in America's Largest Protestant Denomination* (Lanham, MD: Rowman & Littlefield, 2007). For a discussion on gender and the SBC conflict, see Elizabeth H. Flowers, *Into the Pulpit: Southern Baptist Women & Power Since World War II* (Chapel Hill: University of North Carolina Press, 2012); and Craig T. Friend, *Southern Masculinity: Perspectives on Manhood in the South Since Reconstruction* (Athens: University of Georgia Press, 2009).

13. SBC Statement of Faith, "I. The Scriptures," The Baptist Faith & Message 2000, accessed September 16, 2020, https://bfm.sbc.net/bfm2000/.

14. SBC Statement of Faith, "XVIII. The Family," The Baptist Faith & Message, accessed September 16, 2020, https://bfm.sbc.net/bfm2000/.

15. Horizon Communities in Prison, *Participant's Manual: Emphasizing Growth through Transition and Education in the Rehabilitation Process* (March 25, 2014), 15.

16. In many of the dorms, these families have group names. For example, in the faith-based dorm at Tomoka CI, the families are named St. Paul, St. Peter, St. James, St. John, St. Luke. St. Matthew, St. Mark, and St. Timothy. In the character-based dorm, they are named Unity, Testament, Ambitious, Charisma, Integrity, Journey, Potential, and Redemption.

17. Jeremy Travis, Bruce Western, and Steve Redburn, *The Growth of Incarceration in the United States: Exploring Causes and Consequences* (Washington, DC: National Academies Press, 2014).

18. Mustafa Emirbayer and Ira J. Cohen, eds., *Emile Durkheim: Sociologist of Modernity* (Chichester: John Wiley & Sons, 2008), 45.

19. Louie L. Wainwright, "Director's Message," *Correctional Compass* 4, no. 10 (October 1966): 1.

20. Adam Nagourney, "Dole Attacks on Crime, but Clinton Is Ready," *New York Times*, September 17, 1996, https://www.nytimes.com/1996/09/17/us/dole-attacks-on-crime-but-clinton-is-ready.html.

21. Michelle Alexander, *The New Jim Crow: Mass Incarceration in the Age of Colorblindness* (New York: New Press, 2010).

22. Alexander, 2.

23. David C. Anderson, *Crime and the Politics of Hysteria: How the Willie Horton Story Changed American Justice* (New York: Times Books, 1995).

24. Roger Simon, "How a Murderer and Rapist Became the Bush Campaign's Most Valuable Player," *Baltimore Sun*, November 11, 1990, http://articles.baltimoresun

.com/1990-11-11/features/1990315149_1_willie-horton-fournier-michael-dukakis. Additionally, the Horton affair added a racial element to the race, as Horton, a dark-skinned black rapist, tapped unsettled American anxieties about the "black face" of crime. Democrats hoped to silence the issue, and they accused Republicans of stoking racism, but these allegations of racism did not stop an otherwise successful campaign. See Maureen Dowd, "Bush Says Dukakis's Desperation Prompted Accusations of Racism," *New York Times*, October 25, 1989, http://www.nytimes.com/1988/10/25/us/bush-says-dukakis-s-desperation-prompted-accusations-of-racism.html. For a discussion of the racial issues and the Horton affair, see Jon Hurwitz and Mark Peffley, "Playing the Race Card in the Post–Willie Horton Era: The Impact of Racialized Code Words on Support for Punitive Crime Policy," *Public Opinion Quarterly* 69, no.1 (Spring 2005): 99–112.

25. See James Forman Jr., "Racial Critiques of Mass Incarceration: Beyond the New Jim Crow," *New York University Law Review* 87, no. 21 (2012): 21–69.

26. Tanya Erzen, "Testimonial Politics: The Christian Right's Faith-Based Approach to Marriage and Imprisonment," *American Quarterly* 59, no. 3 (September 2007), 1000.

27. Wendy Brown argued that neoliberalism downplays the roles of institutional oppression like racial hierarchies. She wrote, "If there is no such thing as society, but only individuals and families oriented by markets and morals, then there is no such thing as social power generating hierarchies, exclusion, and violence, let along subjectivity at the sites of class, gender, or race." See Wendy Brown, *In the Ruins of Neoliberalism: The Rise of Antidemocratic Politics in the West* (New York: Columbia University Press, 2019), 41.

28. See Wendy Brown, "Neoliberalism's Frankenstein: Authoritarian Freedom in Twenty-First Century 'Democracies,'" *Critical Times* 1, no. 1 (2018): 60–79.

29. Heather Schoenfeld, *Building the Prison State: Race & the Politics of Mass Incarceration* (Chicago: University of Chicago Press, 2018).

30. See David Harvey, *A Brief History of Neoliberalism* (New York: Oxford University Press, 2007); and Kevin Lewis O'Neill, *Secure the Soul: Christian Piety and Gang Prevention in Guatemala* (Berkeley: University of California Press, 2015).

31. Michael Omi and Howard Winant, *Racial Formations in the United States from the 1960s to the 1990s* (New York: Routledge, 1994), 147.

32. William E. Connolly, *Capitalism and Christianity, American Style* (Durham, NC: Duke University Press, 2008).

33. See Olive Banks. *Becoming a Feminist: The Social Origins of "First Wave" Feminism* (Athens: University of Georgia Press, 1986); Maureen Moynagh and Nancy Forestell, eds., *Documenting First Wave Feminisms: Transnational Collaborations and Crosscurrents* (Toronto: University of Toronto Press, 2012); and Pat Jalland, *Women, Marriage and Politics 1860–1914* (New York: Oxford University Press, 1986).

34. See Stephanie Gilmore and Sara Evans, eds., *Feminist Coalitions: Historical Perspectives on Second-Wave Feminism in the United States* (Urbana: University of Illinois Press, 2008).

35. R. Marie Griffith, *Moral Combat: How Sex Divided American Christians and Fractured American Politics* (New York: Basic Books, 2017).

36. Michel Foucault, *The Foucault Effect: Studies in Governmentality*, ed. Graham Burchell, Colin Gordon, and Peter Miller (Chicago: University of Chicago Press, 1991), 100.

37. Wendy Brown argues the emphasis on the family as a central social institution is itself consistent with neoliberalism. See Brown, *In the Ruins of Neoliberalism*. See also Melinda Cooper, *Family Values: Between Neoliberalism and the New Social Conservatism* (New York: Zone Books, 2019), 11–12.

38. Lawtey CI Chaplaincy, "Godly Marriage Principles: God's Indestructible Plan for Marriage," December 4, 2013.

39. Lawtey CI Chaplaincy.

40. Lawtey CI Chaplaincy.

41. Kelsy Burke, *Christians under Covers: Evangelicals and Sexual Pleasure on the Internet* (Berkeley: University of California Press, 2016); Jessica Johnson, *Biblical Porn: Affect, Labor, and Pastor Mark Driscoll's Evangelical Empire* (Durham, NC: Duke University Press, 2018).

42. Tim LaHaye and Beverly LaHaye, *The Act of Marriage: The Beauty of Sexual Love* (Grand Rapids, MI: Zondervan, 1976). Regarding Tim LaHaye, LaHaye is the coauthor the bestselling *Left Behind* novels, which according to Andrew Strombeck reinforced neoliberalism. See Andrew Strombeck, "Invest in Jesus: Neoliberalism and the Left Behind Novels," *Cultural Critique* 64 (Autumn 2006): 161–95.

43. Burke, *Christians under Covers*.

44. Lawtey CI Chaplaincy, "Godly Marriage Principles." Amy DeRogatis elaborates on this idea in *Saving Sex: Sexuality and Salvation in American Evangelicalism* (New York: Oxford University Press, 2014).

45. Lawtey CI Chaplaincy, "Godly Marriage Principles."

46. Lawtey CI Chaplaincy.

47. Lawtey CI Chaplaincy.

48. Lawtey CI Chaplaincy.

49. Lawtey CI Chaplaincy.

50. See Southern Baptist Convention, "The Baptist Faith and Message: The 2000 Baptist Faith and Message," accessed December 2014, https://bfm.sbc.net/bfm2000/.

51. I have compiled the biographical information for Dr. Robert Lewis from autobiographical statements in his *Teaching Manhood to Men*, accessed April 2, 2014, http://mensfraternity.com/assets/documents/teaching_manhood.pdf; from various comments in *33 The Series*; and from the biographies at his companies' websites, accessed March 24, 2014, http://www.authenticmanhood.com/about and http://mensfraternity.com/dr_robert_lewis/.

52. *33 The Series: A Man and His Design* (Nashville: Fellowship Associates, 2012), 88.

53. Lewis discusses this group in *Teaching Manhood to Men*.

54. *33 The Series*, 6.

55. The Authentic Manhood program emerged conterminously with the more well-known Promise Keepers. Almost immediately, the Promise Keepers were a commercial success as they filled arenas with men who gathered together to explore the theological implications of biblical masculinity. The Authentic Manhood

movement was never as popular as the Promise Keepers; however, where Promise Keepers peaked in the mid-1990s and have since struggled financially, Authentic Manhood has experienced a slower, more organic, and according to the architects of Authentic Manhood, more sustainable growth pattern. See Edwin S. Gaustad and Mark A. Noll, *A Documentary History of Religion in America* (Grand Rapids, MI: W. B. Eerdmans, 2003); John D. Spalding. "Bonding in the Bleachers: A Visit to the Promise Keepers," *Christian Century* 113, no. 8 (March 6, 1996): 260–66; and Rhys H. Williams, *Promise Keepers and the New Masculinity: Private Lives and Public Morality* (Lanham, MD: Lexington Books, 2001).

56. See Talal Asad, *Formations of Secularism: Christianity, Islam, Modernity* (Stanford, CA: Stanford University Press, 2003); Saba Mahmood, *Politics of Piety: The Islamic Revival and the Feminist Subject* (Princeton, NJ: Princeton University Press, 2011); John Lardas Modern, *Secularism in Antebellum America* (Chicago: University of Chicago Press, 2011); Tracy Fessenden, *Culture and Redemption: Religion, the Secular, and American Literature* (Princeton, NJ: Princeton University Press, 2013); Joan Wallach Scott, *Sex and Secularism* (Princeton, NJ: Princeton University Press, 2017); Chad E. Seales, *The Spectacular Spectacle: Performing Religion in A Southern Town* (New York: Oxford University Press, 2013).

57. Richard Collier, "A Hard Time to Be a Father?: Reassessing the Relationship between Law, Policy, and Family (Practices)," *Journal of Law and Society* 28, no. 4 (December 2001): 520–45.

58. See Nancy C. Dowd, *Redefining Fatherhood* (New York: New York University Press, 2000); and Martha Albertson Fineman, *The Neutered Mother, The Sexual Family and Other Twentieth Century Tragedies* (New York: Routledge, 1995).

59. Melinda Cooper, "All in the Family Debt: How Neoliberals and Conservatives Came Together to Undo the Welfare State," *Boston Review*, May 31, 2017, 2.

60. See Steven Block, Christopher A. Brown, Louis M. Barretti, Erin Walker, Michael Yudt, and Ralph Fretz, "A Mixed-Method Assessment of a Parenting Program for Incarcerated Fathers," *Journal of Correctional Education* 65, no. 1 (2014): 50–67; "Assessing the Impact of the InsideOut Dad Program on Newark Community Education Center Residents," Rutgers University, Economic Development Research Group (December, 2012); and Susan Kennedy Spain, "InsideOut Dad Program in Maryland and Ohio Prisons Evaluation Report," National Fatherhood Initiative (2005).

61. "Complete Program Kit: InsideOut Dad (2nd ed.)," National Fatherhood Initiative, accessed May 2018, https://store.fatherhood.org/insideout-dad-programs/.

62. "Complete Program Kit: InsideOut Dad (2nd ed.)."

63. William Wright (chaplain at Lawtey CI) in discussion with the author, June 2014.

64. For an introduction to pro-LGBTQ theologies of Christianity and Islam, see, respectively, Patrick S. Cheng, *Radical Love: Introduction to Queer Theology* (New York: Seabury Books, 2011); and Afdhere Jama, *Queer Jihad: LGBT Muslims on Coming Out, Activism, and the Faith* (West Hollywood, CA: Oracle Releasing, 2013). Wright is correct, however, that members of other major religions similarly teach gender submission. For a discussion of submission theology in the Nation of Islam,

see Ula Yvette Taylor, *The Promise of Patriarchy: Women and the Nation of Islam* (Chapel Hill: University of North Carolina Press, 2017).

65. William Wright (Chaplain at Lawtey CI) in discussion with the author, June 2014.

66. Wright (Chaplain at Lawtey CI) in discussion with the author.

67. E. Ann Carson and Elizabeth Anderson, "Prisoners in 2015," U.S. Department of Justice, Office of Justice Programs, Bureau of Justice Statistics (December 2106), NCJ 250229.

68. "Women in the Criminal Justice System: Briefing Sheets," The Sentencing Project, May 2007, https://www.sentencingproject.org/publications/women-in-the-criminal-justice-system-briefing-sheets/, 1.

69. "Women in the Criminal Justice System," 2.

70. Carson and Anderson, "Prisoners in 2015," 14.

71. Irene Wilson (inmate in Florida's Department of Corrections) in discussion with the author, June 2014. While Irene Wilson is not a mother, an increasing number of female inmates are mothers. For a discussion of incarcerated mothers, see Renny Golden, *War on the Family: Mothers in Prison and the Families They Leave Behind* (New York: Routledge, 2005). For a discussion of incarcerated women more broadly, see Rickie Solinger, Paula C. Johnson, Martha L. Raimon, Tina Reynolds, and Ruby C. Tapia, eds., *Interrupted Life: Experiences of Incarcerated Women in the United States* (Berkeley: University of California Press, 2010); Vernetta D. Young, *Women Behind Bars: Gender and Race in US Prisons* (Boulder, CO: Lynne Rienner, 2006); and Barbara H. Zaitzow and Jim Thomas, *Women in Prison: Gender and Social Control* (Boulder, CO: Lynne Rienner, 2003).

72. Annexes are prisons built onto existing prisons. Sometimes a prison will add a dorm or cell block, but an annex is a major expansion that typically doubles the prison's size.

73. LGBTQ rights are undoubtedly related to issues of gender, and while I mentioned them briefly in the previous section, I include them in a separate section because perhaps no social or cultural issues are more maligned and attacked in FCBIs than homosexuality, gay rights, gay marriage, and LGBTQ issues in general. The previous section in this chapter documented the processes by which particular theories about gender and the relationship between husband and wife circulate and become unquestioned truth in Florida's FCBIs. That same process not only circulates heteronormativity but includes a virulent hostility to homosexuality and LGBTQ issues more broadly.

74. Obergefell v. Hodges, 576 U. S. 1 (2015).

75. This resembles what Leslie Dorrough Smith described as chaos rhetoric. According to Smith, chaos rhetoric is a discourse common in the New Christian Right, which describes the world as engulfed in chaos. See Leslie Dorrough Smith, *Righteous Rhetoric: Sex, Speech, and the Politics of Concerned Women for America* (New York: Oxford University Press, 2014). This fear of chaos informs actions, as it implies overt political action. As Frank Furedi argued, fear is always pedagogical (see Frank Furedi, *Politics of Fear: Beyond Left and Right* [New York: Continuum, 2005]).

76. Yahweh Ben Yahweh, *From Poverty to Riches*, TV series, 1991, "Show Four." Lecture from June 24, 1990.

77. Ben Yahweh.

78. Jia Noel (inmate in Florida's Department of Corrections) in discussion with the author, June 2014.

79. Florida Administrative Code 33–602.101.10.

80. Much has been written about gender performativity, but Butler's *Gender Trouble* remains the classic text on this issue. See Judith Butler, *Gender Trouble: Feminism and the Subversion of Identity* (New York: Routledge, 1990).

81. Unless otherwise noted, all quotations from and information about Chaplain Karen Moffett obtained from Karen Moffett (former Other Personnel Services chaplain at Lawtey CI) in discussion with the author, May 2014.

82. Daryl Townsend (founder, Off the Chain Ministries, and volunteer at various prisons in Florida) in discussion with the author, May 2014.

83. William Wright (chaplain at Lawtey CI) in discussion with the author, June 2014.

84. Wright (chaplain at Lawtey CI) in discussion with the author, June 2014.

85. Marci Hamilton, *God vs. the Gavel: Religion and the Rule of Law* (New York: Cambridge University Press, 2005), esp. pp. 189–98. For additional information on religious exemptions, see Sandra H. Johnson "At Law: Discrimination and the Religious Workplace," *Hastings Center Report* 42, no. 6 (2012): 10–11; and Richard Schragger and Micah Schwartzman, "Against Religious Institutionalism," *Virginia Law Review* 99, no. 5 (2013): 917–85.

86. See Harvey, *Brief History of Neoliberalism* for an analysis of neoliberalism's opposition to organized and protected labor.

87. Brown, *In the Ruins of Neoliberalism*, 12. For additional information on the compatibility of the New Christian Right and neoliberalism, see Nancy MacLean, *Democracy in Chains: The Deep History of the Religious Right's Stealth Plan for America* (New York: Penguin, 2017); Michael Lienech, *Redeeming America: Piety and Politics in the New Christian Right* (Chapel Hill: University of North Carolina Press, 1993); Susan Harding, *The Book of Jerry Falwell: Fundamentalist Language and Politics* (Princeton, NJ: Princeton University Press, 2000); Linda Kintz, *Between Jesus and the Market: The Emotions that Matter in Right-Wing America* (Durham, NC: Duke University Press, 1997); and Bethany Moreton, *To Serve God and Wal-Mart: The Making of Christian Free Enterprise* (Cambridge, MA: Harvard University Press, 2009).

88. MacLean, *Democracy in Chains*, xxvii.

89. MacLean, xxvii.

90. Neoliberal economist Gary Becker explicitly linked the decline in morality to the expanded welfare state. See Gary Becker, *A Treatise on Government* (Cambridge, MA: Harvard University Press, 1993).

91. Brown, *In the Ruins of Neoliberalism*, 39.

92. Melinda Cooper, "All in the Family Debt: How Neoliberals and Conservatives Came Together to Undo the Welfare State," *Boston Review*, May 31, 2017, 2.

93. Cooper, "All in the Family Debt," 2.

94. See Jean Comaroff and John L. Comaroff, "Millennial Capitalism: First Thoughts on a Second Coming," *Public Culture* 12, no. 2 (2000): 291–343.

Chapter Six

1. Personal correspondence, Nancy O'Brien. "Thank You for Attending the Tallahassee, FL Day of Champions," Bill Glass Champions for Life (June 11, 2014).

2. Bill Glass (founder, Bill Glass Ministries), in discussion with the author, May 2014. For additional autobiographical information, see also Bill Glass, *Blitzed by Blessings: A Journey to Strengthening Your Inner Core* (Charleston, SC: Advantage Media Group, 2010).

3. For the most recent report, see Bill Glass: Behind the Walls, *Behind the Walls Annual Report, 2016* (Duncanville, Texas, 2016). The total expenses for 2016 were $2,534,793. Behind the Walls completed twenty-nine events in prisons and forty-six events in youth facilities.

4. For additional information on interpolation, see Judith Butler in *The Psychic Life of Power* (Stanford, CA: Stanford University Press, 1997).

5. "Timeline: 1868–1876," Florida Department of Corrections, accessed June 2015, dc.state.f.us/ oth/timeline/index.html (page removed).

6. Department of Agriculture Prison Division, *Eighteenth Biennial Report of the Prison Division of the Department of Agriculture of the State of Florida for the Years 1923 and 1924* (Tallahassee, Florida), 78.

7. Department of Agriculture Prison Division, *Twenty-Ninth Biennial Report of the Prison Division of the Department of Agriculture of the State of Florida for the Years 1945 and 1946* (Tallahassee, Florida), 65.

8. Department of Agriculture Prison Division, *Twenty-Ninth Biennial Report*, 18. Florida's young correctional system was originally administered by the Department of Agriculture.

9. Specifically, the chaplains contacted local churches, where they recruited new volunteers, both lay and ordained (Louie L. Wainwright, "Director's Message," *Correctional Compass* 4, no. 12 [December 1966], 1). They also encouraged incarcerated people to establish ties with a minister of the person's choice in his hometown (Florida Division of Corrections, *Sixth Biennial Report: July 1, 1966–June 30, 1968*, 16). What resulted was an informal army of religious volunteers who provided Florida's prisons with valuable services and free labor. Prison administrators routinely honored these volunteers with various appreciation ceremonies, including the "Volunteer of the Year" award, which almost without exception went to a religious volunteer active in one or more of Florida's prisons.

10. Robert Wuthnow, *The Restructuring of American Religion: Society and Faith Since World War II* (Princeton, NJ: Princeton University Press, 1988).

11. Florida Division of Corrections, *Eighth Biennial Report: July 1, 1970 to June 30, 1972*, 46.

12. "Chaplaincy Services," *Correctional Compass* 12, no. 2 (March 1974): 2.

13. Campus Crusade for Christ was active in Florida's prisons by January 1978. See "Leadership Seminar, Crusades Set for Inmates and Chaplains," *Correctional Compass* 4, no. 1 (January 1978): 2.

14. George W. Bush, "Foreword by President George W. Bush," *Rallying the Armies of Compassion* (Washington, DC: U.S. Congressional Budget Office, 2001), 4. Martin Olasky embraced this concept as he provided additional justification and support for mobilizing "armies of compassion." See Martin Olasky, *The Tragedy of American Compassion* (Wheaton, IL: Crossway, 2008); and Martin Olasky, *Compassionate Conservatism: What It Is, What It Does, and How It Can Transform America* (New York: Free Press, 2000).

15. Byron Johnson discusses how many Christians are reluctant to take any government funding, fearing it would compromise their independence. See Byron Johnson, *More God, Less Crime: Why Faith Matters and How It Could Matter More* (West Conshohocken, PA: Templeton, 2011).

16. Biographical information obtained from Bob Rumbley and Mary Rumbley, in conversation with the author, July 2015.

17. Daryl Townsend (founder, Off the Chain Ministries, and volunteer at various prisons in Florida), in discussion with the author, May 2014.

18. Tina Roberts (warden, Hernando Correctional Institution), in conversation with the author, June 2014.

19. For information about Lowell Annex, see http://www.dc.state.fl.us/ci/367 .html.

20. These statistics gathered from conversation with Chaplain Faithe Liburd (chaplain at Lowell Annex) and Gustavo Mazorra (warden at Lowell Annex), June 2014.

21. Office of Program Policy Analysis and Government Accountability (OPPAGA), "Faith- and Character-Based Prison Initiative Yields Institutional Benefits; Effect on Recidivism Modest" (Tallahassee, FL: OPPAGA, 2009), 4.

22. Rex Henry (chaplain at Hernando Correctional Institution), in conversation with the author, June 2014.

23. Allison DeFoor (proponent of Florida's faith-based correctional program), in conversation with the author, June 2014; and James Crosby (former Florida Department of Corrections secretary), in discussion with the author, June 2014.

24. These statistics gathered from conversations with Chaplain Steve Fox and Warden James Coker from Wakulla CI.

25. OPPAGA, "Faith- and Character-Based Prison Initiative Yields Institutional Benefits," 5.

26. According to Independent Sector, the figure of $25.43 is the per-hour benefit or cost of volunteer time in April 2019. "Independent Sector Releases New Value of Volunteer Time of $25.43 Per Hour," Independent Section, April 11, 2019, https://independentsector.org/news-post/new-value-volunteer-time-2019/.

27. Application available at http://fldocjobs.com/volunteer/dc5-601a.pdf.

28. Florida Department of Corrections Volunteer Services, *Volunteer Training Manual*, 2013, http://fldocjobs.com/volunteer/training.pdf.

29. Alex Taylor (head chaplain, Florida Department of Corrections), in discussion with the author, February 2014.

30. Alan Cooperman, "An Infusion of Religious Funds in Fla. Prisons," *Washington Post*, April 25, 2004, https://www.washingtonpost.com/archive/politics/2004/04/25/an-infusion-of-religious-funds-in-fla-prisons/8360ca26-fd46-4a32-872d-6e6a1fe155e9/.

31. For additional information on this program, see the official website for Authentic Manhood. www.authenticmanhood.com.

32. For additional information on the John 3:16 Marketing Network, see http://john316mn.blogspot.com/.

33. Lorilyn Roberts, "John 3:16 Authors Join Prisoners in Novel Florida Initiative to Boost Reading and Job Skills," *John 3:16 Marketing Network* (blog), July 30, 2014, http://john316mn.blogspot.com/2014/07/john-316-authors-join-prisoners-in.html.

34. Information about Faith Radio's relationship with Wakulla CI obtained primarily from Chaplain Steve Fox, although several incarcerated people also discussed the program.

35. Faith Radio has an official doctrinal statement that aligns it with the NCR. To access their statement, see "Our Mission," Faith Radio, accessed September 16, 2020, https://faithradio.us/about-us/our-mission/.

36. For additional information about the partnership between Faith Radio and Wakulla CI, see "Prison Ministry," Faith Radio, accessed September 16, 2020, https://faithradio.us/missions/prison-ministry/; and Galcom International, USA, Inc., "Finding True Freedom behind Prison Walls," October 2011, www.galcomusa.com/pdf/Oct2011Eltr.pdf.

37. Noel Gilli (inmate in Florida's Department of Corrections), in discussion with the author, January 2015.

38. See Jeremy Travis, "Reflections on the Reentry Movement," *Federal Sentencing Reporter* 20, no. 2 (2007): 1–4.

39. Nathan James, "Offender Reentry: Correctional Statistics, Reintegration into the Community, and Recidivism," *Congressional Research Service* (2015), 12.

40. Henry J. Steadman, Fred C. Osher, Pamela Clark Robbins, Brian Case, and Steven Samuels, "Prevalence of Serious Mental Illness among Jail Inmates," *Psychiatric Services* 60, no. 6 (2009): 761–65; and Craig W. Haney, *Reforming Punishment: Psychological Limits to the Pains of Imprisonment* (Washington, DC: American Psychological Association Books, 2006).

41. See Jangho Yoon, "Effect of Increased Private Share of Inpatient Psychiatric Resources on Jail Population Growth: Evidence from the United States," *Social Science and Medicine* 72, no. 4 (2011): 447–55. As Lauren-Brooke Eisen noted, "More mentally ill people are in the nation's prisons than in its mental hospitals" (Lauren-Brooke Eisen, *Inside Private Prisons: An American Dilemma in the Age of Mass Incarceration* [New York: Columbia University Press, 2018], 14).

42. See Ingrid A. Binswanger, Patrick M. Krueger, and John F. Steiner. "Prevalence of Chronic Medical Conditions among Jail and Prison Inmates in the U.S.A. Compared with the General Population," *Journal of Epidemiology and Community Health*

63, no. 11 (2009): 912–19; Centers for Disease Control and Prevention, "STDs in Persons Entering Corrections Facilities" (2011); Theodore M. Hammett, "HIV/AIDS and other Infectious Diseases among Correctional Inmates: Transmission, Burden, and an Appropriate Response," *American Journal of Public Health* 96, no. 6 (2006): 974–78; Theodore M. Hammett, "Sexually Transmitted Diseases and Incarceration," *Current Opinion in Infectious Diseases* 22, no. 1 (2009): 77–81; Maria R. Khan, Matthew W. Epperson, and Samuel R. Friedman, "Incarceration, Sex with an STI- or HIV-Infected Partner, and Infection with an STI or HIV in Bushwick, Brooklyn, NY: A Social Network Perspective," *American Journal of Public Health* 101, no. 6 (2011): 1110–17; Daniel P. Mears, Laura Winterfield, John Hunsaker, Gretchen E. Moore, and Ruth White, *Drug Treatment in the Criminal Justice System: The Current State of Knowledge* (Washington, DC: Urban Institute Press, 2002); and Andrew P. Wilper, Steffie Woolhandler, J Wesley Boyd, Karen E Lasser, Danny McCormick, David H. Bor, and David U. Himmelstein, "The Health and Health Care of U.S. Prisoners: Results of a Nationwide Survey," *American Journal of Public Health* 99, no. 4 (2009): 666–72.

43. Jeremy Travis, Bruce Western, and Steve Redburn, *The Growth of Incarceration in the United States: Exploring Causes and Consequences* (Washington, DC: National Academies Press, 2014).

44. See Donald Clemmer, *The Prison Community* (New York: Rinehart, 1958).

45. John Irwin, *The Warehouse Prison: Disposal of the New Dangerous Class* (Los Angeles, CA: Roxbury, 2005).

46. See Jeremy Travis, *But They All Came Back: Facing the Challenges of Prisoner Reentry* (Washington, DC: Urban Institute Press, 2005). For additional information on reentry, see Marc Mauer and Meda Chesney-Lind, eds., *Invisible Punishment: The Collateral Consequences of Mass Imprisonment* (New York: Free Press, 2002).

47. See Kamala Mallik-Kane and Christy Visher, *Health and Prisoner Reentry: How Physical, Mental, and Substance Abuse Conditions Shape the Process of Reintegration* (Washington, DC: Urban Institute Press, 2008); and Amanda Geller and Allyson Walker, "Partner Incarceration and Women's Housing Insecurity" (working Paper 1373, Princeton University, Woodrow Wilson School of Public and International Affairs, Center for Research on Child Wellbeing, 2012).

48. See Shawn D. Bushway, Michael A. Stoll, and David Weiman, eds., *Barriers to Reentry? The Labor Market for Released Prisoners in Post-Industrial America* (New York: Russell Sage Foundation, 2007); and Christy Visher, Sara Debus, and Jennifer Yahner, "Employment after Prison: A Longitudinal Study of Former Prisoners," *Justice Quarterly* 28, no. 5 (2011): 698–718.

49. Joan Petersilia, *When Prisoners Come Home: Parole and Prisoner Reentry* (New York: Oxford University Press, 2003), 53.

50. Binswanger, Krueger, and Steiner, "Prevalence of Chronic Medical Conditions."

51. Bob Rumbley and Mary Rumbley, in conversation with the author, July 2015.

52. The last time I visited Care Tallahassee, the residents were grilling a boar that Bob Rumbley shot and killed earlier that morning at his home.

Conclusion

1. All quotes from Jeb Bush from "Inauguration Speech," *Tallahassee Democrat*, January 6, 1999, 11A.

2. John Cassidy, "What Type of Conservative Is Jeb Bush?," *New Yorker*, February 10, 2015, https://www.newyorker.com/news/john-cassidy/type-conservative-jeb-bush.

3. See Melissa Rogers, "President Trump Just Unveiled a New White House 'Faith' Office. It Actually Weakens Religious Freedom," *Washington Post*, May 14, 2018, https://www.washingtonpost.com/news/acts-of-faith/wp/2018/05/14/president-trump-just-unveiled-a-new-white-house-faith-office-it-actually-weakens-religious-freedom/.

4. See Winnifred Sullivan, *Prison Religion: Faith-Based Reform and the Constitution* (Princeton, NJ: Princeton University Press, 2009); and Tanya Erzen, *God in Captivity: The Rise of Faith-Based Prison Ministries in the Age of Mass Incarceration* (Boston: Beacon, 2017).

Index

Violent Crime Control and Law Enforcement Act, 35

volunteers: discipline, 190–92; and faith-based correctional reform, 45, 53, 58–59, 60–63; in FCBIs, 78, 97–99, 115–16, 122, 134–35, 146–47, 163–64, 171–97, 230n22; in Florida's prisons, 174–77; labor, 180–85; material goods, 185–90; in prisons, 44–45, 50, 52, 81; reentry, 192–96

Wainwright, Louie, 16–18, 40; search, 41, 42, 48–49, 174

Wakulla Annex, 67, 82, 192

Wakulla Correctional Institution, 1–2; administrators and chaplain, 77, 88, 107, 188; classes, 106, 108, 113, 116, 120, 130, 161–62, 164; culture inside, 91, 158; history of, 67–68, 77, 178; incarcerated residents, 88–91, 101, 108–9, 120, 130, 136–38, 161–62; religious minorities, 78–79, 84, 101, 160–61; volunteers, 44, 83, 105, 130, 138, 171, 178, 182, 195

war on drugs, 31–33, 142

war on poverty, 25

waterboarding, 75

welfare: neoliberalism, 11–12, 145; reform, 2, 29–31, 34–35, 38–40, 193; religious reform, 22, 38–40, 60, 129, 169, 174, 180

White, Dale, 105

White House Faith and Opportunity Initiative, 200

White House Office of Faith-Based and Community Initiatives, 3, 99

White House Office of Faith-Based and Neighborhood Partnerships, 200

Wicca/Wiccans, 78–79, 84, 163, 183

Wilson, James Q., 25, 37

Winthrop, John, 30

women, incarcerated, 33, 67, 95–96, 138, 139, 146, 152, 153–57, 181–82

Workbook, 72, 85–87, 113

Wright, William, 64, 72, 80, 149, 151–52, 165, 168

Yahweh ben Yahweh, 160–61